Merrill Reese

"IT'S GOOOOOOD!"

by Merrill Reese
with Mark Eckel

SPORTS PUBLISHING INC.
Champaign, IL 61820

©1998 Merrill Reese
All rights reserved.

Director of Production, book design: Susan M.McKinney
Dustjacket design: Joe Buck

ISBN: 1-58261-000-2
Library of Congress Catalog Card Number:98-86641

Sports Publishing Inc.
804 N. Neil
Champaign, IL 61820
www.SportsPublishingInc.com

Printed in the United States.

To Cindy — For your love, understanding, support and inspiration.
To Nolan and Ida — For making it all worthwhile.
To Mom — For pointing me in the right direction, nagging (every now and then) and for encouraging me to reach for the stars.
In memory of Dr. Nathan Reese.

Contents

Foreword

Merrill Reese and I have been friends for over 20 years. Initially, what I found most surprising about Merrill was his size. He has this big, booming voice. I mean a big voice. But when I met him face to face, he was on the small size; only 5-9, and at the most, 140 pounds. His voice just doesn't fit his size. But you know what they say, size doesn't matter.

I didn't know it at the time, but the example I watched Merrill set as the consummate broadcaster when I played actually guided me when I later entered the broadcast arena. Merrill is always prepared. And Merrill always enjoys his work, that makes a difference. A difference you can see, and hear during the broadcast. I remember traveling with Merrill when I played, and he was always studying on the plane. He prepared for his broadcast like a player prepared to play the game. It was serious business. In the hotel, the night before the game, I would always see Merrill with his crew, and they were preparing and planning. Again, Sunday morning, at breakfast, he was preparing.

I met Merrill in 1977 when I first came to the Eagles from Los Angeles. He was the color commentator, and Charlie Swift was the play-by-play man. We did a lot of interviews then for his pregame, and postgame shows. When he became the play-by-play man the following year, we not only did interviews but co-hosted a Celebrity Sports Talk show every Friday night at The Eagles Nest, my golf club in Sewell, New Jersey. We would have guests from all over the sports world, not just Eagles players, but golfers, tennis players, and once a professional polo player from Brazil who spoke very little English. But Merrill's professionalism made it fun. I always knew Merrill would do what it took to insure an interesting and accurate show. Working with Merrill helped me learn to listen as an interviewer. He let the guest do the talking, and he responded appropriately, When a guest was not communicative, he had the skill to keep the show interesting.

I truly believe it was all of those shows that I did with Merrill that prepared me for my own career in broadcasting. He taught me that you have to be prepared, you have to give it everything you've got, and you have to have fun. In my work at ESPN, I try to emulate how Merrill has always approached his work — with honesty, hard work, and homework.

I was ecstatic when I learned that Merrill was doing this book. He has so many behind-the-scene stories to convey. He can give his readers a perspective of the game that no one else can possibly offer. Merrill, born and raised in Philadelphia, has been with the Eagles for over two decades. There are a lot of stories to tell...and Merrill Reese is the one to tell them. As you read the chapters of Merrill's experiences, I'm certain you'll agree.

—Ron Jaworski

Introduction

I always get the "here he goes again" look from Nolan and Ida when I talk about my job. The truth is, I love it, and would like my teenagers to seek out a worthwhile target and attack it with the same passion.

One thing broadcasters miss, however, is having a meaningful memento — a tangible record of what they have experienced — the frustrations and the rewards.

Oh, I have a few footballs signed by "All-Pros" and the sneakers Billie Jean King wore while winning a Wimbledon title but nothing that really represents all of my 21 years in the Eagles broadcast booth.

I've thought about a book for years. Something would happen and I'd think, "What a chapter this would make." But two minutes later my attention would focus on another more pressing area of my life.

Often I would speak at a luncheon or at a banquet and my friend and business partner, Pat T. Deon, would coax me to put my experiences down on paper. My agent and attorney, Lloyd Remick, has been in my corner for years and he challenged me to come up with an outline — a road map for a book. I gave him excuses until I ran dry.

Finally, I asked *Trenton Times* Eagles beat writer, Mark Eckel, to join me in this project. Mark has been an eyewitness to all that concerns the Eagles since 1985 and nobody covers the team with more knowledge, insight, wit, and meticulous attention to details.

This spring I spent countless hours taping the episodes of my life and when the motor showed signs of slowing down, Mark was there to "rev it up" with the perfect question to push me into a higher gear.

I'll always be deeply indebted to Dean Tyler who gave me by big break at WIP years ago, and to Ken Stevens and Tim Sabean who have made the last six years at WYSP truly special.

The fans in the Delaware Valley have been unbelievable. Despite their national reputation as "boo birds", they're great. No fans anywhere care more about their team and follow their team with greater passion. Conveying my enthusiasm to them for at least 20 games a year and sensing their response has been the greatest reward of all.

—Merrill Reese

Stan's Last Game

December 21, 1997, Landover, Maryland. — All along I tried to hide my emotions. Ever since Stan Walters, my broadcast partner for the past 14 years and a player I watched for seven years before that, told me this would be his last year in the booth, I tried to take it all in stride.

In the beginning, when Stan informed me he was moving to London with his wife, Kathy and their two children, I didn't believe it. Call it denial, if you will. But every year or so, it seemed Stan said he was leaving, and for 13 straight years he came back. Even the past two years when he moved from his home in the Philadelphia suburb of West Chester to Atlanta, he still flew back to Philadelphia for every home game, and met us at every road game. I told myself he would again, somehow.

Later, as it became a reality that he really was going to leave, I rationalized that the opportunity was too enticing for his family. Kathy was going to become the President of the European Division for Kimberly-Clark, and a once-a-week job as my color analyst on Eagles games wasn't quite enough for Stan to stay. Although if the roles were reversed, I couldn't imagine any job, anywhere, that would make me want to leave my role as play-by-play man.

Finally, the day had arrived. It was Stan's final game, and I wasn't sure how I would react. The Eagles were about to conclude their worst season since 1986, and their most disappointing since longer than that. This season finale was against the Washington Redskins at brand-new Jack Kent Cooke Stadium. As far as the playoffs, or anything else associated with the team, the game had little meaning. For Stan and I, it meant 14 years of a unique partnership was about to come to an end.

People might find it hard to believe that the two of us had become so close over the years. Stan was a 6-foot-5, 280-pound former All-Pro left tackle who came across in the booth the same way he did on the field, with reckless abandon. And I am just a little shorter, a little lighter, and a little less reckless. But if you ever saw the movie "Twins" you can relate. Stan had Arnold Schwarzenegger's size and Danny DeVito's demeanor. I was the other way around, although I wish they had gotten Tom Cruise for one of the roles.

Before the game began I was worried that it was going to get too emotional, but it really didn't. Our station, WYSP, dedicated most of the pre-game show to Stan. All week I had taped interviews with the people who knew Stan best—Rusty Sweeney, the equipment manager; Mike Dougherty, the video director; Ken Iman, Stan's one-time offensive line coach; and some former players. I had them all tape messages for Stan and they were played during the show.

The guys back in Philadelphia, the regulars on the pregame show, Tom Cardella, Johnny Sample, and John DeBella, also paid on-air tributes to Stan and brought him on for a good portion of the hour-long affair.

Even the night before, we had a dinner at the hotel for him. The entire WYSP crew was there and a couple of local writers and television guys stopped by to say their good-byes. The Eagles head coach Ray Rhodes, who hit it off with Stan right from the beginning, also came by and gave a very heartwarming send off. Ray loved to tell the story of the one game they played against each other when Stan was with the Eagles and Ray was a cornerback for the Giants, and how Stan threw a block at him that he still feels today. It was a good time, but it still wasn't setting in for me.

But during the pregame, we all sat there in the booth, and with Stan on the pregame show, they started to play excerpts of the two of us through the years. I guess you could call it the best of Stan. Right in the middle of it, Stan looked at me and I looked at him and the two of us started to cry. Tears just streamed down our faces. It had all finally hit the both of us right there. It was uncontrollable. It was the first time the realization had hit me. This really was Stan's last game.

Again, you have to understand, Stan and I were more than just broadcast partners, we were close friends. During the year we would spend countless hours on the phone. We would do a game together, be on the air for three hours or longer, and then I would go home, the phone would ring, and it would be Stan. He would just want to talk about that one play in the third quarter that turned the game around, or did I think they were in trouble after a tough loss? My wife, Cindy, would say to me, "Haven't you guys talked yourselves out by now?" She understands a lot about the demands of the job, but this part she has never quite figured out.

This was a relationship I cherished and here it was about to end. I was losing my partner. And the two of us were crying. And finally Stan turned to me and said, "These people in Washington are looking in this booth right now and they must think that this team stinks so badly, that the radio guys cry before they go on the air." We started laughing so hard that the emotion switched, and we got through the game without any other incidents.

But the more I think about it, it was just a strange day. The game itself was sloppy and the same things that killed the Eagles all season—penalties, poor special teams play—killed them again and they lost by three points. But the entire weekend was strange. For the first time ever the Eagles took a train to Washington. Every other year we had taken a bus, or I had even driven down with one of the other guys. But this year we were all on the train, and it gave me time to reflect back on all the good times and all the games Stan and I had done together.

I remembered back to Stan's first game. It was the 1984 preseason at Detroit, in the Silverdome. Actually, I thought back to Stan's last game as a player. Stan tried to retire after the strike-shortened 1982 season. But new head coach Marion Campbell found out in training camp how much they needed him. The man who was supposed to take Stan's place, Dean Miraldi, a high 1981 draft pick, hurt his knee and would be out for the season. So the Eagles went to Stan and talked him out of retirement with a pretty good contract offer. The offer included a clause that the team would build a barn behind Stan's house. This was before the day of big-time signing bonuses. But Stan made it clear it would be for just one more year. He's told me since that he should have stayed retired.

So we were in St. Louis for the final game of 1983, and I was as cold as I've ever been in my life. Forget Green Bay, Chicago, Minnesota before the dome, this day in St. Louis was frigid. It was a terrible season, under Campbell, and this was the last game. The pressbox wasn't heated, and our producer Jerry Rosset, got all the commercials in early, so he could huddle in the men's room and keep warm. I was in agony the entire game. My tongue actually froze up and I had trouble moving my lips. That's how cold it was.

Bill Bergey, the former Eagles All-Pro linebacker, was in his second, and what would be his final, year as the color man on the broadcast. Cary Pahagian, a 26-year-old from New England, was hired as the new program director at WIP (which broadcast the Eagles games until 1992 when WYSP took over). Pahagian, who lasted all of two years at the station before he returned to the Boston area, wanted to put his stamp on the broadcast. It didn't matter that he had little, if any, knowledge of the Eagles or their history, and didn't know Bill Bergey from Billy Penn. That happens a lot in the radio business. Everyone likes something different and everyone wants their own input. That's how Cary was and he wanted a new color man. He wanted his own guy, and there was nothing I could do to convince him otherwise. And I tried.

Finally, I did get him to leave Bill in the booth until the end of the season. I was hoping, as time passed, he would have other things to worry about, and would have left us alone. But at the end of the season he wanted his new guy. He was dead serious.

I never told Bill. Again, I was hoping it would pass and didn't want him to work under impossible conditions. Cary flat out told me to find someone else, and he'd let Bergey finish the season. If not, he would find someone else and he would start immediately. I knew Stan was retiring and knew he wanted to get into radio. He was doing a show called "On the Line with Stan Walters," for WFIL, another local AM station, that season. It wasn't 100 percent set, but it looked like it was going to get done after the season and Stan would take over the following year.

Here we were, the worst day of the season, the coldest day ever. Stan didn't even play that game, because with a 5-10 record in a season going nowhere it was time to see some young players. He was on the sideline and our postgame interview was with him, since his career had just ended. And Bergey asked him, "Stan, now that you're retired and through playing, what are you going to do?" I thought, "This is incredible." It was a tough situation. I felt for Bill and I knew how Stan must have felt, too. He certainly couldn't say, "Well Bill, first I'm going to take your job as the color man."

The first time Stan and I actually worked together was at

Temple Stadium. The Temple Owls had what they called their Cherry and White Game in the spring, and Stan and I did a "practice" broadcast. And we were terrible together. We stepped on each other's lines; it was a real mess.

We worked together in training camp, trying to get better, and our first Eagles game was that preseason game in Detroit. I thought back to how nervous Stan was that night. This giant of a man, who had played for 13 years and taken on some of the best pass-rushing defensive linemen in the game, was tremendously nervous as he sat next to me in the booth.

Then again, I'm always nervous. To this day I get nervous. When I go out to do the first game of next season I'll be nervous. I'm a basket case. People don't realize it; I try my best not to let it show, and I don't think it does, but I'm a wreck. When I wake up Sunday mornings during the season I know there's a game, because I can feel it in the pit of my stomach. It's even worse for night games, because then I live with it all day.

A long time ago I remember talking before a Phillies game with Tony Taylor, who was pacing around the dugout. I asked him if he always got nervous before a game, and he said, "absolutely." He told me this means so much to him that he has to be nervous. That when you didn't feel the butterflies any longer, it was time to quit. That it would no longer be important.

To this day, I can feel it from the time I wake up. It's not the same when I do a daily update, or the coach's show, or a talk show. But a game is different. I feel I prepare all week, the same way the players do. I receive the clippings from the visiting team and I read everything written about that team, all the features, all their past game stories. I might only use 30 percent of it, but my theory has always been overprepare, underdeliver. I'll go through game tapes, coach's tapes. I want to see every formation the team runs. I don't want to get surprised. I want to know that I've seen that before and be able to describe it to the listener. Then there's number memorization. My son, Nolan, will go around the house with flash cards and call out numbers of the other team and I'll give him names. It's really tough during the preseason when teams carry 80-man rosters and half the guys are only known to their mothers.

So I've read all the stories, memorized the numbers, hung around the team all week at practice and in the locker room. I'm sure some broadcasters just show up game day, but I live there all week. I want to be around to know every little thing that's happening with the team. I live with this team from the first day of training camp until the last day of the season.

When it's game day, I wake up with the butterflies in my stomach and I go through the same preparation whether we're home or on the road. I take a hot bath and practice what's called psychocybernetics. Billie Jean King told me about it when I telecast the Freedoms (the defunct Philadelphia World Team Tennis franchise) years ago. The theory is that the difference between real and imaginary is not really different in our frame of reference. If we visualize ourselves succeeding at something we would get the same confidence as actually succeeding. I don't know if I buy it 100 percent. But I think to a degree it is true.

Billie Jean used to tell me before she went to Wimbledon she would sit quietly in a dimly lit room and visualize herself winning point after point, smelling the freshly cut center-court grass, and immerse herself into the entire atmosphere. It certainly worked for her. She set a record for total Wimbledon titles. She played perhaps the biggest game in history for women's tennis when she defeated Bobby Riggs at the Houston Astrodome in what was called the Battle of the Sexes. Nobody, but nobody, was more adept at handling pressure and making it work for her than Billie Jean.

So I lie back in this hot tub and I envision myself calling the game, not plays necessarily. But if the Eagles are playing Dallas, I see No. 22 and it's Emmitt Smith getting a handoff, or I see No. 88 and it's Michael Irvin catching a pass. I go through all the identifications as I'm relaxing, envisioning all of this taking place, so that in a couple of hours when I'm at the stadium and 60,000 people are screaming, and my producer is telling me to get ready for a spot, and Stan is tapping on my shoulder, I can keep my focus.

I go through this every week. Then when I'm finished, I take a shower. And I have the same pregame meal. I don't want to think about should I have this, or should I have that. I have the same thing. I have a stack of pancakes. It used to be a three-egg cheese omelet with a toasted English muffin, but that was too high in fat content. So it's been a stack of pancakes with a little syrup and a cup of tea. I leave for the stadium three and a half hours before kickoff. The drive from my house in Fort Washington to the Stadium in South Philadelphia takes a little more than a half hour. But I leave at 9:30 for a 1 o'clock game, because I want to know if for some reason my car breaks down, I can walk to the game and still get there on time. On the road I take the team bus, so I know the game isn't going to start without me.

Once I get to the game, I'll walk around the field a little bit. I like to see how the wind is blowing, what the temperature is like, if the grass is wet, or if the turf is hard. I'll watch the kickers closely, and see how they're kicking. I want to know what their range is. When I get to the booth, I'll look across the field and call the yards, you know, 5-10-15-20-25-30-35-40-45-midfield-45-40-35-30-25-20-15-10-5-touchdown. That's just to limber up my tongue and make sure everything is in working order. I know this sounds insane. But I really do this.

About a half hour or so before the game, the anxiety will start to build. Then we'll get a "10 minutes before air time" call from our producer Joe McPeak, and then five minutes. Then as he counts it down, when he gets to 30 seconds, you can feel it. Finally he'll tap me on the shoulder and, as he does that, all the nervousness, all the tension is gone. And for the next three hours I'm floating, just floating.

And it's been that way for 21 years.

Growing Up Merrill

Maybe I should have known what was in store for me when, as a child actor, I would play catch with a well-known adult actor named Jimmy Stewart, who had already won an Academy Award for his "Philadelphia Story."

Mine would come later, much later.

My father, Nathan, was a dentist and we lived behind his office at 441 S. 56th St. in West Philadelphia. My mother, Helen, was a former kindergarten teacher who loved the entertainment business and actually owned a dancing studio at one time. Show business was in her blood. Soon it would be in mine, even though I would have preferred a transfusion at that time. Sports wasn't an all-consuming passion in our house, not yet anyway, but there was usually a game on the radio.

I remember times when I wandered into my father's office waiting room and tried to get somebody there to go out and have a catch with me, and my father would politely walk me back to our living room, and I would knock over a lamp, or something. But in that living room, I'll never forget, we had this great big console radio. I would just be glued to that radio. In the spring it would be Phillies baseball and in the fall, my great passion, football. I loved football. My first love was Penn football, which was broadcast by Byrum Saam, who was better known as the voice of the Phillies for several years.

Penn was a national power in the late 40s. The Quakers were a top 10 team that drew 60,000 people to Franklin Field every week, which was about triple what the Eagles drew at Shibe Park on the same weekends. You think back how times have changed and how the Ivy League, which once dominated college football, is now Division I-AA. But back then it was Penn, not Penn State, that was the top college team in the area.

My childhood hero was Reds Bagnell, Penn's All-American tailback. My grandmother gave me a white football jersey and sewed two blue No. 4s on it, because that was Reds' number, 44. I grew to know these people and in my mind saw them through Saam's radio broadcast. I visualized what was going on by what I heard. When Navy, another power in those days, would come to Franklin Field, I could see the blue Navy uniforms and I would let my mind formulate pictures. Even as a kid of four or five years old, I would be spellbound by these games that came through the radio.

I remember when my parents took me to a Penn game at Franklin Field and all those images that I had conjured in my mind actually came alive. And while I loved it, it really wasn't any more exciting to me then when I sat at home and listened to By Saam tell me all about it on the radio. People sometimes tell me now how they enjoy listening to our broadcast, and how they will turn down the sound on the television, or just listen to us, instead of watching television. I'm always flattered by that, but I know what they mean, I was the same way. I loved listening to games on the radio.

Of course, if you asked me what I wanted to be back then, I would have told you, Reds Bagnell. I wanted to be a football star too. That was my dream.

My mother had other plans. She loved the dance and was into ballet and other things like that. So at a very early age she would take my younger sister Carole and me, actually dragged Carole and me around, to singing, dancing and dramatics lessons. It was probably good for Carole, because her one chance at football ended in near disaster.

I had my own uniform that I loved to wear whenever I had the chance to play. Well, I felt Carole should have one as well. Unbeknownst to my parents, I saved my money and went out and bought her a uniform, complete with shoulder pads and the works. My father took us to the park to play one day, and I tackled Carole, bloodied her lip and knocked out her first tooth. From there it was back to the drama lessons.

And I hated it. I fought it most of the time. But I knew as soon as it was over I could go home and get into what I called my "alley" clothes and live my dream of being the next Reds Bagnell, carrying the ball through the concrete pavements between the row houses. I would just leave Carole home, safe and sound.

Those were dreams. The reality was I was becoming a child actor. I went to a place called Mae Desmond's for my dramatic lessons. Mae Desmond was a former actress who put on shows for the area schools. The first one I remembered was Snow White and the Seven Dwarfs, and I think I played Happy, which would have really been a stretch.

What I enjoyed more were the radio dramas, which were very popular back then. I did a show called "Let's Pretend" and we would do classic plays, like David Copperfield, on Sunday mornings. I was too young to sit and read a script naturally, so my mother would sit with me during the week and she helped me memorize what would sometimes be a 26-page script.

From there I got connected with the Al Paul Lefton Advertising Agency, which is still a very big agency in Philadelphia. They would call me for various jobs and off I would go, leaving my Reds Bagnell dream in the alley. I had a small role on one television show called the Sealtest Big Top, which was a circus show. But what I remember most about the show was that the clown in the circus was played by Ed McMahon. So that's one thing I have in common with Johnny Carson.

There was another show called M&Ms Candy Carnival, and the show opened every week with a tight shot of me as I yelled "Hey kids, it's time for M&Ms Candy Carnival." I did another show every Friday night called Six Gun Cinema. The star was a local actor called Chuck Wagon Pete. His real name was Pete Boyle and his son is Peter Boyle, the well-known movie and television actor who currently plays the father on the hit sitcom Everybody Loves Raymond. I did a lot of the commercials during the western movies that Chuck Wagon Pete would introduce. Now remember, most commercials were live, and that led to some unusual experiences.

There were two memorable episodes, both for a cereal called Ranger Joe. The cereal was a sugar-coated puffed wheat that came in a plastic bag, like a potato chip bag. Ranger Joe was also the central figure in this western show that featured a skit every week done around the ranch.

Well, I was on the ranch with Ranger Joe and a couple of his friends and they would break out their guitars and burst into song every so often. I never did any of that. This particular skit involved robbers who broke into the ranch house. I had a pet deer named Prancer, and as the outlaws broke in, I was supposed to dive in front of my deer and yell, "Shoot me, but don't shoot Prancer!" Well the outlaws came in, and off to the side of our set was the deer, who wouldn't move. The bandits came in with their guns blazing, and they are looking for the deer, and nobody said anything. So I jumped in front of this 300-pound cowboy named Cookie, who looked a lot like Hoss from Bonanza, but wasn't actually Dan Blocker, and yelled, "Shoot me, but don't shoot Cookie!"

The other one was a live commercial for the cereal where there was an off-camera announcer who said, "Johnny comes home from school." And I walked in through the backdoor. "And Johnny wants a snack. What does he want? He wants his Ranger Joe cereal." At which point I took a step stool, walked over to the cabinet, and pulled out the bag of Ranger Joe. But the bag wasn't opened, it was sealed. And I pulled, and I tore, and the bag just would not open. And the announcer was dead silent, because he didn't know what to say. Finally I ripped the bag open with my teeth and cereal flew all over the studio. The announcer burst into laughter and the screen went blank. But that was live television.

I also got some bit parts in movies that were filmed locally. I was an extra in the Cecil B. DeMille movie "The Greatest Show on Earth", a wonderful film that won the Academy Award for Best Picture in 1952 and had a celebrated cast that included Charlton Heston, Cornel Wilde, Dorothy Lamour, Jimmy Stewart and Betty Hutton. Some of the circus scenes were shot at Old Lighthouse Field in Philadelphia and I had a part where I was just a kid in the crowd. Because my mind was still on sports, I always brought my ball and glove with me wherever I went, and I didn't know anything about movie stars then. There was this nice guy who played a clown in the movie and during the lunch break he would have a catch with me. One day my mother saw us and asked me, "Do you know who that was you were having a catch with?" I said yeah, "He's my friend, he plays a clown in the movie." She said, "That's Jimmy Stewart." To me he was just a nice guy, with a pretty good arm, who wanted to have a catch.

I would have never thought this at the time, but all the live work, the commercials, the acting, really helped me. It taught me how to somehow avert disaster, which can often happen during a broadcast. There are times when you have technical problems, or you just have to fill dead air. Even the dramatic lessons, which I never wanted to do, probably helped me learn to express myself in a way that my emotions could come through. I could be emphatic, or enthusiastic, and let that show from a vocal standpoint.

In any event, by the time I was 11 or 12, my acting career ended. We weren't in Hollywood where there was filming all the time. And the need for teenagers, or preteens, wasn't as great as it was for child actors. And believe me, I didn't mind giving it up. As much as it may have helped me, I could finally go back to playing in the alley, pretending to be Reds Bagnell, and listening to my heroes on the radio.

It was also right around that time that I realized I wasn't going to grow to be 6-foot-3, and I did not have the ability to become the football star I wanted to be. So what was the next best thing, I wondered. I would be a broadcaster. What could be better than that? So that became my dream.

I listened to every Phillies game from spring training to the end of the season. Gene Kelly was their main announcer. He was a huge man, about 6-foot-8, and had become a local celebrity. You could turn on the radio and when you heard Gene Kelly's voice you knew if the Phillies won or lost. I just loved listening to him.

Every year the Phillies had a contest through one of the sponsors, a junior sportscaster contest. You had to write in 100 words or less why you wanted to be a sportscaster. The top 10 finalists would be brought to Connie Mack Stadium and would be put in a booth to actually tape part of a game. The best one out of the 10 would then get to do one actual inning of a Phillies game with Gene Kelly.

For about six years, I would get all excited and I would write why I wanted to be a sportscaster. It would be the best letter I could write, and every day I would run home from school and check the mailbox to see if I had won. I never won. I never even got to be a finalist. One of the finalists one year was Phil Jasner, a friend of mine, who has been the *Daily News* beat writer for the 76ers for almost 20 years. And the winner of the contest another year was a kid from Harrisburg named Andy Musser, who of course later became a Phillies broadcaster.

One year I finally got frustrated enough and I wrote a personal letter to Gene Kelly before the season started. That summer I received a letter postmarked St. Louis. I had no idea what it was. Who did I know in St. Louis? When I opened it, I was stunned. It was from Gene Kelly. Obviously he sent it to me from a road trip, when the Phillies played the Cardinals. I cherished that letter. I still have it, believe it or not. In it he told me how to prepare myself properly. He used an old quote that he attributed to Branch Rickey: "Luck is the residue of hard work."

That letter was the greatest inspiration to me. I carried that letter around with me wherever I went. That Gene Kelly actually wrote me a letter was mind-boggling to me. It made such an impression on me that in my high school yearbook under ambition it read, "wants to be a sportscaster like Gene Kelly."

When I was in college I worked on the radio station, WRTI, and we had a banquet at the end of each year. My freshman year, the speaker at our banquet was Gene Kelly, who had just been fired by the Phillies. I was chosen to be the sports director, which I didn't know about until Gene Kelly read it during his announcements. I almost passed out. Not just because I had gotten the position that I wanted, but because it was announced to me by him.

Moments later, I had what I call my defining moment. I began to see what life was all about. I went up to Gene and, in my naivete, asked him how he thought the Phillies would do this year. And he turned to me, and I remember this like it was yesterday. He said, "To be honest with you, kid, I don't worry about the Phillies. I worry about Gene Kelly. And besides, I root for people, not teams." I couldn't believe this. Wasn't his whole life the Phillies? Didn't he live and die with the Phillies like I did? I was hurt. I was crushed. Those statements ruined that night, which should have been a great night, for me.

Eventually, years later I realized that what he told me was what so many of us feel when we start to analyze and look at our jobs and what we're around.

My path would cross with my idol, Gene Kelly, one more time. One last time. I had just come out of the Navy, as a naval public affairs officer, and I was looking for a job. After the Phillies fired him, Kelly had gone to Cincinnati where he broadcast the Reds games for a few years. But he moved back to the area as the sports director of a new television station, Channel 48.

I went to see him, and while he couldn't give me a paid job, he let me help him. How did I help him? I drove him places. He had been injured and wasn't in great health at the time, and I became his driver. I would pick him up at Channel 48 and drive him to the airport to pick up video. Or I would take him to the stadium for a game. And while I never got paid, I learned from him. He would tell me stories as I drove, and I would pick up on his wisdom.

One day, a rainy day, we got stuck on the expressway in a traffic jam. I was tired, we were caught in traffic, and Gene Kelly looked over at me and said, "Who would have ever thought that me, Gene Kelly, would need a ride from you Merrill Reese, a nothing."

I'll never forget those words. At that point I drove him back to Channel 48. I said good-bye and never saw him, or spoke to him, again. That was how my relationship with Gene Kelly ended. Can you imagine what that did to me at that point? It was like a building toppled on my head. My hero, the man I wanted to be like, had just called me a nothing.

That was also kind of how I felt when I went to high school at Overbrook High, where Wilt Chamberlain had been a basketball star years earlier. I was younger than most of my classmates, because somewhere along the line I had been skipped a year. Still I had fostered hopes of making the basketball team. As much as I liked football and baseball, basketball reigned in Overbrook Park where we now lived. We played in the Lamberton Schoolyard before school, during lunch, and after school.

I felt there was no reason I wouldn't be able to make the varsity team as a 10th grader. So, with all the confidence from my days on the schoolyards, I went out for the team. The first time the coach put me in, we were having a scrimmage, I took a pass at the right of the key and fired a 15-foot jumper. Swish. I looked over at the coach, Paul Ward, and he wasn't even looking. He was talking to some guy. The next time down court, I found someone cutting toward the basket, fed him with a perfect pass for an easy layup. I looked over and Paul Ward had yet to look in my direction. I felt then I might be fighting a losing battle. The next day the list came out and it read: The following will return to practice. My name wasn't on it. My dream of playing basketball for Overbrook High lasted one day.

I realized then that basketball players at Overbrook were recruited from all around the city. There were tryouts, but the team was picked in the summer. Three of our five starters that year eventually made it to the NBA, Wayne Hightower, Walli Jones and Walt Hazzard. It was just an incredible school for basketball.

High school wasn't a particularly special time for me, however. There are probably several people who went to school with me who didn't even know I was there. I was quiet. I didn't get involved with the student council, or any of the drama clubs. I did my work, got decent grades, and I sat in the classroom and day-dreamed a lot about becoming a broadcaster. My friends would laugh at me when I told them that's what I was going to do. And even though my self-confidence wasn't extremely high, that was the one thing I knew I was going to accomplish. I knew I was going to fulfill my dream.

Maybe it's because when I was four years old, five years old, six years old, I would come into the house in tears. Kids would tease me and tell me Merrill was a girl's name. And I would cry and ask my mother, "Why couldn't you have named me Bobby, or Billy, or Mike? Why did you name me Merrill? And she said, "I named you Merrill, because it's a good name. And one day Merrill Reese is going to be famous."

Me and the Coz

Like the slogan says, I could have gone anywhere, but I chose Temple.

Seriously, my father had died suddenly my senior year of high school, and I really didn't want to go too far from home. Temple had a good communications program and that was what my major was going to be. This was my career path; I wanted to be a broadcaster. Specifically, I wanted to be a sportscaster.

Communications was becoming a popular major and I was one of a large class that year at Temple. We all came in with stars in our eyes. We were all going to be the next Bill Campbell, or the next By Saam, or so we all thought.

I did what I was supposed to do and tried to get on the student station, WRTI. There was both an AM station and an FM station at the time. The FM station, 90.1, you could hear throughout the city. The AM station was basically wireless and went to the dorms and that was about it. You left the campus and you were out of the range of the station. There were a couple of freshmen who were thought to be more mature and had more ability, and they would make the FM station. Of course, I was on the AM station.

I would come in every Wednesday with my box of 45 rpm records and introduce each record as I played them. What I really wanted to do was sports, but at least I was doing something. The sports director at WRTI-FM was a senior named Tom Cardella and I'm sure I followed him around enough and bothered him enough that finally late in the spring, tired of my nagging him, he let me do a Temple-Villanova baseball game. Truth is he probably couldn't find anyone else who wanted to drive all the way out to Villanova to broadcast a baseball game into a tape recorder. They didn't have what we call broadcast lines then.

So I brought my big, old, reel-to-reel tape recorder that weighed about 60 pounds and had all kinds of extension cords and I set up along the first-base line and got ready to do the game. And, of course, I was nervous as I could be. I was scared to death. It was my first chance to do a live play-by-play game. Temple had a pitcher named Don Flynn. And the first thing I said was, "I look down and I see Don Mound warming up on the Flynn." With that start I was off and running. There was no way I was going to miss.

But that got me immersed into the sports world. For some reason, Tom took a liking to me and let me do a sports show, and more and more games. By the end of my freshman year, I was named the sports director. Tom had graduated and I was his replacement. Years later, Tom and I remain close friends and he hosts both the Eagles' pregame and postgame shows on WYSP.

Another thing happened that summer between my freshman and sophomore year; my voice had dropped about three octaves. I sounded significantly different than I did the year before. People often ask me, "How does that voice come out of that body?" Of course on the air I'm more emphatic than I am when I ask my wife, "What's for dinner?" Although there have been times when I've come home from a game, still pumped up, and Cindy will ask me about something. I start to answer her, and she will interrupt and say, "Merrill, you're not on the air, you're home."

That fall I had to get ready for Temple football. There was a pep rally that was being held at the Sullivan Library on campus and that was a good opportunity to get involved with the team. The cheerleaders were there, the band was there, and as the players were being introduced, they announced a fullback who got up and talked. And before you knew it this guy had the entire crowd in hysterics. He told outlandish stories and outrageous jokes that just had everyone crying from laughing so hard. That was the first time I laid eyes on Bill Cosby.

Bill was also a sophomore, but he was older. He had been out of school, in the military for a few years, and then came back to Temple. I remember I asked him that day if he would like to do a radio show with me. We could tape it Fridays, and it would air that night, and again right before the game as sort of a pregame show. We would call it the Bill Cosby Show.

Bill agreed and we did it every Friday. More times than not the show would end with me laughing uncontrollably as he would just take off on some story or another. We would always start off talking about Temple football and the upcoming game, but Bill would then go off in another direction and tell another of his incredible stories. He was just so funny. He didn't need a script, or writers. He was just naturally funny.

It wasn't hard to see then that his future was in comedy, not in football. He was a decent fullback on a decent Temple team, and he was a good athlete. He was also a high jump champion. But he was a comic genius. You could tell that about him the moment you met him. I was not the least bit surprised when he made it as big as he did in the entertainment business. I often wonder if he was surprised that I eventually became the Eagles' play-by-play man.

The following season, our junior year, Bill got suspended from the team. Temple had played a game at Hofstra, on Long Island, and that night Bill was scheduled to do a show in New York City at Catch a Rising Star, a club for young, aspiring comedians. He convinced the bus driver to let him off in New York on the way home. But because of some insurance regulation that every player must return with the team, he was suspended. Not long after that, he decided to leave school.

We had lunch together before he left and I tried to talk him out of it. I told him what a mistake he was making, and how important it was for him to get his degree. He told me he was leaving. He said that he had thought about it for a long time, even before the suspension, and had made up his mind. He wasn't a kid. He was probably in his mid-20s by then, and he felt his future was in entertainment and the time was now. I pleaded with him, but he didn't listen. He left, and by that summer he was appearing on "The Tonight Show" with Johnny Carson. So it was probably a good thing he didn't take my advice. Later, after he became a success he did finish school and even got his Masters degree.

Our paths crossed occasionally after that. He really got into tennis and I got together with him a few times in 1974 when I was involved with the Philadelphia Freedoms. We were together once in Houston, and a couple of times he called when he was back in Philadelphia and we would go out and play tennis. Another time he was at an Eagles game and he stopped by the broadcast booth and went on with us for a few minutes.

With my pre-game partner gone, I was alone, but back at it. I broadcast Temple football and Temple basketball and anything else they would let me do. Ron Herman, who became a very good friend of mine, helped me with my practice broadcasts at South Hall and mostly carried the 60-pound tape recorder around for me.

My junior year, Temple's basketball team began the season 7-0 and was about to play the University of Kentucky in Lexington. WRTI had never done a road game before, but we decided because of the magnitude of the game, both teams were in the top 10, we would try. I went to the Temple Alumni Association to see if we could get financing for the trip and they said sure. I mean this was a big game. And if we didn't go, it wouldn't have been heard anywhere in Philadelphia. There was no ESPN back then, no national college game of the week, and no commercial station did Temple games. So my first road trip was set.

I was excited. This was going to be my first time on an airplane. But it snowed the night before we left and all the flights were cancelled. So instead we boarded a train for what would be a 26-hour train ride to Lexington. The train actually killed a person on the way there, hit a guy crossing the tracks, and that delayed the trip even longer. My color analyst was Phil Jasner, who also worked for the *Temple News*. What I still remember most about that trip was when I saw Harry Litwack, the legendary Temple coach, shaking hands at the morning shoot-around with the Kentucky coach, Adolph Rupp, the all-time legend and "The Man in the Brown Suit." And he was in that brown suit.

It hit me then that this was a part of history, and that as a broadcaster you can also be a part of that history. Very few people got a chance to see this kind of thing this close up and there I was a part of it. Temple lost the game, and we flew home the next day. But if I didn't have enough inspiration for my dream already, being there in Lexington and broadcasting that game just added fuel to my fire. This was what I was going to do the rest of my life. No doubt about it.

In the communications major, there was more than just the radio station. We had to take courses like radio drama, which really doesn't exist any longer. But we had this course, and for a project I produced a radio drama called "Wings that Couldn't be Clipped", the story of the 1960 Eagles. Did I have a one-track mind? I had one kid play Norm Van Brocklin and another kid play Chuck Bednarik, and I, of course, was the narrator. It was probably the worst thing ever put together.

But I remember that 1960 team so fondly, the last Eagles team to ever win a NFL Championship. I can never forget that team, or that season. A friend of mine, Elliott Alexander, and I drove out to the airport the night of December 4, 1960 to welcome the team back after they had beaten the St. Louis Cardinals, raised their record to 9-1, and clinched the Eastern Division Championship. Elliott and I thought it was going to be great. We would see the Eagles players up close. We were even going to pretend to be reporters and ask them questions about the game. When we got there, there were thousands of people already there. The place was mobbed. But we saw Van Brocklin, and Bednarik and Tommy McDonald all get off the plane. It was a sight. Who would have believed that 20 years later when the Eagles finally made it back to a Championship Game, Super Bowl XV, I would be on the plane with them, instead of a fan waiting in the airport.

I applied that year for a ticket to the Championship Game against the Green Bay Packers at Franklin Field. There was a lottery, and I was chosen. I got one ticket. And I went by myself, took a bus, and the subway, and walked, and sat in the farthest corner of the horseshoe at Franklin Field, one row from the wall. It was the end zone where Tommy McDonald scored his touchdown and slid into a snow bank. And I was there screaming as the Eagles beat the Packers, 17-13, and won what would be their last championship.

People talk about quarterbacks and all of the great ones, but I believe that in 1960, Van Brocklin was as great as any I've ever seen. He didn't have the arm strength of say, Randall Cunningham, or Dan Marino. He didn't run like Steve Young, or have the overall athletic ability of John Elway. But as a field general, as the total quarterback, he was unbelievable. He could look at a player with a glance and have the effect that a coach could have. He inspired the team around him. I never saw a quarterback do for a team what he did for the Eagles in 1960.

The following year my mother bought me a season ticket to the Eagles as a present. It was for seven games and it cost $35.00. Imagine that, a season ticket for $35.00. One ticket to one game cost more than that now.

Bill Campbell was the Eagles radio voice then and he was wonderful. When I think back, it's hard for me to believe that the Bill Campbell I listened to, and idolized, is now a close, personal friend of mine.

While I sat in my seat, with my friend Ron Herman, the same guy who carried the tape recorder around for me, I would every now and then focus my binoculars up on the booth and Bill Campbell. Sure I would watch the players, like everyone else, but at times I would move toward the radio booth and perhaps I dreamt a little bit. "Some day, some day, that's going to be me." I told myself.

The old saying goes that if you can dream it, you can be it, and I certainly did dream it. And it was a dream. Like most kids dream of hitting the game-winning home run, or scoring the game-winning touchdown, I was past that point by now. This was my dream. If you had asked me at that time if one day would I be broadcasting NFL games, I would have said yes, because I wanted it more than anything else in the entire world. And I was willing to make any sacrifices to achieve that. There wasn't anything that was going to hold me back. I felt like I wasn't going to be denied.

Now, if you asked me a few years later when I began searching for my first job if I was going to one day get there, the response would have been different. There were many, many days when I thought that this big dream was disappearing and that it was only a dream. And maybe it was time to put away childhood dreams and get on with my life.

From Pottstown to WIP

When I finished at Temple and ended my career on the college station, I was ready to conquer the world. I quickly found out I couldn't conquer Coatesville, Pennsylvania.

After a tour of duty in the Naval reserves, I was anxious to fulfill my dream of becoming a broadcaster. I was loaded with confidence and sent out enough resumes, I thought, that I would have my pick of jobs.

In between, I stopped at every television and radio station in Philadelphia, but the result was always the same. I could not get past the receptionist's desk. I could not even get an interview, never mind a job. The best I got was an application form that probably went straight to a wastepaper basket.

That confidence I had began to wane. It had been a while since I had actually been on the air and I began to wonder if I could still do it. Maybe Gene Kelly was right. Maybe I was a nothing.

As I was growing up every summer was spent in Ventnor, a small suburb just outside of Atlantic City where my mother and her four sisters shared a beach house. This summer I was down there again and an old friend of mine, Steve Berger, had a show on WOND radio that he did from a booth in front of the old Steel Pier. He was on every night from 11 o'clock to one in the morning. I would sit in the shore house every night and listen to the Phillies game on the radio and take notes. I'd also copy down all the rest of the baseball scores around the league. Then, every night at 11:30

and 12:30 Steve would let me come on and give five minutes of sports news. My family thought this was my job, and I never told them I wasn't getting paid a dime to do this. I'm not even sure the station knew I was doing this. And if they did, what did they care? They were getting a guy to come on and do five minutes of sports and they weren't paying him.

That's how it went almost the entire summer. I would play tennis every day and try to get in as many tournaments as I could. I would listen to Phillies games at night and do my five-minute sports shows. Then I would go out to eat at an all-night restaurant called Sambo's with Steve and a friend of his, some guy named Gene Hart, who wanted to talk about hockey all the time. Gene continued to talk about hockey and became the legendary voice of the Flyers.

My grandmother was the only one down at the shore who seemed to be on to me. Every once and again, her hand would grab my hand and she would stuff a $10, or $20 bill into it. It was her way of saying, "I know you need the money." The rest of the family thought I was getting paid for my "sports job." As far as a real job was concerned, the prospects continued to grow dimmer. I had been out of the service for over a year now and people began to wonder. What was I going to do the rest of my life? I had the same questions. Maybe this dream of mine was just that, a dream. I especially felt that way after an interview with a radio station in Coatesville, Pennsylvania.

Jerry Rosset, another friend of mine who later became a producer at WIP and is now an attorney, heard about some job openings at WCOJ in Coatesville, a small town in Chester County. We got an appointment to meet with the owner of the station and drove out there on just a terrible, rainy day. We found the station, which was located on the second floor above a Pontiac dealership, and raced into the building and up the stairs. We were drenched. Jerry's glasses were fogged to the point he couldn't see, and he asked the receptionist if there were any paper towels. She pointed toward the towels a few feet away. Jerry stumbled over, reached down and picked up what he thought was a paper towel. Instead, it was one of those old mimeograph sheets of paper. I was not paying a lot of attention, trying to dry off myself, but I saw him wipe his glasses and his face with this paper and everything turned purple.

Now, the owner of the station, William Halperin walked out and Jerry reached out with his purple hand to shake hands with him. I was about ready to die at this point. As the two of them attempted to get clean, I went to audition in this booth. Halperin came out a few minutes after I was finished, and told me I wasn't ready and that I should start somewhere small. I wasn't ready for something this big, and he wasn't sure I ever would be. Jerry never even got an audition.

We walked back to the car, now oblivious to the pouring rain. If Coatesville was too big, what was smaller than Coatesville? Where should we go from there? Was it time to give up?

Ironically, about 10 years ago I was a speaker at a dinner to honor former Eagles coach Dick Vermeil, and at the end of the dinner, this little, older man came up to me and said, "Merrill, my name is William Halperin, and I just wanted to say I was wrong."

Just about when I was ready to believe what Halperin told me, Tom Cardella, my old friend from Temple, heard that a station in Pottstown was looking for somebody to do high school football games every Saturday afternoon. Why not? Let's give it a try. We drove out to Pottstown, another small Pennsylvania town not far from Valley Forge, and met with the owner of WPAZ, Herb Scott. By this time, I had heard "no" so often my confidence was shot. Herb Scott looked at me and said, "I'd give you a shot to do the games, but you look like you might have a nervous breakdown."

On the way home, Tom told me I had to get tougher. I needed to get my confidence back. He said I could do this, but I needed to believe in myself again. That Friday I got a phone call from Herb Scott and he said he couldn't find anyone to do this game. It was either me or dead air. Those were his exact words. So much for the confidence booster I sought. So Tom and I went out that Saturday afternoon and did a Pottsgrove/Springford High School football game and split quarters. Tom did play-by-play and I did color for two quarters and I did play-by-play and Tom did color for two quarters. We made it through, and by the end of the game I felt pretty good again. It was the best I felt since I left college.

Monday, Herb Scott called back and said he wanted to meet with me. He wanted to hire me full-time. The guy they had, the one full-timer, had just joined the service and there was an opening. I said sure, and he said, "Great, can you start tomorrow, Alan?" And I said, "Excuse me, Mr. Scott, that's Merrill, Merrill Reese." He said, "No, I don't like Merrill. Let's use your middle name, Alan, you'll be Alan Reese on this station." At that point he could have called me Betty Reese, it wouldn't have mattered. The job paid $65 a week, and until they got a Sunday person, I would work seven days a week. And for about six months, I worked seven days a week.

I started every morning at 10 o'clock and worked until 4:30 in the winter, and until 7:30 in the summer. I did just about everything. We had a newsman, but there were times I filled in for him, or he would leave me the news. One of my first assignments was a fire engine parade from nearby Collegeville. It was two hours, and for those two hours I described fire engines. I was trying to figure out different ways to say, "Here comes another red one."

But the motto of that station was, "If it's sold, it's on the air." There was a time around Christmas when the station had so many commercials that I counted them, and we had 63 minutes of commercials that had to go on in the span of one hour. I asked Herb, "How could we do this? There's more commercial time, than actual time." He said, "Read fast." The station made money, that was certain.

Another show I did was called Highland Garden of Memories, which was a local cemetery. They would play organ music in the background and I would read death notices over the air. They say everything in your life prepares you for something, that everything is a learning experience. And I have to tell you that the organ music and death notices eventually prepared me to describe the last seven games of the Eagles 1994 season.

My sports work there, other than the few high school football games I did when I first started, was Little League baseball. We did a game almost every night. And, of course, the game was always sponsored, which is why we did it. One night, I was at the ballpark and the clouds opened, the thunder roared, and it started to pour and it didn't stop. I went to the phone, called the station, and told them there wasn't going to be a game. It was rained out. Whoever it was at the station that night told me, "There has to be a game. It's already sponsored." I went back to the stands, sat there in the rain, by myself, and made up a game. I have to tell you there were a lot of 1-2-3 innings and the final score was 1-0.

I lasted there 11 months before I heard about a station called WBCB in Levittown, Pennsylvania; Bucks County. The station was looking for a newscaster and it seemed like a better job. I auditioned there and it went well. They offered me the job, and I told them I was making more than I really was in Pottstown and I needed at least $100 a week to start. They offered me $102.50, and I thought I had just pulled off a major coup. When you hear about the terrific signing bonuses football players get today—well none of them could have felt as good as I did when I walked out of there with a $102.50

salary. I was on top of the world. And best of all, I could go back to being Merrill Reese again.

One of the things I got to do at WBCB was President Nixon's 1968 campaign, when it swung through Bucks County. There was also a famous murder case in Levittown that gained national attention and some of my reports made it to the big stations. I stayed in Levittown for 22 months, and along the way still found my share of disappointment. I auditioned for a job at KYW radio in Philadelphia, and was told by their news director, Reginald Laite, that I did not have the sound they were looking for. That I didn't have the sound that was needed in a major market. He told me if I wanted to stay at a small station, that was fine. But I'd never make it to a larger market. Again, I was crushed. I thought after Pottstown and Levittown that I was ready, that my dream was alive, and then I was told again that I was nothing.

Back in Levittown, I went back to work, but lacked the enthusiasm I had before. Don Kirby, the station manager, noticed something was wrong and asked me about it. I told him what Laite said and he shook his head and told me that was just one man's opinion. He said everyone there thought I was doing great and that all the feedback he had gotten was positive. He told me not to get down, that one day I would make it.

Finally Rick Friedman, who worked part time at WBCB with me, had gotten a job in the city at WWDB. Rick called me and told me there was an opening and asked if I would be interested. I was, and I was hired. I wasn't there yet, but at least I was nearby. WWDB was an FM station that was in the same building and had the same ownership as another station, WHAT, which was a rhythm and blues station. I would do the news for both stations. It was kind of unique, because I would sit in the same booth and read the news rather conservatively for WWDB, and then without moving, I would read the news with this uptempo style for WHAT.

What I wanted was to do was a sports show, but every time I asked, I was told they weren't interested in a sports show. Finally, I offered to do a sports show for the station on my own time. I wouldn't be paid extra. All of a sudden it was a good idea. So I did a five-minute sports show every morning at 7:30 and again at 4:30. I didn't care that I wasn't paid. I just wanted to get involved in a sports show.

Most of the disc jockeys at WHAT were African-American. One who I became friends with was Sonny Hopson, who was very close to a lot of the local black athletes. You never knew who might stop in at the station to just hang out with Sonny. Dick Allen, the Phillies big-time power hitter, was always dropping by and the two of us became friendly as well. There was a time when Allen was supposedly AWOL from the team and nobody knew where he was, and he was with us at the station. I was actually quoted in a *Philadelphia Bulletin* story saying that I had seen Dick that day, and he was around.

Another player who often stopped by was Herb Adderly, the one-time All-Pro for Green Bay and Dallas, who lived in the area during the offseason and still does. Adderly actually told me, right after Vince Lombardi retired, that he was not going back to Green Bay and was going to demand a trade. I asked him if I could report this. He said, "Sure." And I broke the story that Herb Adderly wanted out of Green Bay and was going to be traded.

I enjoyed what I was doing. I would get to go to some games. But it appeared that my career had hit its peak. It wasn't my dream, but it wasn't bad. It was broadcasting, but it wasn't play-by-play. Al Shrier, the Temple sports information director whom I remained friends with after I had graduated, called me one day and told me WIP was looking for a summer replacement for Charlie Swift, the Eagles' play-by-play man and the station's sports director. Swift had gotten a lot of vacation time and took it all at once in the summer before the football season started. I figured I had nothing to lose, why not give it a shot?

I called Dean Tyler, who was the program director at WIP, and he set up an interview/audition for me. Dean was honest with me, and told me everyone in the city and some outside of the city wanted this job. WIP was the epitome. I remember when I was in college we used to pretend we were on WIP. That was where you wanted to be. WIP was the New York Yankees. They were the No. 1 station in Philadelphia and had the No. 1 profit margin in the country. It was the big time.

I had my audition, and a few months went by and I didn't hear anything. I figured it was just another rejection. Then around the beginning of April, I got a call from Dean Tyler's secretary asking me if I could come back for a second interview. I did, and again I heard nothing. Finally, around the beginning of June I got another call and I went back for a third time. I was sitting in the lobby when Charlie Swift, himself, walked by. He called me over and started to tell me things like, "Here's where I want my mail. And when you go on at 6:30..." He could probably tell by the puzzled look on my face, but he stopped and said, "Didn't anybody tell you? You got the job."

I couldn't believe it. I was prepared to give up my full-time job at WWDB just to work the summer at WIP. But when I went back to WWDB, they said it was OK. I could do both. I gave up my morning sports at WWDB. But I worked the mornings at WIP. I would get there around 4 o'clock and go on the air with the sports at 6. I would then update the sports at 7, 8, and 9. In between I would plan for the next day. I taped interviews, whatever had to be done. I would leave WIP at 11, drove down the Expressway to WWDB, and do the news from noon to eight. Then I would go home and collapse from exhaustion.

The morning man at WIP was one of the most famous broadcasters in the history of the city, Ken Garland. He had the No. 1 ratings. Everyone listened to him. He was the media star in the city. Just the thought of working with him was enough to make me nervous, and of course I was a nervous wreck. Everything I had worked for, everything I had ever wanted, was here. I was going to work at WIP. All I could think to myself was, "Don't blow it now."

I mean there I was 25 yards away from Ken Garland, the most powerful man in radio. One word from Ken Garland to a station manager could make you or break you. If Garland didn't like you, you could be taken off the air in a second. What if Ken Garland thought about me the same way that Reginald Laite did? I would be finished. But all I know is when that light went on, I did my sports and I let it all out. I did it at a fever pitch, full of enthusiasm, I gave it everything I had. And as I said, "I'm Merrill Reese. It's 6:05 and it's time for the Ken Garland Show." Ken came on without an opening and the first words he said were, "Wow. If I'm Charlie, I'd hurry back from vacation." That was the greatest endorsement I had ever gotten.

Within the next few weeks, before Charlie got back from vacation, Dean Tyler had asked me if I would be interested in doing the Eagles' pregame and postgame shows. That was like asking a kid if he would like to be locked in a candy store overnight. It took all of about a second for me to say yes.

I began to do the shows in the preseason of 1972 and before long I was asked if I would also do the Ed Khayat Show every Monday night. Khayat was the Eagles head coach, who had taken over for the fired Jerry Williams early in the 1971 season. That coach's show proved to be one of the most important things I ever did in my career.

It was a terrible year for the Eagles in 1972. They finished 2-11-1 and Khayat was fired at the end of the season. You can say what you want about Ed, but he was a great man. I mean a truly good human being. People would call with questions on the show and he would answer whatever the question was. He even did the show the day after he was fired. It was up to him. He was fired that morning and he could have easily said, "Forget it I just got fired, I'm not going to do a show." But we did the show, and it was fiery. The callers were tough. They called him everything you might imagine. And he took it all, and never said anything against the organization. Over that one year, the two of us became pretty close.

Mike McCormack was hired to replace Khayat, and he was the hot assistant coach that year. He was on George Allen's staff with the Redskins, and he was a former All-Pro lineman before that. So there was excitement as the Eagles headed into the 1973 season. I was still doing the pregame show and the postgame show. But you could feel that there was a sense of excitement around the team. Roman Gabriel was the quarterback and the Eagles had what they called the Fire High Gang, led by wide receiver Harold Carmichael and tight end Charle Young. McCormack went just 5-8-1 that first year, but the team had shown improvement. The following year the Eagles went 7-7 and won their last three games.

There was a player's strike before the 1975 season, and that tore the team apart. Gabriel, who was the team's leader, the player they called The Messiah, crossed the picket line during the strike and it ripped the team apart. Ironically, compared to the way Buddy Ryan held his team together and brought it together during the strike of 1987, McCormack's team was ripped apart by the strike of 1975. It was never the same for him after that, and he was fired at the end of a dismal 4-10 season.

During that '75 season there was one incident that I feel I have to mention. It was after a terrible 42-3 Monday Night loss to the Rams. It was the most one-sided Monday Night game ever. The day after the game, McCormack was asked at his press conference by Tom Brookshier, the former Eagles player and then a television man, "How many dogs do you have on this football team?" McCormack said, "I don't have any dogs. I'm not calling anybody a dog." Brookshier came back and asked, "You know, guys who aren't giving everything they have." McCormack answered the way most coaches would, but never called the team dogs. The next day the headline was "McCormack Calls Team Dogs." If it wasn't over for McCormack before that, it was then. The players did quit. His control was gone.

For me, things were going a lot better than they were for the Eagles. In 1974, I became the play-by-play man and director of communications for the Philadelphia Freedoms, the World Team Tennis Franchise that played its season from May to August. I also did a show with Billie Jean King and telecast the games on Channel 29. I kept my job with WIP doing the Eagles' pregame and postgame shows as well as other part-time work, but eventually had to give up WWDB.

My old friendship with Ed Khayat paid off for me in huge dividends the final game of that 1974 season. Khayat had become an assistant coach with the Detroit Lions and they were in town to play the Eagles. The Saturday night before the game, I got a telephone call at home. It was Ed and he wanted to know if I wanted to get together at the Marriott Hotel for dinner. Sure, I thought, it would be great to see Ed again and talk some football with him. I never imagined how important this dinner would be. We ate, had a couple of drinks, and talked, mostly about football and his team, the Lions, and how they were playing. And I asked him questions, just because I wanted to know. And he told me everything about every player. It was great. I was a fountain of knowledge on the Detroit Lions.

The next day as I got ready to go to the station to do the pregame show, the phone rang again. This time it was Dean Tyler. He said, "Don't go to the station. Al Pollard (Charlie Swift's color analyst and a former Eagles player) is sick. He might not be able to make the game. Could you do the color?" I told him, "Sure." I sat there for a half hour and it felt like two days. Dean called back and said, "Go to the stadium. Al is too sick to do the game."

This was it. My first chance in the booth and, of course, I was nervous. But so was Dean Tyler. This was his call. All he knew was I could do a good sportscast, he didn't know if I could do color or not, and frankly, neither did I. About a minute before air time, Dean said, "Are you set?" And I said, "Just one thing, is it still three for a field goal?" We all laughed and then off we went. But I really did a good job, because I had just spent hours with the Detroit assistant coach who told me everything I needed to know about the team. I said some things that people couldn't believe I knew.

In the spring of 1975, WWDB called me and asked me if I would come back. The station went to an all-talk format and wanted me to be the sports director. The Freedoms folded after their one year of existence, and the offer was too good to pass up. I added one stipulation. I wanted WWDB to add some football so I could do play-by-play. They picked up the University of Pennsylvania, which happened to be coached by Harry Gamble, who would eventually become the President of the Eagles. And my spotter that year was a very quiet kid, who never had much to say, named Howard Eskin.

Right before the 1976 season, Al Pollard told WIP he was tired of being the color analyst. He had started a business, and it was going well and he wanted to spend more time with that. The station called me, and I fully believe it was because of that one game in 1974, and offered me the color job. There was no doubt in my mind I got that job because of the dinner I had with Ed Khayat that night before the game.

A Swift Tragedy

There were all kinds of expectations in 1977, both for me and the Eagles. Dick Vermeil was in his second year as head coach. He had just acquired quarterback Ron Jaworski in a major trade, and I was the new color analyst.

Twelve games into what turned out to be another losing season for the team, my dream finally came true. Except it was more of a nightmare.

We had just gotten back from Dallas after a 24-14 loss dropped the Eagles to a dismal 3-9 in a season that was expected to be a lot better. As on most trips, Charlie and I sat together on the plane ride home. We talked about the game and the season. We were kind of happy that it was almost over, and that the last two games of the season were both at home. We got off the plane, and I said, "See you next week, Charlie." He said, "Sure kid."

Except I never saw Charlie again.

Wednesday morning about 3:30 my phone rang. I got up around 4:30 every morning anyway, because I was still doing the morning show at WWDB. So it wasn't that strange to get a call at that time. It could have been someone at the station. Sometimes they would call me to just to make sure I was awake. This time it was Tim Early, a good friend of Charlie's. He said, and I'll never forget his words, "Merrill, Tim Early, Charlie's dead."

Those five words repeated over and over in my head and I couldn't believe it. He said it again, "Charlie's dead. He killed himself." I was shook. I still couldn't believe those words I heard. It couldn't be true. Tim went on to give me the details. Charlie shot himself in the head. His wife had found him in their apartment. This was just unbelievable. How? Why? There were a million things going through my mind and none of it made any sense. I got up, got dressed, and drove into WWDB. I wrote a piece dedicated to Charlie and read it on the air. It went like this.

"I've never had a sledge hammer hit me in the heart, but I know what it feels like. I found out suddenly this morning when I learned of the death of Charlie Swift, my partner on the Eagles broadcasts, and the sports director of WIP. I was saying to some people just the other day, as a matter of fact I was bragging, that in our Eagles broadcast booth there is no tension. That there was a feeling of friendship and warmth and most of all respect that existed all the time, not just when the mike was turned on. When I came out of college I had a lot of promises from a lot of people. They were all going to open doors and pave the way to great success. But promises were made by many people as a demonstration of their importance. There was never any intention of keeping them.

"Charlie Swift never made any promises. He wasn't a man of idle words. But when he said something you knew he meant it. In a business of professional personalities, Charlie was something greater. He was sincerity, on the air and off the air. You didn't automatically become Charlie Swift's friend. You earned his friendship. And when you earned it you had it for life. He was a loyal person. He was imbedded with old world virtues like loyalty, devotion, dedication, honesty. When he didn't like something you knew it immediately. His eyes became steel gray and you were quickly and emphatically told exactly what and why. But when he did like something there was a glowing joy he exuded. He didn't have to say a thing.

"Six years ago I was selected by WIP to fill in for Charlie as his summer replacement. As the time approached I worried because, while our philosophy was the same, our delivery styles varied greatly. If you round up 100 sports directors and find out what they tell their substitutes, it would probably go something like, keep it straight, just read the stories and give the scores. That wasn't the case with this guy, because Charlie Swift had no insecurities about his own abilities, none whatsoever. He left me with these words and even this morning they echo through my ears. 'Do things your way. Don't try to be me or anyone else. We hired you, because we like your work. So come on strong and don't stop.' That carried right into last summer before my first Eagles broadcast. He gave me confidence. In fact, he pounded it into me. Not that I didn't believe I could do that job, but when the number one man tells you that he's 100 percent behind you . . . the rest is easy.

"Charlie Swift set an example with his own meticulous preparation. I've seen people, believe me I have, who toss out a few cliches and ask "who's playing" off the mike. Not this guy. He came prepared with a solid background of the game, and his facts and figures and numbers and tendencies long under control. Play-by-play broadcasts aren't made on Sunday, they're made during the week with hour upon hour of preparation. Sunday is the day for fun, for using what you've learned. Charlie Swift, the person, was one of a kind. He enjoyed each day. He lived it to the fullest. He loved to laugh and when he did everyone felt good. He had the ability to bring happiness to a lot of people. He was a good listener and established a lasting rapport with so many athletes, not based on their on-field abilities, but on his feelings for them as human beings. When Charlie befriended you, you didn't have to keep scoring touchdowns to keep his friendship. When your playing days were over, the friendship didn't end. He was a man of depth, enormous depth and feeling and a love of people. That was who Charlie Swift was. Right now my hands are still cold. So are my feet. And my head is feeling very light. My heart is very heavy."

That's what I read on the air that morning. It was one of the worst mornings of my life.

Shortly after I was finished, I got a call from WIP. Bruce Holberg, who had replaced Dean Tyler as program director, wanted me to come down to the station. You know, it's strange, but from the moment Tim Early called me and told me about Charlie until the time Bruce Holberg called, I sensed that I was about to take over in the booth as the play-by-play man, but I never thought about it. I was in too much shock over the whole thing.

I had a good professional relationship with Charlie. I was deeply grateful to him. He was secure enough to allow another announcer, who basically at heart was another play-by-play man, in the booth. He could have easily stopped that. One word from him and I wouldn't have gotten the color job. He gave his approval. Charlie always treated me well. Off the air, Charlie was very quiet; he was a man of few words. And he was a little guy, about 5-feet-4 with a razor sharp crewcut, he looked like the quintessential marine. He just had that look. He rarely smiled, and his steel blue eyes looked right through you at times. Even on the air, his style was very sound, as sound as anyone I've ever been around. You sat next to him and watched him work and you picked up certain things. Just the way he set formations, or tracked the team as they came out of the huddle. He was not very emotional, not particularly dramatic, but he was solid, very solid. He gave you a very strong rendition of what happened on each play. He wasn't the kind of announcer who people mimicked. I wish I had a dime for every Merrill Reese impersonator. Stations have even had sound-alike contests. But there was nothing unusual about Charlie. His only catch-phrase, if you could call it that, was when he made a mistake he would say, "Check that," and give the correction. That was it. "Check that." And Charlie would always correct his mistakes. He told me once that during the course of a broadcast you say hundreds and hundreds of things, some aren't always going to be right. You can't be perfect.

And as much as he helped me and as much as I admired him, we weren't close friends, nothing like Stan and I became. We rarely went out to dinner together. We never had breakfast together. There were times when I wouldn't even see him from the time we arrived in a city until we got to the booth before the game. He went his way, and I went my way. Even during the week, we would occasionally bump into each other, but it was never more then for a moment.

All I could think about was, "Why did this happen? How could this happen?" as I drove over to WIP to meet with Bruce Holberg, who I really didn't know that well. He took over for Dean Tyler earlier that year and more or less inherited me. I had no idea how he felt about me.

Everyone at WIP that morning was in tears. People just wandered around with their heads down. This was a guy who everyone saw every day for the past 10 years, or so. And just like that he was gone. And the way it happened—nobody could have imagined that. There wasn't anyone I knew, or anyone around the station, who saw this coming.

I walked into Bruce's office and the first thing he said was, "We all feel badly, but we have a game on Sunday. Who's doing the color?" I took that to mean I was doing the play-by-play. You know, when I got the color job, I felt I would do it for a couple of years and then eventually land a play-by-play job somewhere else. Believe it or not I even got a letter once from KRLD in Dallas, who had gotten a tape I sent, it read that they would keep me in my mind if there was ever an opening. Can you imagine if I had ever been the voice of the Cowboys?

But I always wanted to be a play-by-play man. And I felt when that opportunity came it would be a time for rejoicing. I would have finally made it. Here, I was being told that I was about to do NFL play-by-play, my dream had come true, and it was under the worst possible circumstances.

That entire 1977 season was filled with that kind of roller coaster emotions. Personally, I couldn't wait until the season began. I had made it to the Eagles broadcast booth. I hadn't fulfilled my dream to be the play-by-play man, but as the color analyst I was as close as you could get.

All offseason I prepared like you wouldn't believe. I bought every football book on the market. I even got my hands on a real NFL playbook and read that to try and understand the game better. Remember, my only game in the booth came after an intense night of talking football with Ed Khayat. I couldn't count on that to happen every week. But I was going to train myself to know every technical aspect of the game. I wasn't a former player like a lot of analysts are, especially today, but I was going to know as much. I talked to every assistant coach during training camp and got them to tell me every aspect of their position. I would watch tape with them, actually it was film back then. I remember the first preseason game I did, it was a bus trip up to the Meadowlands against the Jets. The week before the game I made it a point to write three facts about every player on the roster. It was a strategy I kept for the rest of that season. Whenever a player did something, I would be able to spout off something about him. It sounded like an ad-lib, but really it was a thought-out plan.

The team had as high hopes as I did. Dick Vermeil was in his second year as head coach and you had the sense that after all the losing, 13 sub .500 seasons in the span of 16 years, maybe there was hope. There was faith in Vermeil. He had a certain charisma that made you think he was going to do well under any circumstances. The team had just engineered a major trade. They sent All-Pro tight end Charle Young to the Rams for a quarterback named Ron Jaworski.

Young and the Eagles had reached a stalemate in their contract talks, and it appeared it just wasn't going to get done. The agent was Howard Slusher, who had earned the nickname "Hold

'Em Out Howard" because of his tactical approach to contracts. At the same time, the Rams had not signed Jaworski yet, either. I didn't know a lot about Jaworski at the time of the trade. I had seen him a few times on television with the Rams, but that was it. He had a big-time arm, I knew that. That was how he got his nickname, the "Polish Rifle."

This was a big trade. Although back then it wasn't treated with the same media attention it would have gotten today. The beat writers who covered the team then kept everything pretty straight. It was like a wire report would be today. And the columnists didn't really make much of a big deal about it, either. Of course, there wasn't a 24-hour sports talk radio station around where callers got a chance to voice their opinions. If that kind of trade happened today, where an All-Pro tight end was traded for a strong-armed quarterback, you would have all kinds of opinions about it. Half the people would have loved it, the other half would have hated it. Back then everyone just accepted it.

Charle Young was a great player. He was the No. 1 draft pick out of Southern Cal in 1973, went to the Pro Bowl three straight years in 1974, 1975, and 1976. This was a special kind of player, a dominant kind of player. He might not have been as good a tight end as Keith Jackson became, but he was very good. And Vermeil traded him for a quarterback, who had basically been the Rams' backup. It was a bold move. But the Eagles still wouldn't have been to a Super Bowl if it wasn't for that move. People talk about all you need to win: a good defense, good corners, a good line; but what you really need is a quarterback. You have to have a good quarterback. And Jaworski was more than just a good quarterback, he was a leader. And that's what the Eagles needed.

Now as the season prepared to close, another losing season, I needed to find a color analyst. The first name that entered my mind was my old friend, Herb Adderly, who lived in Atlantic City. Herb had been retired for five years, after a brilliant 12-year career, nine with Green Bay and the final three in Dallas. And he had done some college games on WCAU, so he had experience in the booth. I called him and he said, "absolutely."

Herb and I actually drove out together to Delaware County for Charlie's funeral Friday morning. We never even talked about the game that week. Again, we were both still stunned at what had happened. That Saturday, the day before the game, I wanted to just stay at home and relax. But instead I went to the annual dog show at the Civic Center. I loved the dog show, and still do. It was a good way to take my mind off everything that had happened. I knew if I stayed home, I would have thought too much about Charlie and the game, and I would have cracked. So it was better for me to get out and do something and take my mind off it all. I came home that night and said to myself, "This is it." It was a horrible way to take over. And if there was any way I could have brought Charlie back, I would, and would have given up my dream in a second. It was just the worst possible circumstance you could have imagined.

And the moment for which I had geared my entire life was now less than 24 hours away.

It's My Job . . . For Now

The broadcast booth that Sunday morning, December 11, 1977, was very quiet. Everyone was there, our producer and my good friend Jerry Rosset, our statistician Jack Edelstein, my spotter Bill Werndl, and Herb. But it wasn't the way it normally is before a game. We were there to work that day, not to have fun.

My opening was not, "Hello, everybody welcome to the Eagles and New York Giants..." My opening was another tribute to Charlie Swift. And just before we went on, the public address announcer asked for a moment of silence and Charlie's name and picture went up on the scoreboard. All the Eagles players had been instructed to turn around and face the broadcast booth.

Every eye was now on me, as I was about to go on the air for the first time as play-by-play man. I can still feel the shakiness and the nervousness of that moment. My knees were clanging together like hammers against cold steel; I just hoped I could say something. I was as close to being speechless as I've ever been. My chest was a base drum and my knees were the symbols. Herb reached over and, with his left arm, squeezed my left shoulder. Just then Jerry tapped me on my right shoulder, which is the cue to start. And I began the tribute to Charlie.

"Good afternoon, everyone. This is Merrill Reese and today the Eagles meet the Giants here at Veterans Stadium. By now you all know of the untimely death of Charlie Swift. Charlie was the voice of the Eagles since 1969. He was admired and respected by so many people in sports and in broadcasting. He had thousands of fans in every walk of life. Charlie Swift was a warm, caring, compassionate human being who was more than a partner to me in this booth. He was a friend. Handling the color commentary today is another friend of Charlie's, a man we spoke about during last week's broadcast from Dallas. The former All-Pro defensive back of the Green Bay Packers and Dallas Cowboys, Herb Adderly. Herb, thank you for joining us."

And as I got to the last few words, I began to choke up, but I got through it and we went to a break. After the commercial we came back to the game, and I was fine. It was like I had picked up from my days as the Penn play-by-play man. I felt I belonged.

There were two things about the game that I remember most. There was an Eagles rookie, a returnman, who brought a kickoff back for his first NFL touchdown. That was Wilbert Montgomery, and I would go on to broadcast every touchdown of his career, all 58. Montgomery was traded to Detroit in 1985, but played just one season and never scored for the Lions. The other occurred late in the game. The Eagles trailed 14-10, but were down near the Giants goal line. Jaworski faked a handoff and bootlegged around left end for a touchdown, and the Eagles won, 17-14.

The following week was a messy day against the Jets. It just poured rain the entire day. It was the last game of the season between the 4-9 Eagles and the 3-10 Jets, and only 19,000 people bothered to come. The Eagles won 27-0 and ended the season with a two-game win streak.

I was on the same kind of roll. I had been complimented after both of my performances and had felt that I had done a good job. Of course, I was never too confident. I had learned early in this business never to assume anything. You often hear that a certain broadcaster is "so insecure." Well, in this business as I learned, you're never too secure. There isn't a broadcaster in this business who can't be replaced. We can all be replaced in the blink of an eye, and it's happened to some of the best.

I've always felt that I have to be at my best. And I knock on wood when I say this, but I've never missed a game (it's 339 straight, not counting preseason, going into the 1998 season). And I never intend to miss a game. I've worked sick. I've worked with a 103 temperature. I worked the 1992 playoff game in New Orleans, I don't know if I had food poisoning, or what, but I woke up green. I was so sick I don't know how I made it through that game. But I had eaten a Caesar salad the night before, and I've never had a Caesar salad again.

In 1985, Cindy was expecting our second child. Our son, Nolan, was born safely during the offseason of 1982. We had a Friday night preseason game at Ohio State. Earlier that day, I'll never forget it, the Eagles traded Wilbert Montgomery to Detroit for a linebacker named Garry Cobb.

I spoke to Cindy that day at home and she told me she was starting to feel some discomfort. I told her to hang on. We were flying home that night, and I would appreciate it if she could wait until tomorrow. As it turned out she didn't have the baby that day, or the next day. That night I told her, "Listen the season starts in two weeks, September 8. There's one more preseason game, Thursday night at home against Detroit. Have the baby any day in that two-week span, but Thursday."

Sure enough, Thursday morning I woke up to go do my morning show at WIP, and Cindy said, "Merrill, I think I'm having contractions." I said, "But it's Thursday." It didn't matter. This was it. I called Stan at home, because at times he would fill in for me doing the morning show. I told him Cindy was having the baby, and asked him if he could fill in for me. Fortunately, he could, and off I went to the hospital with Cindy. Ken Garland was on the air that morning, and announced that Cindy Reese was having a baby, so Stan Walters was filling in for Merrill Reese. Cindy called her doctor to tell him we were on our way and he said, "Where have you been? Ken Garland told the world you were having the baby. I've been waiting to hear from you."

Cindy packed her bag and I packed my bag, my briefcase, my green blazer for the game, and all the rest of my things. It looked like I had more stuff with me than she did. We got to the hospital, the doctor examined Cindy and said, "It looks like you'll have the baby some time this evening." Then, he looked at me and said, "Wait a minute. What time is the game, tonight? What time do you have to leave?" I told him I should leave the hospital around 3:30, or so. Cindy had a natural child birth with Nolan and planned to do the same this time.

The doctor said, "I'll give you a choice. I can break your water and give you Pitocin and an epidural, and Merrill I'll guarantee you're at the stadium on time." Cindy said, "Let's do it." At 3 o'clock Ida was born, I was there, and a half hour later I was on my way to the stadium. I announced her birth on the air before the game and that night, after the game, I went back and spent the night with Cindy and our new daughter.

It was close, but I've never missed a game. I've learned to work under all kinds of circumstances. You don't miss a game, because you live with the fear that they will like your replacement more than you. And that winter of 1978, the job was far from mine. Bruce Holberg called me in after the season, and let me know there were a lot of candidates. Believe it or not, they had over 100 applicants the week that Charlie died. There were resumes piling up in the offices before his funeral. All Bruce Holberg told me was, "You did a great job, and we're happy with you. But there are a lot of candidates. You're one of them, but there are a lot."

This was December. I heard nothing all through January and February. As each day passed, I got a little more nervous and a little less confident. It seemed every night I was having dreams about it. I can't tell you how many times I actually dreamt I had the job, and actually saw Bruce Holberg bringing me in and telling me the job was mine. And then I would wake up and feel so disappointed that it was just a dream. Conversely, there were many nights when I would dream that I didn't get the job and wake up the next morning and have a feeling of relief. I was so consumed that it was on my mind even while I slept. I not only didn't have any assurances that I was getting the job, I didn't have any assurances that I was going to get my old job back as the color analyst. There were no promises at all.

One day in March as I read the *Philadelphia Bulletin* I felt a terrible pain in the pit of my stomach. There was a column the paper ran on a regular basis by Bob Vetrone called Buck the Bartender. It was kind of an around the town sports notes column. One of his notes that day was, "Don't be surprised if a very familiar name resurfaces as the voice of the Eagles." My heart dropped. I knew that wasn't me. I wasn't that familiar and I wouldn't have to resurface.

That night I went to a college basketball game at the Palestra and I saw Bob there. I asked him, "Who is it?" He said, "I'll tell you, but please don't tell anyone. I just talked to Al Meltzer, and he told me he was offered the job."

Al Meltzer had been sports director at Channel 3. He had done Big 5 college basketball. Before that he had done the Buffalo Bills games on radio during O.J. Simpson's years. At that point, he was an anchor in Chicago. Some often wonder if Joe Piscopo, who was also in Chicago at the same time, didn't copy his sports bit from Al. But word was that Al wanted to come back to Philadelphia. I believe that WIP wanted a big name, and Al was a big name. Heck, he was, and still is, Big Al. He was a major name. If he was hired to come back as the voice of the Eagles, it would have gotten a major publicity news splash. Much bigger than Merrill Reese being hired.

I had this information and I didn't know what to do with it. I thought all night and came up with a plan. The next morning I went in to WIP. I went to the general manager Don Kelly's office. Don and I always got along. He was always very nice to me and very complimentary of my work. I told Don I was at the Palestra last night, and I heard from a security guard that Al Meltzer was coming back to do the Eagles games. As I said that, Don Kelly's eyes grew wide and he said to me, "Well, we made an offer to Al. There's a great sales value there. Al is supposed to get back to us. But since this is already out there, I'm going to press him for an answer by next week."

From what I believe, Al was also waiting to hear from Channel 10, which was thinking of hiring him as sports director. So Al was making WIP wait until he heard from Channel 10. Now he had to make a decision, and make a decision in the next week.

I was still working at WWDB doing a morning show with Wynn Moore, and Jack O'Reilly. Wynn read in the paper one day where the famous Troc, an old burlesque house which became a strip joint, was closing down. Wynn and Jack were talking about this and how they couldn't believe it. And I innocently asked, "What's the Troc?" They could not believe I had never heard of the Troc, or had never been to the Troc. Wynn had an idea. What if we purchased all the seats to the last two shows and we invited our listeners to come, and we showed you what the Troc was all about. He did it. He bought it out, and sold tickets to the listeners for $10 a ticket. He was swamped. He could have gotten $50 a ticket.

Wynn didn't stop there. He hired a band, a touring act, and a couple of strippers and they actually taught us some old vaudeville routines. They even had me sing "A Pretty Girl is Like a Melody" while one of the strippers performed. We did this for the two nights. After the first night, we brought 50 of the listeners with us after the show for a Chinese dinner down in Chinatown. I got home around 2:30 in the morning, and I still had to get up for the morning show. This turned out to be one of the most successful radio promotions of its time. And in between the two nights, the most successful moment of my life.

I finally fell deeply asleep Friday afternoon, even though I knew I had another show that night. The phone rang. I answered it groggily and it was Bruce Holberg and he said, "Merrill, we want you to be voice of the Eagles and sports director of WIP." And I said, "That's great." He said, "Can you come in Monday and sign the contract?" I said "How about now?" Monday, he said, was fine.

I was so excited. But I was physically exhausted and went back to sleep. Monday morning I went to WWDB and told them about the offer, and they kind of expected that I was going to get the job. Now as I drove down the expressway from WWDB to WIP, all of a sudden I broke into a cold sweat. What if it had been a dream? I was in such a deep sleep when he called me. And I had so many dreams about this. What if this was another dream? I had just quit my job and I had this awful feeling I was going to walk into Bruce Holberg's office and he was going to tell me the job wasn't mine. That Al Meltzer had decided to take it. Fortunately, when I got there it was real. I signed the contract and I was the Eagles play-by-play man. The dream, my real dream, had come true.

Dick Vermeil, Now And . . . Then

After 14 years of losing the same dinner bet to Stan, I finally won it when Dick Vermeil came back to become the head coach of the St. Louis Rams in 1997. I thought I had won it a couple of years earlier.

When Dick Vermeil announced his teary retirement at the end of the strike-shortened 1982 season, I told Stan he would come back and coach again. Stan, who had played for Dick for seven years, said, "No way."

But at the end of the 1994 Eagles season, it became pretty obvious that Rich Kotite was going to be fired by the team's new owner Jeffrey Lurie. Every owner would like to hire his own coach, and the fact that the Eagles fell apart that year and lost their final seven games just made it easier for Lurie.

Right before the last game of the season in Cincinnati on Christmas Eve, a story broke in the *Trenton Times* that the Eagles were interested in Dick Vermeil to come back and be their head coach and general manager. By game time it had been picked up everywhere, and Joe Banner, the team's vice president and Lurie's right-hand man, told me there was indeed some interest. He said the situation would be investigated. He would not tell me anymore than that.

The reason I thought Dick would some day be back on the sidelines, not necessarily with the Eagles but back in the league, was because he was born to coach. Some people are put on this Earth to do certain things, and I believed Dick Vermeil was put here to coach. I felt over the years he had become a pretty good broadcaster for ABC, but he was an outstanding coach. He was the quintessential coach. And I always felt he retired at much too early an age. Coaching wasn't something that you could get out of your blood that easily, and even though I was wrong for all those years, I was always convinced he would come back.

Vermeil had a chance in the late '80s to coach the Atlanta Falcons, but he turned them down. What I was told by Carl Peterson, Dick's good friend and the Kansas City Chiefs President and general manager, was that had Rankin Smith, the late Falcons owner, gotten Dick Vermeil to fly down there and meet with him, he would have not turned down the job. Instead, everything was done long distance. If Dick had been down there and walked around the stadium and gotten involved, I believed he would have taken the job.

Jeffrey Lurie had him in town and almost had him as his first head coach. Vermeil actually announced what appeared to be a tearful almost-good-bye on television to his partner, Brent Musburger, during the NFL playoff game they did that year. Musburger and Vermeil actually talked openly about the Eagles job, and Vermeil went on to say nice things about Lurie. It looked like the deal was all but done.

Then, suddenly, it broke down. There were some high monetary demands made by Vermeil's agent, and some issues of control that got involved, which seemed to kill the deal. But after it apparently died, it flared up again on a Thursday night. According to reports, the money part had been worked out and all that was left was the point on control. I fully expected a call Friday morning from the Eagles to announce a press conference. Instead Saturday morning, during a mid-winter heat wave, I got beeped at a tennis lesson with Nolan. I wore my beeper that day, because again I thought I might get called for a press conference that would announce Dick Vermeil as the new head coach.

There was not a press conference that day. The Eagles had called to say all talks with Vermeil had ended, and they would now continue their search for a new head coach. My heart sunk. I truly believed Dick Vermeil would have been a successful head coach · with the team. And, while a lot of people do not agree with me on this, I still think Vermeil is going to win with the Rams.

The big question about Vermeil and his comeback was could he be the same coach he was in 1995 that he was when he arrived in 1977? I thought he could. I felt he would have learned from his mistakes. Dick Vermeil was a driven person with a strong engine. I hoped his approach was more moderate today than it was with the Eagles the first time. And I felt it was. Look at how he tried to get Lawrence Phillips, the Rams running back and their first pick in the 1995 draft, straightened out. He failed, and they released him. But in the old days he might not have cut Phillips and would have given him another chance, and yet another chance. Where the game has changed the most in the time Vermeil was gone was that a coach used to get a five-year plan. Those days are gone. With free agency, a coach has to win now. The guy Vermeil took over for in St. Louis, Rich Brooks, was fired after just two years. Dick, surely, was aware of that.

There was one major difference about the Philadelphia Eagles team that Dick could have returned to in 1995 from the one he left in 1982. There was no 24-hour sports talk radio in 1982. Every move he made then was not scrutinized all day by talk show hosts and callers. Dick's own radio show back then was done from his office. There was not a live audience at a restaurant the way there is today for the Ray Rhodes Show. I don't know how talk radio would have affected Dick Vermeil. I would like to think it would not have had an affect on him as much as it would have had an affect on how the public saw him. He would have been under that microscope for 24 hours a day, seven days a week, and every flaw would have been exposed for public scrutiny.

Vermeil put himself under that microscope for the seven years he spent in Philadelphia between 1976-82. The Eagles were a bad team, a team that had just fallen apart in 1975, not a lot unlike the team in 1994 for that matter. Mike McCormack was fired the day after the final game of the season, ironically a 26-3 win over Washington. I talked to Mike that day, and he said he felt he had the rug pulled out from under him. He told me how he felt he had entered that season as a lame duck coach and never had a chance. That was the first time I heard a coach refer to the last year of his contract as a lame duck year.

There were a lot of names and a lot of rumors that floated around after McCormack was fired. The number-one coach the Eagles wanted in 1976 was Joe Paterno. I believe they actually made him a very lucrative offer to leave Penn State, but of course he turned them down. Paterno was the guy who Eagles owner Leonard Tose really wanted. Another coach who really wanted the job was Allie Sherman, the former Giants coach and a former Eagles player. But he never had a shot. The guy who almost got it was Joe Restic, the Harvard coach, who ran this unique multiple set offense. They brought Restic in and interviewed him on a Friday afternoon. The deal was so close to being completed that the front office told Jimmy Gallagher, who was the public relations man at the time, to get things ready for a press conference. Restic was going to be named the new head coach.

Restic, however, backed off a bit. He wanted to go back to Boston and discuss the entire situation with his wife and family. But he promised them he would get back to them first thing Monday morning. By then it was too late.

Saturday, Tose and Jim Murray, the team's vice president and Tose's right-hand man, decided they would fly to California and would meet with Dick Vermeil. First let me explain a little bit about Murray. He rose through the ranks of the Eagles as a public relations man; but he was always more than that. He was a deal maker. He had a tremendous amount of charisma. He could trouble-shoot. He could soothe the most aggressive feelings. He made things happen. He never got involved in actual personnel decisions. He never told the coach to take a left tackle or to not take a wide receiver. He handled the contracts, the big contracts. And the deals he did always turned out where the player thought he got a good deal, and the team felt it got a good deal, that was the way Murray was. And the best thing about him was he was Tose's buffer. There were so many times when Leonard Tose would want to make a hasty decision about his coach, or a player, and Murray would step in and handle the situation. There were not enough Jim Murrays around.

Anyway, Tose and Murray flew to Los Angeles and met with Vermeil who had just guided UCLA to the Rose Bowl title. After a long meeting that went well into the night and the next morning, Vermeil thanked them, but decided he would stay in California. He was a California guy through and through. He grew up in California, was the quarterback of his high school team, married his high-school sweetheart, the captain of the cheerleaders. He even had the Hollywood look. If they made a movie about him, Robert Redford would play the lead role.

Sunday, Tose and Murray were about to fly home when Vermeil called them and caught them in the hotel. He told them he had changed his mind and he wanted the job. He had talked to some close friends that morning and they had convinced him that the Eagles offer was too good. It was a great opportunity for him. The three of them flew back together that afternoon and there was a press conference Monday that announced Dick Vermeil as the head coach. Nobody ever found out what happened to Joe Restic.

Despite the Rose Bowl win, there was early skepticism about Vermeil. He was a college coach from California, but this was the NFL. It did not go over real well with everyone in Philadelphia. There were cynics and there were doubters. Ironically, when Mike McCormack was hired three years earlier, he was the guy with the right credentials. He was a former Pro Bowl player. He had been in the presence of Paul Brown and Chuck Noll, and was the top assistant on the staff of George Allen in Washington. He had risen through the ranks the way a coach was supposed to rise. Vermeil was a coach with some NFL experience, as a special teams coach with the Rams, but he was only 37 years old. There were plenty of reasons to doubt him.

Mine were erased the day of his press conference. I had never been in a room with a man who exuded that kind of spark, that kind of forcefulness, that kind of enthusiasm. He just excited everyone. He told everyone it would not happen overnight, but that it would happen. He promised the job would be done. And everyone believed him. Even when his first team in 1976 went through a five-game losing streak and finished the year with the same 4-10 record that got McCormack fired, not one person questioned Vermeil. There was that much confidence in him.

And that confidence came from the fact that Vermeil and his staff worked so hard; they were tireless. It's possible to work hard and not win. But Vermeil had the other qualities as well. It would have shocked me if he did not win. It took time. Vermeil's second year was another losing season. The team went 5-9, but the blowouts were gone. They didn't lose 46-3 any longer. The games were at least competitive. And those final two games of 1977, ironically my first two games as play-by-play man, were wins over the Giants and Jets.

If you have to point to where it all turned around for Vermeil's teams, I would say it was the acquisition of Jaworski. You have to have a quarterback in place. Look at the teams that have been successful and every one of them had a good quarterback. Another factor came at running back. In 1977, the Eagles did not have a draft pick until the fifth round because of past trades during the McCormack Era. They had traded their first rounder for Bill Bergey, the second rounder for running back James McAlister, who played one season, the third-rounder for guard John Niland, a player at the tail end of his career and the fourth-rounder for Cliff Frazier, who never made the roster. In the sixth round, however, they drafted a back from Abilene Christian named Wilbert Montgomery.

All Montgomery did primarily his rookie year was return kick-offs, and he led the NFL in average yards per return. Until the final game of the season—the game in the rain against the Jets. That game was a preview of the Eagles' future. Montgomery got his first major opportunity as a running back and carried 22 times for 103 yards and two touchdowns. With Jaworski at quarterback and Montgomery at running back to go with a defense that was getting better every week, Vermeil was on his way.

In 1978, the NFL expanded its schedule to 16 games, and cut the number of preseason games from six to four. Except that the Eagles played five preseason games that season because they were in the Hall of Fame Game in Canton, Ohio. They beat Miami that day and Vince Papale caught a touchdown pass. Papale, who became a fan favorite, more or less epitomized the Dick Vermeil Eagles. He was not a great player by any means. He did not even play college football. He was a local kid who went to St. Joe's and played for the Philadelphia Bell. He was not very big, but he had some speed and a whole lot of desire. Vermeil made him a symbol. He wanted to show the rest of the team that nothing was impossible. That if you worked hard enough, tried hard enough, anything could happen. This walk-on kid with no college experience, could make an NFL roster.

During that '78 preseason you could see it coming together. Jaworski at quarterback, and Montgomery at running back, were set. Stan, and Jerry Sizemore, who had moved outside from guard, gave the team two reliable tackles who would eventually both go to the Pro Bowl. Dick brought in an old veteran guard named Woody Peoples, whose best days were gone, but had enough left and could still pass block as well any guard in the league. The tight end was Keith Krepfle, a kid from Iowa State who didn't even play high school football, but was recruited because he was so tough on the high school basketball team. The defense was built around Bill Bergey, a linebacker acquired from Cincinnati who cost the Eagles their first-round draft picks in 1977 and 1978 and their second-round pick in 1978. As a matter of fact, during the draft Bergey's name was cursed around the Eagles offices because they wanted those picks. And he would bounce into what they call the war room, or the draft room, and would announce "Your No. 1 pick is here." They wanted to kill him. But without Bergey that defense would not have been the same. If Bergey was the brawn of the defense, fellow linebacker John Bunting was the brain of the defense. He made all the reads and all the calls and put everyone in the right position. I thought then, and still do now, that Bunting would make a very good head coach in the league. Vermeil must agree, because he has him on his staff in St. Louis and appointed him co-defensive coordinator for the 1998 season.

The Eagles made the playoffs that season for the first time since the league went to a playoff format. Back in 1960, when they last won the championship, it was just a one-shot title game between the winner of the Eastern Division and the winner of the Western Division. Along the way in 1979, however, they lost their field goal kicker, Nick Mike-Mayer, on a botched extra point attempt in a game against the Giants that became known as the Miracle of the Meadowlands.

Mike-Mayer's loss, however, turned into a nightmare. Vermeil turned to punter Mike Michel as his kicker for the last five games of the season. Michel never had a chance to try a field goal and missed at least one extra point in all five games. Vermeil continued to have faith in Michel, which turned out to be a gross miscalculation. The year before he had gone through a slew of kickers, and didn't want to do that again. For a guy who was so prepared at all times, this was a terrible mistake to go into a playoff game without a kicker.

Michel missed another extra point and was wide right on a 33-yard field goal attempt with 13 seconds left, and the Eagles lost the NFC wild card game to the Atlanta Falcons, 14-13. On that plane ride home, Christmas Eve, there was not a lot of Christmas joy being spread. Michel just sat there with his head in his hands and Vermeil went back and sat next to him. He told him he was a punter and that this was a difficult spot for him. Of course, the following training camp Michel was cut. The new kicker was a third-round draft pick from Texas A&M named Tony Franklin, who kicked barefoot, and the punter was an eighth-round pick from South Carolina named Max Runager.

The game in 1979 that I felt defined this team was a game in Dallas on Monday Night Football. The Eagles had not won in Dallas since 1965. Here it was 1979 and they were in Dallas in front of a national television audience. The Eagles were 6-4, but had lost three straight games after an impressive 6-1 start. Jaworski made a great play in that game on a third-down-and-one situation where he faked a handoff to Montgomery, which everyone expected, and threw long for Carmichael. Another huge play came when Jaworski was shaken up and John Walton came in and connected on a long pass to Charlie Smith. But the biggest play may have been a 59-yard field goal by Franklin, the longest field goal in Eagles history, and the second longest in NFL history.

On the way home that night, Franklin complained to a teammate about a field goal he had missed in the game. Jaworski overheard him and lashed out at him. "We won tonight, rookie. This isn't about you or me. We just won a huge game. I don't want to hear your whining." That was the first time I had heard Jaworski show that leadership quality to that extent.

But Franklin was a character. He and Vermeil went at it more than once in their four years together. When Vermeil drafted Franklin he said, "I drafted him because he's a great kicker and he's not a flake." That was what he said. Every coach thought his kicker was a flake. That he was not a real football player, just a kicker, a player that you had to have on the team. Vermeil wasn't any different in that regard.

I got to know Franklin that summer before the season began. I was married now and living in an apartment complex that had a huge pool. Franklin came by one Saturday afternoon with Bill Werndl and he held court with a dozen single women. You might have thought he was the star of the team instead of the rookie kicker. But that was the way he was. He was so confident in himself; he felt he was the game's greatest kicker. It did not take long for that confidence to turn into arrogance and for it to get on the nerves of his teammates.

When he walked into the locker room one of the players would pop a tape into the stereo and it would play, "If I were an Oscar Meyer wiener..." The point was Franklin was a hot dog. It had gotten so bad that Vermeil pulled a few veterans aside and told them to take it easy on the kid. One time Franklin won a game with a crucial field goal and after the game told the press he was confident because his holder was Ron Jaworski and it was great to have your best friend as your holder. Ron told me the next day, "Why did he have to call me his best friend?"

In the playoff loss to Tampa Bay in 1979, for some reason Tony's father was on the sidelines that day, Franklin's big moment came. The Eagles had just scored to cut Tampa's lead to 24-17 with three minutes left in the game. The decision came down to either try an onsides kick, or kick deep and hope that the defense held. Vermeil decided to kick deep. Franklin decided to kick onsides, and did. Tampa Bay recovered and held on to win the game. Vermeil wanted to kill him and I was surprised he didn't. And that was the way the 1979 season ended, again in disappointment.

The 1979 season began for me on a great note. Just before the season I had gotten married. My sister, Carole, knew Cindy and set us up on a blind date two years earlier. We went out that one night, and I told her I would give her a call. But I lived in Andorra and she lived in Wallingford, Delaware County and it was some time before we got together again. About a year later, my sister and brother-in-law invited me over for dinner after the season had ended. I thought to myself, who should I bring? I remembered that Cindy lived out in that area and geographically it would make sense. I called her and asked her. She said yes, and we had a great time with my sister and her husband. When I dropped her off that night she joked that she would hear from me again next year. I said, "How about next week?" And from that time on we stayed together.

Cindy and I will celebrate our 20th anniversary next year and I could not be happier. It takes a lot to be married to a guy who is rarely around for six months out of the year and when he is around is consumed with what formation the Washington Redskins run, or what numbers the Dallas Cowboys offensive linemen are wearing. Cindy has been great through all of it, and has been a special inspiration to me.

She went with us to the Super Bowl in New Orleans after the 1980 season and has traveled with me a few other times. That Super Bowl season was just incredible. The Eagles played Dallas the final game of the regular season and would clinch the NFC East title as long as they did not lose by more than 24 points. At one point in the game they were behind 35-10, but came back and lost 35-27, which was good enough. That was the only time in my 21 years where I saw a team lose a game and celebrate afterwards. It was a crazy scene that day in Dallas.

But that "loss" enabled the Eagles to host the Cowboys in the NFC Championship game. First they beat the Minnesota Vikings, 31-16, in the conference semifinals, while Dallas beat the Los Angeles Rams, 34-13, in the wild-card game and the Atlanta Falcons, 30-27, in the other conference semifinal.

Vermeil took the team to Tampa to practice the week before the title game. Every day after practice, Vermeil moaned and groaned about how the Eagles were so battered and bruised, and how Dallas outmanned them at almost every position. He found every negative match-up and played it up to the press. But the Saturday night before the game, at the team meeting, he told the players, "Now we've got them right where we want them. You are ready. You can beat the Dallas Cowboys. Tomorrow, if you all do your jobs, by tomorrow night we'll be headed to the Super Bowl." When he was finished, every player could not wait until he hit that field the next day. That was Vermeil at his best, his absolute best and he was never as effective again.

The Eagles, of course, lost the Super Bowl. The 1981 season started with six straight wins, but ended with another playoff loss. There was a win over New Orleans that year that stood out. Vermeil ripped into the team after the game, and a lot of players told me that "winning wasn't even fun anymore." Vermeil was so focused on his mission to get back to the Super Bowl, he might have overdone it. The players started to tune out. That euphoric feeling that propelled the team to new heights, seemed to fade away. From that New Orleans game on, I saw trouble and knew it was not going to be the same.

During that 1981 season, we came back after a tough loss on the road. Jack Edelstein, who was on the trip, called me at home late that night and told me Leonard Tose wanted to see me first thing Monday morning. Jack and Leonard were very good friends, but he did not tell Jack what he wanted, just that he wanted to see me. All I thought was, what did I do? Had I said something I shouldn't have said? Why did Leonard Tose want me in his office? I was hired by WIP, but of course with the approval of the Eagles. I did not sleep all night.

The next morning I went to the stadium and took the elevator up to the owner's office. Leonard was there when I walked in and told me to sit down. He asked me, "What did you think of the play calling in yesterday's game?" I thought to myself, I can't touch this one. I gave him some noncommittal answer. The last thing I wanted to do was get between the owner and the coach. In my job I have to walk a fine line. You cannot get between a player and a coach, and you certainly cannot get between the coach and the owner. Tose then said, "Well, I'll tell you what I thought of the play calling." And he ranted and he raved. And he paced and he smoked one cigarette after another. This went on for about a half hour. When he was finished, he thanked me and said, "This is what I wanted to say to Dick. But if I did he would kill me."

Tose and Vermeil had a special relationship. It was unique. Vermeil knew how to play Tose. He began every press conference after a win with words about how he could not have done this without the ownership behind him and always gave the front office credit for every move the team made. It was the complete opposite of what would happen with Buddy Ryan as coach and Norman Braman as owner.

Vermeil and Tose went through the awful strike year of 1982 together. Only nine games were played that season and the Eagles won just three. The season started with a great game against Joe Theisman and the Washington Redskins, and the Eagles lost in overtime, 37-34. The next week the Eagles went to Cleveland and won, 24-21, on a touchdown pass from Jaworski to Leroy Harris. Then the strike hit and it became a war zone. Today, Leonard is remembered as an owner who loved his players, but during that strike he was hated the same as every other owner. The players were bitter.

The strike bothered Leonard more than most people. He took it personally, and so did Vermeil. Dick talked a lot that year about stress. It had gotten that bad. There were no games from September 19 to November 21, thank God there were no replacement games, and Vermeil said he had a chance to see the real world. He and his wife, Carol, had gone out. He saw the leaves change colors. And he began to realize what kind of toll the game took on him.

For me, with no games to broadcast, I lost a great deal of money. I was fortunate that WIP picked up Penn games on Saturdays and I was able to work and recoup some money, but not enough. Prior to the season, Nolan was born, and Dick sent him a no-cut, no-trade contract for $1 million a season that goes into effect in 2003. That might be the minimum salary then, but wait until I show up at the stadium with Nolan that year and ask for a buyout. Like his father, Nolan is more of a tennis player than a football player.

When the strike ended, I was elated to get back to work. The players were not; the strike killed them. Vermeil worked them well into the night the day they returned, but it didn't help. They were not the same team. Vermeil, as it turned out, was not the same coach. There was one day when I thought to myself, maybe he had enough. It was something he had said, or the way he said it. But I thought again, that maybe he was just frustrated by the strike, and after an offseason he would come back refreshed and ready to go for 1983.

Instead, about a month after the season had ended, I got a call around 1:30 in the morning from a player who told me he had just come back from Vermeil's house, and they talked and Dick was going to resign Monday afternoon. I asked him if I went on the air with this in the morning, would I be safe. If it was wrong, I would lose my job. The player said, "You can go with it." I led the entire newscast that day with the word that Vermeil would announce that he was through coaching the Eagles.

The phones went berserk. Word spread all over town. The Eagles would not confirm the story. WCAU, which broadcast the Dick Vermeil show, denied the story and said there would be a show that night. During all of this, the same player called me back around 10:30 and said Marion Campbell would be hired to replace Dick. And I reported that as well. Finally, by 1:30 the Eagles had announced that there would be a press conference.

Dick, who had stood at the same podium seven years earlier with those Robert Redford looks and that battle cry that rocked the city, was here again and looked like he had aged much more than seven years, and had the weight of the world on his shoulders. And he sobbed and talked about how he was burned out.

Vermeil was the most loyal coach I have ever been around. Most coaches are loyal to a degree, but Dick took it to another level. He brought with him when he came to the Eagles his UCLA quarterback, John Sciara, who was not drafted. Sciara not only made the roster, but Vermeil would use him on third-down plays to run the option. Jaworski hated that. What quarterback wanted to come out of the game on some of the most important plays of the game? But Dick wanted to use Sciara, and more times than not, the option plays did not work. That loyalty may have led to the Eagles' decline at the end of Vermeil's tenure with the team. There were a lot of old guys who he hung onto too long because he cared about them so much. That was a very old team that he turned over to Marion Campbell in 1983. It was a team that had won just four of its last 15 games.

And a team that wouldn't win again for some time.

From Miracle to Disasters

The game that defined, or at least sent the Eagles on their way under Dick Vermeil, occurred November 19, 1978 at the Meadowlands against the New York Giants.

It was just another game, actually a rather boring game, until the final seconds. The Eagles trailed the Giants, 17-12, and the Giants had the ball. The Eagles were out of time outs, and for all intents and purposes the game was over. I was in the broadcast booth with Jim Barniak, and it just so happened that game was picked up by Armed Forces Radio and was broadcast all over the world. I turned to Barniak and said as the Giants went into what is known as the victory series, "Let's see what lies ahead for the Eagles. Next week they will travel to St. Louis to meet the..." Before I said Cardinals, I said "Joe Pisarcik fumbles the football!"

Pisarcik was the Giants quarterback, who later became an Eagle and never lived down this moment the rest of his career, or for that matter the rest of his life. He became an assistant high school coach in South Jersey and was taunted even then about the Miracle of the Meadowlands.

Pisarcik turned to hand off to Larry Csonka and the ball never got there. I saw number 46 pick up the ball out of nowhere and he ran from right to left toward the end zone. I said, "I can't believe it. I can't believe it. I can't believe what I have just witnessed. Joe Pisarcik fumbled the football. He was hit by Charlie Johnson and the ball was picked up by Herman Edwards and run in for a touchdown." Over 20 years later as I retell the story for about the thousandth time, I still can't believe that happened. That was the most remarkable play I have ever broadcast and it happened in my first year as the play-by-play man.

That night, the Giants' offensive coordinator, Bob Gibson, who had the same name as the great baseball pitcher, was fired. At the end of the season, the Giants head coach, John McVeigh, was fired. The Eagles used that win to move ahead of the Giants in the NFC East and eventually into the playoffs for the first time since 1960 as a wild-card team. I received letters after that game from people all over the world who had heard the broadcast. It was the Miracle of the Meadowlands. And it was the most miraculous play I still have ever seen.

If that was the most miraculous play, the entire 1980 season was the most miraculous year. The Eagles finally made it to the Super Bowl, and the game itself was anticlimactic. The Eagles' Super Bowl occurred two weeks earlier when they beat the Dallas Cowboys. At least that was what we tried to tell ourselves after the Super Bowl. The truth was the Dallas game was not the Super Bowl. There was only one Super Bowl and the Eagles lost, and lost badly. It was a disaster.

The Eagles went into the game as a six-point favorite. Everyone thought they would win. They had beaten the Oakland Raiders, 10-7, earlier that season. The Raiders were a wild-card team, who had to upset the San Diego Chargers in the AFC Championship Game to get to New Orleans and Super Bowl XV. The Eagles had trounced Dallas, 20-7, and appeared to be a team of destiny. WIP had already planned a victory parade, and I would be the master of ceremonies for it when the team returned home as Super Bowl champions.

Like the rest of the media, I spent the week before the game in New Orleans with the team. There were millions of media members there. I did daily reports every day, all day, for WIP. Much has been made of the fact of how the Eagles were so tight and the Raiders were so loose before the game and that was why the Raiders won. I have to tell you that while the Raiders were loose, so were the Eagles. I never sensed that the team was not ready, or was nervous, or any of that. I've heard people, who were home and watched the game on television, say that they could tell the Eagles were tight when they were introduced before the game. That was nonsense.

Vermeil had kept the team pretty much under wraps, especially compared to the Raiders who were out on Bourbon Street to all hours most nights. But that was the way Vermeil had been all season. Why should he change now before the most important game of the season? There were the same curfews the week before the NFC Championship Game when the team stayed and practiced in Tampa. Actually, the team stayed on the same routine it had followed most of the season. The team seemed confident to me. I did not see any signs of what would happen in that game.

Of course I was excited and nervous. This was my chance to broadcast the Super Bowl. I did a live radio show from the Hyatt Regency, the league's Super Bowl headquarters. I had all kinds of guests lined up, some players, some assistant coaches, some sportswriters. And we took calls from back home. Well, I was all set and like I said, excited, and we took the first call and the caller said, "Hi, Uncle Merrill, it's Craig."

It was Tom Cardella's son. I took his question, gave him a quick answer and got onto the next call. This was a big-time show, I did not want calls from family and friends. I took the next call and the voice said. "Hi, Merrill, it's Mom. I just want to say I think Dick Vermeil has done a great job and so have you." I was ready to die. Fortunately, the rest of the show went a little better. Unfortunately, the game did not.

It was a beautiful football day and my first thought was, "What a shame to play inside in a dome on such a great day." I hated domes and still do. There was also a huge yellow ribbon tied around the Superdome in honor of the hostages in the Iran crisis.

The game itself was the Raiders' right from the start. Ron Jaworski had a rough game. He was picked off by Raiders linebacker Rod Martin a couple of times. Oakland scored on a long pass from Jim Plunkett to Kenny King. The Eagles had a touchdown pass from Jaworski to Rodney Parker called back on a motion penalty against Harold Carmichael, and to this day he denies he ever moved.

The only brightspot was a Jaworski touchdown pass to tight end Keith Krepfle. But this was a day of bad news. We got a message at halftime that former Eagles head coach Joe Kuharich had passed away that day.

That next morning I had to wake up at 5:30 to do the morning show with Ken Garland. And I did not want to get out of bed. I had never felt so low after a loss. It was painful. What everyone said was it was tough to win the Super Bowl on your first trip there. We told each other that the Eagles would get back again, and the next time they would win. Except there still has not been a next time. There has been a good share of disastrous games. Here are the ones that have hurt the most.

December 24, 1978, Atlanta, Georgia
Falcons 14, Eagles 13

I have to start with the playoff loss to Atlanta in 1978, the Mike Michel game, if you will. It was a damp rainy day in Atlanta, but the Eagles had actually played pretty well. They led 13-0 after three quarters. It should have been, 14-0, but Michel had missed an extra point for the sixth straight game. In the final five minutes, Atlanta quarterback Steve Bartkowski threw two touchdown passes. Jim Mitchell caught the first touchdown with 4:53 left in the game, and Wallace Francis caught what proved to be the winning touchdown with 1:39 left. Ironically, or cruelly, both extra points were kicked by Tim Mazzetti, a former Eagles training camp kicker who was also a bartender at Smokey Joe's, a popular bar just off the campus of the University of Pennsylvania. Jaworski brought the Eagles back in the final minute and drove them to the Atlanta 16 yardline. But with 13 seconds left, Michel missed wide right on a 33-yard field goal attempt and the Eagles lost.

What I remember about the final field goal attempt, was that Jack Buck and Hank Stram were in the booth next to ours and as Michel's kick went up, Buck yelled, "Good." I almost yelled it with him, but I saw that the official had waved it off. I learned that day you cannot watch the kick, you have to watch the official. I yelled, "Oh no, it's no good. The Eagles lose." Players were sprawled all over the field. They could not believe it, either.

That was the second worst ending to a game in all of my 21 years.

September 15, 1997, Dallas, Texas
Cowboys 21, Eagles 20

This was the worst. The Eagles played the Dallas Cowboys on Monday Night Football, the third week of the season. They had just come off a thrilling 10-9 win over the defending Super Bowl champion Green Bay Packers and looked to get to 2-1 on the young season. They dominated the Cowboys early and led, 17-6, at halftime and, 17-9, after three quarters. It was still, 20-15, with a minute to play when Dallas quarterback Troy Aikman found Anthony Miller in the end zone behind Eagles backup safety Tim Watson, for a touchdown. Watson, by the way, was cut the next day.

Still the Eagles were not finished. Ty Detmer took the team down field, just like Jaworski had done in Atlanta. Fred Solomon, who had caught the winning touchdown a week earlier against Green Bay, took a Detmer pass and went 46 yards to the four yard line with four seconds left. Everything was set. Chris Boniol, the Eagles kicker and the former Cowboy, came out to beat his old team with an easy 21-yard field goal. And, inexplicably, the holder Tom Hutton dropped the snap from Steve Everitt. I wondered if he still had time to put it down and get the kick, but he picked it up and ran with it and was tackled. The game was over. That was devastating. And from my point of view, the team never really recovered from that loss and went on to a 6-9-1 season.

But you learn about people in crisis time, and I gained a lot of admiration for Hutton that night. He stood at his locker after the game and answered every question. He took full responsibility for the play and all the blame. Three days later, the Eagles had a bye the following week, Hutton almost purposely stood at his locker again and answered any other questions about the play. That game, as terrible as it was, showed me a lot about Tom Hutton.

It also brought back memories of a similar game in 1981 against Washington when John Sciarra fumbled the snap on what would have been a game-winning 25-yard field goal in the final minute, and the Eagles lost, 15-13.

Like Detmer, Jaworski drove the Eagles from their 20-yard line to the Redskins' seven-yard line. Tony Franklin came out to kick the field goal and Sciarra dropped the ball.

One of the things about this job is you see so many new things, but you also see history repeat. What happened in Dallas was frighteningly close to what had happened against Washington.

If those were the two worst plays, then the next one is the worst quarter.

December 1, 1985, Philadelphia.
Minnesota 28, Eagles 23

This was the game that finished Marion Campbell as head coach once and for all. If there was a chance of him returning after the season, it was gone after this loss.

The Eagles led the Minnesota Vikings, 23-0, with eight minutes left in the fourth quarter and lost, 28-23. When it was 23-0, Stan said on the air it was time for the Eagles to get their starters out of the game, and I agreed. We started to talk about the following week and the Washington Redskins.

And all of a sudden the Vikings scored. And then they scored again and again and again. Wade Wilson came off the bench and threw three touchdown passes, and a guy named Willie Teal returned a Jaworski fumble for a touchdown. It was incredible. Minnesota scored 28 points in eight minutes. Norman Braman entertained the players from the 1948 Championship team that day and was totally embarrassed. If Marion Campbell was not finished before that game, he was after.

As a matter of fact, the two teams met again three weeks later, and Campbell was no longer the Eagles' coach.

December 27, 1981, Philadelphia
Giants 27, Eagles 21

It was not the game itself that was so much a disaster, as the feeling we had afterwards.

The Eagles lost the wild-card game to the Giants, 27-21, after they fell behind, 20-0, thanks to two fumbles by kickoff returner Wally Henry.

What made this one hurt so much was that it was the year after the Super Bowl. Even though the team had struggled through the middle of the season there was hope they would put it back together in the playoffs. They had routed St. Louis, 38-0, the final game of the season and went in on a high. But those fumbles led to a big Giants lead and the team never came back.

And they did not come back to the playoffs for another seven years.

December 31, 1988, Chicago, Illinois
Bears 20, Eagles 12

The Eagles finally made it back to the playoffs and again disaster struck. This time it came by way of Mother Nature. I still think this may have been the best team under Buddy Ryan. A lot of people thought it was still a young team that needed more experience, but I felt they were ready. I thought this was a team that could have gone to the Super Bowl. Instead, they went to the Fog Bowl.

The Eagles opened the playoffs in Chicago against the Bears at Soldier Field. I remember I packed warm clothes for the trip to Chicago in late December, and when we arrived there the temperature was in the 60s. There was a heat wave. It also created a thaw.

Chicago scored first on a touchdown pass to Dennis McKinnon. The Eagles came back, but a touchdown pass from Randall Cunningham to Mike Quick was called back on a motion penalty against Anthony Toney. There was also a questionable spot on a long catch by Eagles wide receiver Ron Johnson. And what should have been another touchdown pass by Cunningham was dropped in the end zone by tight end Keith Jackson. Cunningham put the ball right between the two eights on Jackson's chest and he just dropped it.

Midway through the second quarter, we saw what we thought was a puff of smoke. Stan thought someone had set off a smoke bomb in the stands. It grew, and now it looked like it was a fire. Before we knew what had happened we were totally engulfed in this fog. I could not see anything. We all thought it would clear in a matter of minutes. I looked to my monitor, which I never used, and that was all white. I told people after the game that it was as if they painted the windows white. We could not see through. I tried to listen to the public address announcer who had moved down to the field. It was utter craziness. But the thing was that whoever had the lead when the fog rolled in would win, and that was the Bears.

But one thing I have to add, was that I felt the league did the right thing. I did not think the game should have been stopped. As impossible it was for me to broadcast, the game has to be played. Weather will always be a factor in football, snow, rain, heat in Arizona, whatever. And on this day, fog.

January 5, 1991, Philadelphia
Washington 20, Eagles 6

This was Buddy Ryan's last chance. The Eagles had made the playoffs for the third straight year under Ryan, but had yet to win a playoff game. The rumblings were that if he had lost again, Norman Braman would fire him. Ironically, it was a rule that Braman kept alive that led to the Eagles' 20-6 loss and Ryan's ouster.

The Eagles led 6-0 early in the second quarter when cornerback Ben Smith recovered an Earnest Byner fumble and returned it 94 yards for a touchdown that would have made it 13-0. Instant replay was still in effect that season and replays showed that Byner was down before he fumbled. The Redskins retained possession and went on to score and take a 7-6 lead.

That previous winter at the owners meetings in Orlando, Florida, the league was ready to get rid of replay, and those against it thought they had enough votes. Braman, however, changed his mind and voted to keep replay, which was the one vote the dissenters needed.

Randall Cunningham had one of the worst games of his career that day. Ryan benched him for a series and brought in Jim McMahon, a move for which he was roundly criticized. It didn't matter. After the reversal, the Eagles never did anything again and it did turn out to be Ryan's last game in Philadelphia.

Which was almost as disastrous as the first game of Rich Kotite's career.

September 1, 1991, Green Bay, Wisconsin
Eagles 20, Packers 3

This was a win, 20-3, at Green Bay. Still it was a disaster.

On the first play of the second quarter, Randall Cunningham went down with a knee injury. He was hit by Green Bay linebacker Bryce Paup on a third-down play and had to be helped from the field. You could not tell at the time how serious it was. But just as we were about to go to a commercial break, Eagles public relations man Ron Howard came into the booth and told us Randall was done for the season. He had torn his anterior cruciate ligament and would have surgery the next day. Stan said on the air, "There goes the season."

Even though Jim McMahon won that game, and even though the team went 10-6, Stan was right. Without Randall Cunningham, the team floundered through quarterback after quarterback. McMahon got hurt, and the team turned to Pat Ryan, then rookie Brad Goebel, then Jeff Kemp. It was a disaster.

October 6, 1991, Tampa, Florida
Tampa Bay 14, Eagles 13

When Cunningham went down with the knee injury on opening day, there were several veteran journeymen quarterbacks available to sign. The Eagles picked the worst of the bunch. Ex-Jet Pat Ryan, who head coach Rich Kotite knew from their days together in New York was summoned, from a construction site where he did work as a carpenter, to become McMahon's backup.

By the sixth game of the season, McMahon was hurt, and Ryan was so bad, that rookie Brad Goebel was forced to start against

Tampa Bay. Goebel had been an undrafted player out of Baylor who missed most of his senior year with a broken hand. Now, here he was a starter in the NFL.

The Eagles' defense was great that day, as it was all season. Free safety Wes Hopkins intercepted a pass and recovered two fumbles. Linebacker Seth Joyner scored the Eagles' only touchdown when he recovered a Tampa Bay fumble in the end zone. Still, the Eagles lost 14-13, when the Bucs came back with two late touchdowns in the fourth quarter.

All the Eagles did on offense was hand the ball to running back Heath Sherman, who carried a team-record 35 times for just 89 yards. Sherman carried 12 straight times in the fourth quarter and did not pick up a first down.

On the plane after the game, my eyes met Joyner's and he looked at me and said loud enough for everyone to hear, "Merrill, was that the dumbest coaching you have ever seen?" All I thought was, "Why did he have to say 'Merrill?'"

December 15, 1991, Philadelphia
Dallas 25, Eagles 13

Thanks to the defense, the Eagles were still alive for a playoff berth with two games left in the season. They hosted Dallas, with the winner to clinch a playoff spot and the loser to be eliminated.

Earlier in the season at Dallas, they had crushed the Cowboys, 24-0, and sacked quarterback Troy Aikman 11 times in the game. Now, they entered their most important game of the season, at home, and on a six-game win streak. Again, disaster struck.

This time it came by the way of special teams. First, a fumbled kickoff return led to a Dallas safety. Then with the score 18-13 in the fourth quarter, Cowboys returnman Kelvin Martin brought a punt back 85 yards for a touchdown and a 25-13 win.

Dallas, which would win three of the next five Super Bowls, returned to the playoffs for the first time in five years, and the Eagles would miss them for the first time in four years.

September 24, 1995, Oakland, California
Raiders 48, Eagles 17

The Eagles got back to the playoffs under first-year head coach Ray Rhodes, but it sure didn't look like they would early in Rhodes' rookie season.

It was the fourth game of the season, and Rhodes' team was 1-

2, with home losses to Tampa Bay and San Diego sandwiched around a road win at Arizona.

This game was at Oakland, where the Raiders had relocated after 12 years in Los Angeles. Alameda stadium was not quite ready for football yet, and neither were the Eagles.

In all of my years with Stan, we rarely, if ever, got into any type of arguments or even got on each other's nerves. In that game we did. The Eagles jumped out 17-0 early, and Oakland scored the next 48 points. They scored at will. It was like the Eagles were not even on the field. It was ridiculous.

Late in the fourth quarter, I said on the air that it appeared that the Eagles had quit. Stan gave me a look I had never seen before, and said, "How can you say that?" I said, "It's laughable. They look like the Keystone Cops out there." And they did. Stan became irate. "You can't say that. There's nothing funny about this. You have never been down there on the field." Stan had never said that to me before. I never felt that you had to be a player to understand the game, and especially to broadcast a game. Later, Stan said he was so disgusted that the old player in him came out and he apologized.

November 24, 1996, Tempe, Arizona
Cardinals 30, Eagles 29

Some might have called this one of the most exciting games, and until the final seconds it was. Then, it became another disaster, a disaster in the desert.

The Eagles trailed Arizona, 29-20, with 2:30 left and came back on a kickoff return for a touchdown by Derrick Witherspoon and then recovered an onsides kick that led to a go-ahead field goal by Gary Anderson.

It was 30-29, with 45 seconds on the clock, and the Cardinals out of timeouts. Quarterback Boomer Esiason took his team 66 yards, the final 24 on a touchdown pass to Marcus Dowdell, who got behind Eagles cornerback Troy Vincent for the game-winning touchdown.

It was a terrible loss; one that should have never happened. But it wasn't the worst loss of the season. That came two weeks later.

December 5, 1996, Indianapolis, Indiana
Colts 37, Eagles 10

This was just a horrible game from start to finish. The Eagles played the Colts on one of those special Thursday night ESPN games.

Indianapolis was a battered team. Quarterback Jim Harbaugh was out for the game with an injury, and so were most of his linemen, and half of the team's defense. It did not matter. The Eagles would not have beaten a good college team that night.

It was 7-3, Colts, at the end of the first quarter, and the Eagles did not score again until backup quarterback Mark Rypien threw a touchdown pass to Irving Fryar with eight seconds left to play.

In between, two Colts quarterbacks named Paul Justin and Kerwin Bell tore the Eagles' defense apart. When it was finally finished, the Eagles lost 37-10, and had never looked so bad under Ray Rhodes.

Almost in Phoenix

Tuesdays became my regular day off at WIP, and Stan came in on a weekly basis and did the morning sports. This particular Tuesday, December 11, was not a day off.

The phone rang around 6:30 in the morning. My first thought was I overslept and I had to get to the station. Then, I realized it was Tuesday. It was Stan on the phone and he told me, "Merrill, the Eagles are moving to Phoenix." There had been a story on the Associated Press wire and Stan called me as soon as he saw it.

Ed Wisniewski, the Eagles public relations man at the time, was besieged by phone calls. The team would neither confirm nor deny the story. I told Stan to stay at the station and I would get down to the stadium as soon as I could.

The way it was back then, you could just walk through the Eagles offices at any time of the day. That was how we worked. We would walk in, hang around, and then go out and watch practice. We really didn't have a pressroom. There was a small work area right outside the executive offices where the writers kept their computers and wrote their stories. That was the first time that I was told when I got to the stadium to wait out in the lobby.

Rumors were everywhere, not just in Philadelphia, that Phoenix, Arizona was going to get an NFL franchise. Bart Starr, the Hall of Fame Green Bay Packers quarterback, was the head of one group that wanted to bring an expansion team to the Phoenix area.

Never did I hear the Eagles name mentioned until early in 1984 when their name came up as a possible team that might move to Arizona. Susan Fletcher, Leonard Tose's daughter and a vice president with the team at this point, was rumored to have been in the Phoenix area and had actually looked into the school systems for her children. Of course she denied it to the media. And on November 11 during a game in Miami against the Dolphins, Susan came on the air with Stan and me at the outset of the broadcast and addressed the rumors that had circulated.

I asked her flat out that day if there was any truth to the speculation that the Eagles were one of the teams that was considering a move to Phoenix. She said, "Absolutely not." She was so adamant about it that you had to believe her. And I did.

One day and a month later, it appeared she had lied. Within an hour or so the entire press corp had descended on Veterans Stadium and demanded to know what was happening. Was the team about to move? Where was Leonard Tose? What about what Susan Fletcher had told us? Everyone, like me, had assumed this story died with Fletcher's denials. Now, it was back in the headlines bigger than ever. There was a column that day in the *Arizona Republic* by Bob Hurt that said the Eagles were on their way. It was written as if it the deal were done.

Tose's gambling problems were the story behind the story. He had lost big in Atlantic City at the blackjack tables, and his personal finances had begun to interfere with the team's finances. There was a popular joke after the Eagles lost to the Colts, 22-21, in 1983, that Tose thought the Eagles won. He thought the Colts busted.

Now it all started to make sense. If Tose was forced to sell the team because of his personal debt, a new owner could come from anywhere, including Phoenix, Arizona.

There had been times over the past few years that Leonard Tose had almost sold the Eagles, but each of those times it was to local businessmen. One time there were reports that Ed Snider, the owner of the NHL's Flyers, was very interested in buying the team and had talked to Tose about a deal. Another time Lou Guida, an owner of all of the top standard bred race horses, nearly had a deal done over champagne and hoagies with Tose. And at the last minute, or according to some after the last minute, Tose reneged on the deal.

The Eagles front office remained mum that day. We talked with people from the city who claimed the Eagles lease was binding and couldn't be broken. We talked to players, some of whom thought the move would be good because it would get them closer to home.

Of course the one player who was upset was Ron Jaworski, who had become mired in the Philadelphia area and had started his businesses. He did not want to go west.

That next day I went back to WIP and got called into Mikel Herrington's office. Herrington was the station's new program director and while he acted like he knew sports, he really had very little knowledge of football, or much else. He screamed at me and asked me, "How could you go down to the stadium yesterday?" That forced him to send a news reporter to City Hall to get that angle on it. He actually thought it wasn't that big of a deal. "It was only important to sports fans, and nobody else cared," he told me. Obviously, he did not realize how many of us sports fans there were. Or that the Eagles were the lifeblood of the city.

Word had spread so quickly about this possible move, that I had gotten calls from a few radio stations around the country that wanted to know if the Eagles moved, would I go with them, or would I be interested in a job at another station. I was called by WGN in Chicago which had just acquired the rights to the Bears games. I told them if it happened, if the Eagles moved, I would certainly get back to them. I got another call from a friend in Tampa about a possible job with the Buccaneers radio station. I even got a call from a station in Arizona that had hoped to pick up the Eagles games, and wanted to know if they did would I want to continue to be the play-by-play man.

To be honest, I was worried. I wasn't concerned that I might have to move. When Cindy and I were married, one of the things we talked about was that, in this job, you might have to move sometimes. I am one of the few broadcasters who actually works in the city where I grew up. So that was not a problem. But I enjoyed it here. I have always felt that it was a benefit for me to broadcast the games for the team I lived and died with for so long before I became the play-by-play man. Could I have gone to Chicago or Tampa? Sure. But it would not have been the same for me. I would have worked hard and learned the team and the players, but it would have never been the same for me. It would not have been the Philadelphia Eagles.

Every day more news broke. Some said it was a done deal. The Eagles were gone. Some stories even speculated on which team might move to Philadelphia after the Eagles were in Phoenix. Ironically, the St. Louis Cardinals, who would eventually move to Phoenix, was the one mentioned most prevalently. Others said, or wrote, the team could be saved. At the same time, Tose and the Mayor at the time, Wilson Goode met almost around the clock. I was, of course, the eternal optimist. I went on Channel 3 that Thursday night as a guest during the newscast and I said, "The longer the talks went on with Leonard and the Mayor, the more I thought it would work out and the team would stay." Maybe I was just hoping.

I knew Leonard Tose did not want the Eagles to leave Philadelphia. He never wanted to sell the team, period. He had just incurred such a financial burden that it forced him to sell. Actually, the deal that Leonard turned down from James Monaghan to move to Phoenix was a great deal. He would have moved to Arizona, but he would have retained a percentage of the team and would have been a part of the team's day-to-day operation.

We were in Atlanta on Saturday night, the day before the final game of the 1984 season against the Falcons, when word came from City Hall that a deal had been struck to keep the team in Philadelphia. The deal was a great one for the Eagles. It allowed the team to keep the money from the Super Boxes. It had the city build the Penthouse Suites. It had the city build two practice fields and an indoor bubble. It was some deal, and made the Eagles a very attractive purchase to a buyer who would agree to keep the team in Philadelphia.

That entire scenario during the 1984 season brought up the great debate: Whose team is this? The fans felt the team was theirs and Leonard Tose, or Norman Braman, or Jeffrey Lurie were just caretakers. They felt that the team belonged to them. From a rooting standpoint, an allegiance standpoint, from an interest standpoint, the team does belong to the fans. But in the legal sense the owner was the person who owned the team be it Tose, Braman, or Lurie. Of course, the league has to grant approval for a team to move, but Al Davis has proven that not to be a huge obstacle.

Earlier that year, before the talk of the move Susan Fletcher became very involved in the Eagles organization. Susan certainly did not have a football background. Whatever she knew about football was just whatever she had picked up from her father over the years. She was an attorney with a keen business sense. She started with the team as a legal advisor, but before long she was calling the shots, major shots.

Fletcher took over contract negotiations and gave what at that time were big contracts to strong safety Ray Ellis and defensive end Greg Brown. Those two contracts led to unrest on the team and the virtual dismantling of the defense in 1985 when several players demanded the same kind of money, or even more, as Brown and Ellis had gotten.

One of the reasons for the contracts of Brown and Ellis was the USFL, a new league that wanted to compete with the NFL and tried to steal a lot of their players. The two players were seen at a prizefight with their agent, Lloyd Remick, and Donald Trump, in Atlantic City. And rumors got started that Trump, who owned the USFL's New Jersey Generals, was interested in the two Eagles players. The new summer league had already raided several NFL teams for its players, and taken away some top draft choices, and the Eagles were not about to let it happen to them.

Instead they overpaid two good, but not great players, and sent the rest of the team into upheaval. By 1985, after Tose had sold the team to Norman Braman, linebackers Joel Williams and Jerry Robinson, free safety Wes Hopkins, defensive end Dennis Harrison, and running back Wilbert Montgomery were all contract holdouts. Only Hopkins would ever play for the team again.

Williams sat out the season and was traded to Atlanta. Robinson was traded to Oakland. Harrison was dealt to the Rams, and Montgomery went to Detroit.

Hopkins, however, might have been the most vociferous about the situation. He publicly blasted Ellis' contract and said if Ellis was worth that much, he was worth much more. Later Ellis told me that he felt Wes was his friend, and was hurt that he would use him in his own contract troubles. Why didn't he just ask for a better contract without degrading Ellis?

The trouble was those contracts were paid by Tose and Fletcher and now the team had been sold to Norman Braman. Tose finally did sell the team on March 12 to Braman and his brother-in-law, Ed Liebowitz, a pair of automobile dealership owners from Miami, for $65 million. Despite the sweet new deal that kept the Eagles in Philadelphia and added the luxury boxes, Tose never benefited from any of it.

Leonard Tose was a kind man, a Damon Runyon character. He dressed right off the pages of *Gentlemen's Quarterly*. He traveled in a Rolls Royce. He had a personal pilot who flew him around in a helicopter. There were often times when during a training camp practice at West Chester all action would stop as a helicopter flew overhead and landed in a field behind the practice fields. Leonard emerged and made a grand entrance, again in the best of suits, with his jacket draped over his shoulder and his tie loosened just a bit.

Tose grew up just outside of Norristown, in the Bridgeport area. His father had the Tose truck company and Leonard was involved as it became a big-time business. For a long time he did all the right things and eventually bought the Eagles in 1969 from Jerry Wolman.

Players loved Leonard, because he treated them all like stars. He was a "let the good times roll" kind of guy and was never overly cautious about anything. He threw spectacular parties. And he did a lot of charitable work. He answered the call when Fred Hill, a former Eagle, called and told him his daughter had leukemia. Tose started the "Eagles Fly for Leukemia" program and the Ronald McDonald House. Both still exist today and have raised millions of dollars in the fight against the terrible disease.

Jim Murray, of course, was strongly behind the organization of the program. For the first fundraiser they had, the players actually came in and answered phones in a radiothon that was broadcast on WIP. Leonard called an offensive linemen, Mark Nordquist, up to the podium to make a presentation. And on live radio, Nordquist grabbed the microphone and said, "I want to thank Mr. Tose for having the balls to pull this off." Today, that would not have been a big deal, but back in the late '70s it was. The engineer almost passed out and the program director panicked. But that was Leonard, and one of Leonard's players.

Leonard also treated the media like they were stars. His press luncheons were out of this world. They used to be held in the old Bulletin building where the Eagles offices were at the time. We would come in, and the first thing we would do was watch film with the coach. Then, we would sit down at the conference tables for an incredible meal. We had lobster thermidor, filet mignon, clams on the half shell—you name it. For a Monday Night game once, he served surf and turf with shrimp cocktail at the media buffet. I used to call it Le Bec Bird, a takeoff on the world renowned downtown restaurant Le Bec Fin. It was dangerous covering the Eagles back then, you could gain 25 pounds over the course of the season.

Tose had his share of characters on his teams. The kind of player he would have been if he had played. Flamboyant. Outrageous. Fun-loving. There was a quarterback in training camp one year, a guy named Jim "King" Corcoran, who had played for the Pottstown Firebirds. He showed up at Albright College the first day of camp with speakers that blasted out of his car stereo that proclaimed, "The King is here. The King is here. Long live the King." During his first practice he wiped his hands off on a towel and then flung it back to who he thought was the ballboy. Except it was Jerry Williams, the head coach. Needless to say, the King did not make it to the throne, or to the regular season.

There was Tim Rossovich, a linebacker from Southern Cal, who played from 1968-71. He was more famous for his glass-eating than anything he ever did on the football field. And later he became a Hollywood actor and had a few small roles in some movies.

Guys like Adrian Young and Bill Bradley were wild young men, who loved to party and have a good time. And the owner of the team was the same way. Tose would take groups of friends on a cruise, all expenses paid, all the time. Money was never a factor to him, and it seemed the more he spent on others, the more he enjoyed himself.

When Cindy and I were married I told him that we were having a little party and would love for him to come. He said he would try. Jack Edelstein showed up and said Leonard could not make it, but handed me a card from him. I took the card, put it aside and thought it was nice that he even sent a card. Later that night we opened it and there were ten hundred dollar bills inside. We almost fell over. That was just the way he was.

Leonard told me once that he wished he knew that Charlie Swift was so troubled. He would have done whatever he could to have helped him. Leonard loved to help people, and loved to have fun. And often the two would overlap.

What hurt Leonard almost as much as the Atlantic City casinos, was the 1982 strike. That somewhat colored his attitude about football. And he finally realized that this was a cold hard business as much as it was fun and games for him. The atmosphere before the strike, the free-spending, fun-loving times, were just a little different after the strike. As good as he was to his players, he was criticized just like every owner was by the players during the strike. And even though it finally ended, I believed it really hurt him deeply.

What would Leonard be like today if he still owned the Eagles? It would be different. Back in the '70s and '80s most of the teams were family owned. There was not a corporate atmosphere present. Leonard would still be flamboyant, there was no other way with him. He would be a high-profile owner. But I don't know how he would react to today's NFL. It has become so much more of a business than it was, and I don't think he would have enjoyed himself as much as he did, especially in the late '70s and early '80s.

One story that most people don't know about Leonard Tose was that he had a heart problem. It should not come as a big surprise. He smoked almost non-stop and drank a lot of scotches on the rocks. Jim Murray, as always, was there for Leonard. Unbeknownst to the community, Murray arranged for Leonard to fly to Houston to meet with a well-known heart specialist, Dr. Michael DeBakey. Heart bypasses today have become a lot more commonplace. But back in 1978 they were much riskier. Leonard was to have his Monday, November 20, 1978.

The reason the date has stuck in my mind this long was because the day before Leonard Tose's operation was the day of the Miracle of the Meadowlands. He laid in bed in a Houston hospital that afternoon with a telephone to his ear and listened to our broadcast on WIP. Here he was waiting for a major heart operation and in a weakened condition, and he heard my call of Joe Pisarcik's fumble and Herman Edwards' touchdown. It was a miracle that he made it through that day.

And maybe another miracle that he was able to own the team for 16 incredible seasons.

Starship 12

In 1985, just before the draft, I had a long talk with Lynn Stiles, the Eagles' personnel man at the time. Lynn and I had become pretty close over the years and he trusted me enough to talk about the draft. The team needed an offensive tackle in the worst way, and there were three players the Eagles wanted in the first round. There was Bill Fralic, from Pitt, who figured to be gone by the time the Eagles selected at number nine. The other two were Lomas Brown and Ken Ruettgers. And at least one of them was expected to be on the board when the Eagles drafted.

As the draft unfolded, Fralic went to Atlanta with the second pick. It got down to the seventh pick and both Brown and Ruettgers were still available. It appeared the Eagles would have their choice. And then it all went wrong. Detroit, which had several needs on the defensive side of the ball, decided it could not pass up a great offensive tackle and selected Brown. So, the Eagles would get Ruettgers, a big athletic left tackle from USC—that would be fine. Just then Buffalo, with the eighth pick and no need for a tackle, traded out of the spot with Green Bay, and the Packers selected Ruettgers.

The Eagles panicked. Marion Campbell turned to Stiles and asked, "Who is the next best tackle?" Stiles said, "We can't take a tackle. The top three are gone. But there are some great players out there." Out there were Jerry Rice, Al Toon and a player who the Eagles thought was a guard, but became one of the game's best left tackles, Jim Lachey. The Eagles passed on all of them, and instead went for the tackle they had rated fourth, Kevin Allen, of Indiana. Marion Campbell wanted a tackle. And he got a tackle.

Allen turned out to be perhaps the worst No. 1 draft pick in Eagles history, and that says something. He held out his first training camp, was rushed into the starting lineup on opening day against the Giants and almost got Ron Jaworski killed. After a disastrous rookie year, Buddy Ryan waived him the following training camp. In between, Allen found time to get charged with sexual assault for a crime committed on the beach at Margate, just south of Atlantic City. He went to jail and never played football again.

The Eagles, however, made up for it with their second-round pick that year. Stiles had told me for weeks about this quarterback from Nevada-Las Vegas named Randall Cunningham. He loved him; he thought Cunningham was an incredible athlete. Stiles said he had an arm you would not believe, could run better than a lot of running backs, and was one of the best punters in the country. He was from a small school and had not gotten a lot of publicity, and the only thing he was known for at that time was being the younger brother of Sam "Bam" Cunningham, a star running back for New England. Stiles hoped he would be there in the second round for the Eagles. And he was.

Again Stiles had to fight with Campbell, who wanted UCLA's Steve Bono, a kid from nearby Norristown. Since Campbell had won the first-round fight, Stiles was able to get his way in the second, and the Eagles took Cunningham. Not long after the draft they found out Cunningham had signed a contract with the USFL. Somehow there was a loophole in that contract and the Eagles were able to keep his rights and signed him to an NFL contract.

Cunningham was still a curious pick. He was an unknown, and a vast majority of the fans felt the Eagles had other major needs besides quarterback. Ron Jaworski was not at his peak in 1985, but most agreed he still had some years left. There did not seem to be a reason to select a quarterback so high in the draft. But the team began to lose, and Campbell and Jaworski's relationship began to wane as well. It was compounded by the fact that the offensive line had started to fall apart. Jerry Sizemore and Stan had retired, leaving huge holes at the tackle spots. High draft picks like Dean Miraldi and Rusty Russell were not in the same class. Center Guy Morris, and guards Woody Peoples and Petey Perot, were long gone. The sacks began to pile up, and Jaworski couldn't get away. A mobile quarterback like Cunningham might have had a better chance.

I remember Randall's first day at training camp; it seems like yesterday, not 13 years ago. When I saw him throw his first pass, my jaw dropped. It was clear from that day that this guy was gifted. His arm was like a whip and when he snapped it, the ball just flew in a perfect tight spiral. What you did not know right away was how this tall, slender quarterback could run. Boy, could he run.

All my life I have been fascinated with the quarterback position more than any other position. And I have always thought the quarterback is the most important person on any team in any sport. You can't win the Super Bowl without a great quarterback, or at least a quarterback who had a great season as in the case of Mark Rypien and the Washington Redskins in 1991.

Randall Cunningham played well enough to win a Super Bowl for the Eagles. He has gotten a lot of blame for the team's playoff failures. But I never believed it was all his fault. In all of his years with the Eagles, Cunningham never had an offensive lineman or a running back make it to the Pro Bowl. The only wide receiver to make it was Fred Barnett, and that was only after a few other receivers backed out of the game.

From the end of the 1987 season until his first serious injury in 1991, I thought Randall Cunningham was the best quarterback in football. *Sports Illustrated* had called him the Ultimate Weapon in a cover story they did on him prior to the 1989 season, and they were right. He was a weapon, and his accomplishments seemed limitless. In that time, the most remarkable thing about Randall to me was his durability. He never missed a snap. And beyond that, he never had any minor injuries. Most times you see players, especially quarterbacks, iced up after a game. Randall never did, it was as if he were made of rubber. Mike Schad, a veteran guard on the team, once called him "Gumby" and it was a great nickname. He would take some of the most jarring hits, and bounce right back up and be in the huddle calling the next play.

The early Randall was quiet, almost shy. He came to camp as a rookie in 1985 with a jeri-curl hairdo and a t-shirt he liked to wear that read, "If you want an interview, call my agent." It was as much an advertisement for his agent, Jim Steiner, as it was a statement. I got to know him that summer during the preseason. I noticed he drove a gray, Porsche 944 sports car. I've always loved sports cars, and on the team bus going to a preseason game at the Meadowlands, I turned to him and asked if he wanted to see a copy of *Car and Driver.* He took it and thanked me. He seemed appreciative of both the magazine and just the fact that someone cared enough to offer it to him.

Cunningham opened a lot of eyes in the preseason, mostly with his big arm and his amazing ability to run out of the pocket and gain yards. I called him Ramblin' Randall on the air and the name stuck. In preseason, especially when the backup players are in, you see more broken plays, and Randall was the king of improvisation. There was nothing he did better than make the most of a play gone wrong. But you could also see that he needed time to develop those incredible skills. He certainly was not ready to start yet. Or was he?

The Eagles opened the season at the Meadowlands against the Giants that year, and with Kevin Allen at left tackle, Jaworski was sacked nine times on Sunday, and a tenth time on Monday. That one came from Campbell, who benched his veteran quarterback and named the rookie Cunningham the starter for the second game of the season against the Los Angeles Rams.

It was interesting how the story broke. There was the annual Maxwell Club luncheon that afternoon and nothing was said about a quarterback change. I later did the Marion Campbell Show on WIP. Marion's show was different than most coach's shows. There was no live audience, or even live calls. It was done from his office at the stadium and fans could call during the day and leave a question on a tape. Marion would then choose which questions he wanted to answer on the air, and we would play the tape of the caller. The show was taped from six to seven and played from eight to nine.

That night before we started the show, Marion told me that since the show was taped anyway, and by the time it aired word would be out, he better tell me now. I had no idea what he was going to tell me. And when he said Randall Cunningham was going to be the starter next week against the Rams I was flabbergasted. I turned to Marion and asked him if he was doing this because the new owner, Norman Braman, wanted him to do it. It was the only time I ever saw Marion Campbell get mad. He slammed his fist down on the table and he yelled, "No, damn it. The day an owner tells me who to play, is the day I walk out of here. I'm doing it because I want to do it. I feel it's the right move."

I believe Marion told me the truth that night. Braman most likely did not order him to start Cunningham. But Marion was in a tenuous position. He couldn't feel too good about his future. He had a new owner in town. And I thought Marion did what he thought the owner wanted him to do. Everyone knew Braman liked Cunningham, and was excited about the way he threw the long ball and ran like crazy. Marion did what he thought his boss wanted to see.

Randall's first start was a typical roller coaster ride. He made some good plays and he made a lot of mistakes. He ran 10 times for 90 yards and passed for 214 yards. But he completed just 14 of 34 passes, threw four interceptions and did not get the Eagles in the end zone, as they lost, 17-6. It was clear that he was overmatched. He just was not ready to be a starter, especially not with a quarterback like Ron Jaworski still on the team.

The following week, Randall started again at Washington and the Eagles won, 19-6. The city went wild. A "Star Was Born" the headlines read. When I got home that night, Cindy told me that CBS Radio had called and that they wanted me to go on with Jack Buck and Hank Stram and talk about the game. All they wanted to talk about was Cunningham. I refused to fall into the trap that this was an emergence of a new star. I think they were surprised at my lack of enthusiasm about what the nation had perceived as the changing of the guard in Philadelphia. But I was not sold yet. I believed Randall needed more time.

And that time would come.

Later that season in a game at New Orleans I spotted a familiar face in the pressbox at the Superdome. It was Sid Gillman, who had worked on Dick Vermeil's staff and was in my mind, as well as many others', an offensive genius. I felt Gillman was the best offensive mind and quarterback coach I had ever been around. Here he was in New Orleans, and I couldn't figure out why. When I asked, he told me he was just there on a business trip and brought a few clients to the game. I thought that was strange, and I was right. The very next day it was announced that Gillman would join Campbell's staff as a consultant and to work with Cunningham. And there was no doubt that was Norman Braman's move, because Marion Campbell was not happy. He wanted no part of this move.

Sid Gillman worked with Randall and saw in him incredible gifts. But he wanted him to learn the game. Sid believed the game was played from the neck up, and that Randall, like a lot of young quarterbacks, did not prepare himself enough. Sid wanted you to live football day and night and even in your sleep. He was big on film work and wanted you to watch every aspect of the game and learn it. Sid once gave Randall a film with a piece of paper in the film about a quarter of the way through it. The next day Randall brought the film back. Sid asked if he watched it, and Randall told him he did and that he learned from it. Sid took the film and saw the piece of paper in the same exact spot.

Campbell, Gillman, and the rest of the coaching staff was gone by the start of the 1986 season. Buddy Ryan came in and one of his first moves was to trade for Matt Cavanaugh. Ryan wanted Cavanaugh to be the starter, but it was evident from the first day of camp that he could not beat out Jaworski for the job. What Ryan did with Cunningham, however, was unique. To take advantage of his great arm and improvisational skills, he would put him in the game on third down and long situations. Some people thought that helped make Randall a better quarterback in the long run. That it gave him a chance to make big plays, which was what he did best. I thought it took the Eagles offense out of its continuity and it certainly did not sit well with Jaworski. Early in his Eagles career, he was pulled on third downs by Vermeil for John Sciara, and now late in his career he was being pulled on third downs by Ryan for Cunningham. In any event, it was clear that sooner or later Jaworski was going to be replaced, and Cunningham was going to be the quarterback of this team.

Midway through that season in a game against the Giants, Jaworski broke the index finger on his right hand, and that was the break Ryan needed. Cunningham replaced him, and Jaworski never played for the Eagles again. That offseason the team failed to pick up the option on his contract and he became a free agent. He later signed with Miami as Dan Marino's backup and finished his career in Kansas City, also as a backup. Could he have stayed and been Cunningham's backup? That was a question asked over and over. In my mind, it would not have worked. It was one thing for a long-time starter to go elsewhere and be a backup, it was another to be a back up for the team you took to the Super Bowl.

However, during that 1986 season with Cunningham now in charge, the team played back-to-back games in Seattle and Los Angeles, and Ryan kept the team on the west coast the entire week in between. We flew to Los Angeles after the Seattle game and stayed at the Anaheim Marriott through the week, which happened to be Thanksgiving week. Randall was really upbeat that entire week. He told me he was excited, because his brother Sam, who lived in Los Angeles, was going to have Thanksgiving dinner with him. Both of

Randall's parents had passed away within the span of a year when he was still in high school and Sam was sort of a father figure to him. I saw him early Thanksgiving Day in the lobby of the hotel and he said he was waiting for Sam. I went out that day, and it was kind of weird to be away from home on Thanksgiving and have the temperatures in the mid 70s. But I went out and played tennis and when I got back to the hotel about three hours later, Randall still sat in the lobby waiting for Sam. I can't say for sure that Sam never showed up, but you had to feel sorry for Randall. He was just a sad sight that day.

You could see then how Randall just did not fit in with the rest of his teammates. And even as his stardom grew, he was never one of the guys. And that day, on Thanksgiving Day, he sat alone in a hotel lobby waiting an eternal wait. The crazy thing was he never let his personal life interfere with his professional life. It had to have bothered him what happened with his brother, but that Sunday against the Raiders he played a great game and led the Eagles to a 33-27 overtime upset. Randall passed for 298 yards and three touchdowns and scored the overtime touchdown himself on a one-yard keeper.

In that game, he also made one of the most remarkable passes I have ever seen. It went down on the scoresheet as a 10-yard touchdown pass to Mike Quick, but it was simply incredible. Randall rolled out to his right at full speed, nearly went out of bounds, and threw the ball to the exact opposite corner of the end zone for Quick. He went 53 and a half yards, the width of the field, without any arch.

There were great expectations for Randall in 1987. He had the job. Jaworski was gone. And he had shown signs, like the Raiders game, that he could get it done. Now he had to just gain the consistency, and who knew what he might achieve. I did a radio show that year from Old Original Bookbinders with Randall, Mike Quick, and Reggie White every Friday night at 6 o'clock. I also did a 10-minute interview with Randall every week that ran as part of the pregame show on Sundays.

Randall was very involved in these shows. Most players just wanted to do what they had to do, and get back to something else. I have never seen a player as concerned about his performance in an interview as Randall was. He would come to the WIP trailer during training camp and wanted to listen to the tape. If he didn't like the way it sounded, he wanted to do it over. He wanted it to be perfect every week. And he would ask me several questions about how he should sound, or what he should say. He was very conscientious about this 10-minute interview.

In 1987, after two games, the players went on strike. And this bothered Randall more than it did most of the players. He knew he was coming into his own as a quarterback, and as a star, and to be interrupted for a month by the strike could only hurt his development. He did not, however, let it get in the way of his radio shows. I would be at WIP early in the morning to do my sports reports, and I would get a call from Randall. He would say something like, "Meet me at 16th and Oregon," or at some other secluded place, because he didn't want anyone to know he was doing this. I would meet him at a different locale every week, and I would get in his car and we would tape the interview. It was like some secret covert operation. He really wanted that strike to end, and while he would have never crossed the picket line, he did not like being out of the game for a month.

Randall came back after the strike and it was as if he were never off. He led the Eagles to two consecutive dramatic wins in the final seconds against St. Louis and Washington, and when the team won its final two games of the season against the Jets and Buffalo, you could see that this team was about to make a name for itself. These Buddy Ryan Eagles, with Randall Cunningham at quarterback, had begun to take flight. The team finished 7-8, but throw out the strike replacement games and they were 7-5. And that was how the players looked at it. They were a winning team for the first time since Vermeil had left. And they wanted more.

In 1988 the Eagles won the NFC East. It was their first division title since 1980, and they haven't won another one since. Randall was the NFC Player of the Year and you could sense a bit of a change. He was no longer the shy, introverted player who came to West Chester back in 1985. He didn't get a big head or anything, but all of a sudden he had a lot of hangers-on, guys who just wanted to be with him and be his friend; he started to dress flashier and live a better life. And he wasn't as focused on football, he always wanted to be an entertainer as much as he wanted to be a football player. And now it seemed he cared about being on the Arsenio Hall Show as much as he did Monday Night Football. Randall once left a preseason game at halftime, with Buddy's approval, to go to Whitney Houston's birthday party. Randall wanted to be more than just an All-Pro quarterback, he wanted to be like Magic Johnson, or Michael Jordan. He wanted it all.

Right before the second game of the 1989 season at Washington, the Eagles tore up Randall's modest million dollar contract, and gave him a new one. This was a seven-year extension that paid him over $3 million a year. To celebrate, he went out and threw five touchdown passes in an incredible 42-37 win over the Redskins. Randall had made it to the big time. He was among the highest paid players in the game, and his off-the-field career now included the Randall Cunningham television show, his own version of the Arsenio Hall Show. He had also built a mansion in Moorestown, New Jersey, where he lived, and it was featured on the television show "Life Styles of the Rich and Famous." It had everything, including some private rooms, like the Michael Jackson Room, and Eric's Domain, reserved for Rams running back Eric Dickerson, and other novelties. Randall had started to become what Stan often referred to as Starship 12. You never knew when he would take off, or where he might land.

One of the best moves Ryan made where Cunningham was concerned was the hiring of quarterbacks coach Doug Scovil, who he had worked with when both of them were in Chicago. Scovil was also the head coach at San Diego State before he came to the Eagles with Ryan. Cunningham more than just respected Scovil, he loved the guy. He called him Dougie Fresh, which may have been the name of a rap singer at the time. But Scovil was great for Randall. Doug and I were very good friends as well. He was probably as close a friend as I've ever had among the assistant coaches. He would tell me about Randall and what a bright future he saw for him. The thing was, Randall listened to Doug. He played hard for Doug, and when he had a bad game he felt he let Doug down.

Doug and I played a lot of tennis together. We played every day for a week during a week-long stay in San Diego. The Eagles again had consecutive road games on the west coast, this time Denver and San Diego and Buddy kept the team in La Jolla for a week. One day in San Diego, while we were playing, Doug had to stop several times. He was winded. I told him we could stop, but he wanted to go on. He just said he felt a little light-headed. He sat for a while, but came back and played, he said it was no big deal. And I didn't think much of it, either.

Five weeks later I got a call at home on a Saturday. It was the station and they wanted to let me know one of the Eagles assistant coaches had passed away that morning. It was Doug Scovil. My heart sunk; I couldn't speak. Randall was just as crushed. The Eagles beat the Cowboys the next day, 20-10, but Randall went out there with a heavy heart. He had lost his mentor, his father figure, his biggest fan. Doug believed that Randall would have become the game's best quarterback and that he was on his way.

Randall served as one of the pallbearers at Doug's funeral and also gave the eulogy. As big as Randall had become, with his television show, his own candy bar, the Randall Bar, and his Hollywood friends, Randall still had his insecurities, and losing Scovil just made it worse. Randall was never the same after that. After Doug died, Randall's career took a turn for the worse. He put up big numbers in 1990, but he wasn't the same. Nobody else ever had the affect on him that Doug did.

Randall became more and more concerned with statistics; his statistics, and every other quarterback's statistics. He would sit at his locker and study the league stats. He would be able to tell you where every quarterback was ranked and what their numbers were. It consumed him more than it should have. He once got very upset with Bill Parcells, then the Giants head coach, because Parcells had called him, "One of the top 10 quarterbacks in the league." He felt that was an insult to only be included in the top 10. He said that meant he might only be the 10th best.

Throughout his career, Randall played with the kind of abandon that was reckless to say the least. He felt he could do whatever he wanted and would come back. Maybe he believed what Schad said, that he was Gumby. He was invincible, or so he thought. Randall entered the 1991 season with a streak of 64 consecutive games played, the longest active streak of any quarterback at the time.

Rich Kotite became Cunningham's third head coach, and Zeke Bratkowski became his fourth offensive coordinator in the span of six years, before that 1991 season started. And for Randall it lasted just 15 minutes. On the first play of the second quarter of the opening game against Green Bay, Randall went down, hit like he had been a thousand times before, only this time he did not get up. And he did not come back the rest of the season.

I never thought he was the same after the injury. He worked like crazy to come back and rehabbed every day. But he had lost that sense of invincibility. And when he was injured again two years later, the fourth game of the 1992 season against the Jets, it just doubled his doubts.

Off the field, Randall became even more of an enigma. He was always good to the media, always had time for an interview. Except in his interviews, he would say one thing, and a few minutes later say the complete opposite. He was the "king of contradiction" as one writer called him. Or as another said, "You can never quote Randall out of context, because he's never in context." It had become a joke as to what he might say, or do, next. He meant well, but his intentions were sometimes taken the wrong way. Like at the end of the 1990 season when it was assumed Buddy Ryan was going to be fired. Cunningham openly endorsed Rich Kotite, the offensive coordinator. It appeared at the time that Randall had stabbed Buddy in the back. He later said he was just trying to help Kotite get a job somewhere else, if they were all going to be fired. By the end it seemed he was always involved in a controversy.

There was his infamous one-game benching in 1992 when Kotite announced after a loss to Dallas that he was going to start Jim McMahon against the Raiders, and then bring Randall back the following week against Green Bay. It was the only time I had ever heard a coach make just a one-week change like that. I thought he did it as a benefit to Randall just to give him a week off to sit back and watch. Of course, Randall did not see it that way, and that may have been the beginning of the end between he and Kotite.

Later that year, the Eagles played their biggest game of the season against the Washington Redskins. The winner was in the playoffs. The loser needed to win the following week and hope for other scenarios to take place. As I left the locker room Friday afternoon, Randall sat at his locker by himself. I walked by and said rather casually, "Randall, you're going to have a great game, Sunday." I expected the response to be, "Thanks, Merrill, I'll do my best." Instead, he looked at me and said, "What makes you say that?"

I said something about it being a big game and he loved big games, I mean I was kind of taken aback by it. And he looked at me again and said, "I really think this all comes down to play calling. If Richie calls the best plays, we'll win. If Joe Gibbs calls the best plays, they'll win." Again, I was shocked. I actually had to give him a little pep talk two days before the biggest game of the season. Thank God the Eagles won the game that Sunday, or I would have felt that maybe I messed him up even more.

In 1993, Randall suffered his second major injury; this time a broken leg the third week of the season against the Jets, and he was never the same again. I thought he lost a little after the first injury, but after the second he was a different player. It wasn't his arm. I've always thought that one day when Randall is 93 years old he will still be able to throw the ball on a laser to the far corner of the end zone. But his foot speed, his agility, were not the same. He just couldn't do the things he used to. And as he lost some of his ability, he also lost his confidence.

Some great quarterbacks, like Joe Montana, Steve Young, and Warren Moon, as their physical skills deteriorated, became more mentally involved. Hopefully, that can happen with Randall in Minnesota. You saw him in the playoffs last year win a big game against the Giants. I would love to see his career rebound with the Vikings. But it wasn't going to happen with the Eagles. He needed a change. He sulked. It became evident that he did not want to be here anymore.

When Ray Rhodes took over in 1995 he wanted Randall to be his quarterback. One of the first things Rhodes announced at his press conference was that Randall was his quarterback. And he was for about five games. Rhodes benched him the second half of the second game of the 1995 season in Arizona, but returned him to the lineup the following week against San Diego. After a 1-3 start and a terrible loss to Oakland, that was it. Rodney Peete replaced Randall and started the rest of the season.

Randall became a mess. He packed his locker before the season was over. He wore his Eagles jacket inside out on the sidelines. But still he stole the headlines one more time at the end of the season. Randall's wife, Felicity, was expecting the couple's first child and was due in January. The Eagles made the playoffs, beat Detroit in the wild-card game, and were headed to Dallas for the second round. And it was getting close for Felicity. Randall made it clear to a couple of writers that he was going to be with his wife, no matter what.

The Eagles spent the week before the Cowboys game in Vero Beach, and sure enough, Randall got the call in the middle of the week that Felicity had gone into labor. Ray gave him the go-ahead, and Randall left Florida and flew to his home in Las Vegas. Except he left his playbook behind. And he didn't fly back until after the last practice Friday morning. By that point, when you asked any of the players about Randall, they would just roll their eyes which told you more than you needed to know. He was Starship 12 to them by now, too.

What made this all worse, was that Peete was injured early in the Dallas game and could not play. The pressbox announcer at Texas Stadium said, "Peete was knocked woosey and would not return." The feeling among the rest of us was that they hadn't seen woosey yet. Cunningham went into the game, as unprepared as you could be, and played that way. It was his last game as an Eagle, and it was a shame for him to exit that way.

After 11 years as the Ultimate Weapon, he left as a shadow of that player. He left as an unprepared, seemingly disinterested player who spent the last week of his Eagles career away from the team.

CHAPTER ELEVEN

A Buddy Forever

Buddy Ryan was 12 games into his first season as head coach of the Eagles back in 1986, and like a lot of fans at that time, I had no idea how to take him. Mike McCormack, Dick Vermeil, even Marion Campbell, I had gotten to know very quickly and very easily. Buddy was different. Or at least I thought he was.

We were in Anaheim for the week before the game with the Raiders, and Sam and Lorna Cohen, friends of mine from Philadelphia who had relocated to San Diego, came by to visit. Sam was a huge Eagles fans and, as we sat in the lobby of the Marriott, he asked me what I thought of this Buddy Ryan guy.

I told him the truth. I had been around a lot of coaches and this was the most difficult man I have ever tried to get to know. He was cold and unfriendly and not what I had grown to like in a coach. I met him the day he was hired. I was at his first minicamp in Tampa and his second minicamp back in Philadelphia. I was there every day of training camp and every day during the season. And I felt he didn't know me, or even my name, or what I did.

Just then, almost as if we had it planned, Buddy Ryan walked through the lobby and came right over to us. He looked down at me and said, "Hi Merrill, how's your tennis?" I thought I would pass out. I introduced him to the Cohens, and he sat down and talked football with us for the next hour. From that day on, he was as warm and friendly to me as any coach before or after.

What I finally realized was, with Buddy it took time to acquire his trust, but once you did he was your friend forever. I've already talked about Dick Vermeil and how much I thought of him as a man and as a coach. But Vermeil was so intense during the season. When I had to do a pregame show with Dick, if it was 10 minutes, after five minutes he would start to look at his watch. And as soon as we were finished, he would be gone. Buddy was absolutely the best. Once I had gotten his trust, he told me whatever I wanted to know and always had time for me.

Tom Brookshier, the former Eagles star defensive back, had arrived at WIP as a investor with the new owner, Spectacor. One of Tom's responsibilities was the pregame show and he was supposed to tape an interview every week with Buddy. Once, an hour before the game, we got a panic call in the booth that Tom had forgotten to do the interview. I told them just to fill the time with something else. They said we couldn't, that the show was sold on the basis of a 10-minute interview with Buddy Ryan and we had to have it. Now, we were 55 minutes away from kickoff.

I turned to Stan and said, "I'm not doing this alone, you better come with me, big fellow." Stan and I went down to the coach's office. It was 12:10 by then and the show aired at 12:20. We saw Buddy and told him what had happened. He laughed, and said, "Come on in, let's do it." Neither Stan nor I believed it.

Three weeks later it happened again, exactly the same way. Brookshier again forgot to do the show. I said to Stan, "No way. He was nice enough to do it once. He's not going to do it again. He's going to kill us." We went down to his office. He saw us and laughed again. This time he said, "I just want to make sure Brookshier is paying you guys extra for this."

For all of his gruffness, or supposed gruffness, Buddy Ryan was really one of the nicest people you'd want to meet. If he trusted you, he couldn't do enough for you. And the work he did for local charities, and the help he provided for those charities, has gone unmatched.

When Buddy was hired, it came under some strange circumstances, not unlike the way Vermeil was hired and later, the way Ray Rhodes was hired. The guy who Norman Braman originally wanted was David Shula, the son of Miami Dolphins head coach Don Shula. Actually, the first name I had heard, which came during the season when Marion Campbell's demise was being speculated in the newspapers, was Howard Schnellenberger. Braman knew Schnellenberger when he was the head coach at the University of Miami, and they had been spotted together at different parties in the Miami area.

But with one game left in the season, and just after a road loss to San Diego, there was a story in the *Inquirer* that Braman and Harry Gamble had met with David Shula about becoming the next head coach of the team. The story outlined this lengthy meeting, and the plans to hire the then-26-year-old Shula. Of course, the Eagles would not comment on the story. But that day Marion Campbell resigned and one of his assistants, Fred Bruney, was named interim coach for the final game of the season at Minnesota. The Eagles won that game and Bruney became the only undefeated head coach in team history. Some of the players tried to campaign for Bruney, because players were always afraid of change, and Bruney would have been the safe pick for them. Of course, he had no chance.

Shula was the first choice. And the deal almost got done, but there was a disagreement over the contract. The Eagles had a clause in it that after five years the team would have an option for another five years. Shula did not want the option, and that became a major problem which eventually killed the deal.

In the meantime, Jim Mora became the hot commodity and Braman's second choice. He had been the head coach of the USFL's Philadelphia Stars and had experienced great success at that level. He was also a Dick Vermeil clone as a coach. He had that same California look that Vermeil had and some believed the same passion. And again it looked like it was a done deal.

There was supposedly a press conference planned to announce Mora's hiring, but Hal Smith, the new general manager of WIP, told me to hold off on any news about Mora. He had heard from one of the people he dealt with in the Eagles front office that it was not going to get done. Mora had a problem with the contract as well. His problem stemmed from how much money he could make from outside interests.

Next was Buddy Ryan, the defensive coordinator of the Chicago Bears. The Bears had run through the NFL that 1985 season and were in the Super Bowl. Harry Gamble flew down to New Orleans for the game and to meet with Ryan as soon as it was over. The NFL has a rule that another team cannot talk to a prospective coach until his season was completed. So Ryan could not be approached until after the Super Bowl, and Gamble wanted to be first in line.

Chicago won the game, 46-10, the defensive players hoisted Ryan off on their shoulders and a few days later he was in Philadelphia for a press conference. What I remember most about that press conference, other than that it was held at the Quality Inn—which is not exactly named properly—was how much Ryan seemed to enjoy himself. He could not answer enough questions. While some coaches, especially new ones, would often duck the tough questions or talk around them, Ryan wanted more. He was asked, "How long will it take the team to learn your 46 defense?" Buddy looked down at the reporter and said, "Oh, about 35 minutes."

Buddy didn't give his later infamous Arizona Cardinals speech, that "You have a winner in town." But it was close. He made it clear that he expected to win and he expected to win in a hurry.

That first minicamp in Tampa was crazy. I had never seen a coach just rip up his players the way Buddy did. He called fullback Michael Haddix, "A damn reject guard from the USFL." He called linebacker Dwayne Giles, "An old washerwomen." I thought this guy was certifiable. He was nuts.

Then there was his first draft. Buddy had his own radio show on WCAU and did a program the night before the draft. During the show he was asked about Ohio State running back Keith Byars, who was expected to be a top 10 pick, but was also a question mark because of a broken bone in his foot. Ryan made it clear that Byars was not in his plans. He called him "a medical reject." So with the tenth overall pick in the draft, Ryan chose Keith Byars, running back, Ohio State. It absolutely floored everyone. Some people were upset. How could he lie like that, they asked. I thought it was just another crazy move from a guy I had still not figured out.

In the second round, Ryan took another running back, Anthony Toney, who he also said during that radio show he was going to take in the first round. With his next second-round pick he took a linebacker named Alonzo Johnson, who had tested positive for drugs in college at the University of Florida. Buddy would later admit that was his only mistake, and that, while he did not know much about drugs or drug use, he would learn all he could.

Later in the draft, Ryan selected two unknown players from unheralded schools; Seth Joyner, a linebacker from the University of Texas-El Paso, and Clyde Simmons, a defensive end from Western Carolina. They would turn out to be two of the biggest draft day steals in Eagles history.

Buddy was also very creative on the field, and off. More than once he forced the league to change certain rules. Once, punter John Teltschik, in punt formation, threw a pass high in the air that resembled a punt. That was to draw a pass interference penalty on the defense, who of course thought the ball was kicked. There was also his infamous "Polish punt team", his words not mine. That was where he sent 14, or 15 players onto the field in the final seconds when the Eagles were forced to punt. Back then, the clock ran even if there was a penalty. Ryan's thought was let them call us for too many men on the field. The clock would still run out and with all those men on the field, there was no way the punt would be blocked or returned for a touchdown against us.

Ryan also invented what has become known as voluntary camp, a pre-training camp that lasted about two weeks right before camp was scheduled to start. This was strictly up to the player if he wanted to come to the camp or not. Of course if he didn't come to the camp, he would be traded or released. But that voluntary camp was one of the best innovations by a coach. The Eagles, like some other teams, always had contract holdouts. It was more the norm, or Buddy would say, "the Norman", to have players hold out than it was for them to be in camp on time. So he came up with this camp that gave the players who were not going to be at training camp on time some work, both on the field and in the classroom.

There was also the light side of Buddy Ryan. He was terrible with names, so he would either murder a guy's name, or he gave him a new one. Mike Reichenbach, his middle linebacker in the 46 defense, was Rock-em-back. Seth Joyner, the All-Pro linebacker, was Zeff. Junior Tautalatasi, a late-round running back who stuck for a few years, was Junior Smith. Byron Evans, who later replaced Reichenbach, was simply BNE, his initials.

Buddy told me a story once that I can never forget. I asked him why he got rid of Ken Reeves, a tackle from Texas A&M. Reeves had been injured a few times, but when he played he was decent. Buddy said, "If a cow has a calf, and that calf gets hit by a car, it's bad luck. If that same cow has another calf, and it gets hit by lighting, you shoot the cow."

Then there was the time Tim Kawakami, the beat writer from the *Daily News* and one of Buddy's more loyal supporters, got a little confused. He asked Buddy, "What was it that Steve Kaufusi (a backup defensive end) liked about him?" He meant what did Buddy like about Steve Kaufusi. But without missing a beat, Buddy responded, "I'm short, fat, and good looking."

One of Buddy's biggest problems, however, was his inability to say anything nice about Norman Braman, or Harry Gamble. Worse

than that was his insistence to knock them, at any, and every opportunity. After the first game of the season, a 41-14 loss to Washington, Buddy spoke at the Maxwell Club luncheon and mentioned
that Harry, who was just promoted to President, "must be Braman's
illegitimate son."

The Maxwell club roared with laughter, and the assembled
media had their story for the day. Harry laughed too, but also turned
a bright red. It wouldn't be the last time Buddy embarrassed him.

One of the things I disagreed with Buddy about was his view
of Harry Gamble. For whatever reason, Buddy thought Harry was
out to get him, and it was the farthest thing from the truth.

The greatest misconception was that Harry was not a football
man. That was exactly what he was. He played football, he coached
football at the college level for 14 years, and was an assistant on
Vermeil's staff. He also had a great business mind and had his doc-
torate in business. Harry was well-liked around the league and was
even on the league's competition committee before he retired in
1995. Personally, I've always felt that if Buddy and Harry would
have gotten along better, and if Buddy could have just complimented
the front office every now and then, instead of the insults, it could
have been a great marriage. If he would have just tried a little harder,
I believe Buddy Ryan would have coached this team as long as he
wanted.

Instead, Buddy wanted to run the show, and for the most part
Harry had no problem with that. If nothing else, Buddy had a great
eye for talent. Even his biggest critics had to admit that Buddy knew
personnel, and his drafts were the best the Eagles had before or
since. There were no mistakes picked in the first round under
Buddy's watch. And his late-round picks like Joyner and Simmons
were also a sign of the work he did on the draft.

But this was Buddy's team for five years, and it was right from
the start. In his first training camp at West Chester University the
team had what it called "fan appreciation day." Buddy grabbed the
microphone that day and proclaimed to the thousands in atten-
dance that, "We're going to win the NFC East and we're going to
sweep Dallas, Washington, the Giants, and St. Louis along the way."
They went wild. As it turned out, the Eagles went 1-6-1 in the NFC
East that season and finished in fourth place.

What Buddy did, however, that entire season from his outrageous predictions to his wild quotes, was take all the pressure off a
young, inexperienced team and put it directly on an old, experi-

enced coach. "I can take it," he said later. "They can't, not yet anyway."

You could see the team begin to develop in 1986. They didn't win, but they did improve. An early 41-14 loss to Washington turned into a 21-14 late-season loss to the Redskins. An ugly 35-3 loss to the Giants was trimmed all the way down to 17-14 later in the season. And of course the next-to-last game of the season, Buddy beat Dallas. He always beat Dallas.

He beat the Cowboys again in 1987 in a classic Ryan performance, one that put the Eagles/Cowboys rivalry back in the spotlight.

It started with the players' strike that saw the regular players leave for a month and be replaced by strike players who actually played in three games that season. They were the worst games I've even been associated with as a broadcaster. I've broadcast 339 games in my career plus the preseason and I looked forward to every one of them, except those three strike games. I hated the replacement games, and so did Buddy Ryan.

No other coach in the league made it as clear as Buddy did that he wanted no part of these games. He barely coached the players that were brought in for him; and he, more than any other coach encouraged his players to stay on strike while around the league some veterans had crossed the picket lines. The Eagles were the only team that year that had total unity. "I either wanted them all in, or all out," Ryan said. "But I wanted them together."

That togetherness forged a bond among the Eagles players and Ryan that led to the success the team enjoyed over the following four seasons.

After a strike loss to Dallas, in which the Cowboys used veterans like All-Pro running back Tony Dorsett and quarterback Danny White, and won 41-22, Buddy vowed revenge. He hated Tom Landry anyway, and when Landry put his veterans back in the game late after the score was out of reach, Ryan was furious.

As fate would have it, the first game after the strike ended was at Veterans Stadium against Dallas. All week Ryan hinted that he was going to do something out of the ordinary. He never said what, and we would have never guessed. The Eagles played one of their best games under Buddy to date, and led 30-20 with less than a minute left. With the ball at midfield, he ordered Randall Cunningham to take a knee on first down and again on second down. Dallas had used its final time out, and one more kneel down and the game was over. Except on third down, Cunningham faked the kneeldown, and threw into the end zone for Mike Quick. The surprised Dallas defensive back was called for pass interference, and on first-and-goal from the one yardline, Keith Byars scored to make it 37-20.

It was unprecedented. It was Buddy Ryan. Personally, I loved it; I don't mind saying how much I loved it. I thought back to the days when Dallas linebacker LeeRoy Jordan kicked out Timmy Brown's teeth. I thought back to the days when Dallas regularly blew out the Eagles and never thought twice about it. This was for all those games. For Buddy it was fun. It was revenge. And when it was over he acted like nothing happened. "They opened the can of worms," Ryan said. "We closed it."

But what Ryan had reopened was the great rivalry with the Cowboys. It would continue when Jimmy Johnson replaced Landry. There was the Bounty Bowl and the Snowball Game, and more importantly seven straight wins over the hated Cowboys. And Buddy loved every one of them a little more than the one before. After a close win over a Cowboys team the Eagles should have handled a lot easier in 1990, Ryan said, "They know we're going to beat them, they just don't know how."

That 1987 strike got Buddy in trouble again long after it was over. At the end of the season, in his final press conference, he went over the year and how the team had come back to finish 7-5 in the "real games" and how the strike had killed them because they went 0-3 in those games. He then presented what he called "scab rings", which were actually paper weights, to Joe Woolley, his personnel man and George Azar, Gamble's close friend and assistant. Again, the room went wild with laughter. Woolley, who was used to Buddy's way, accepted his and blushed a bit. Azar hurried out of the room and never actually faced the embarrassment.

At that point, Norman Braman was furious. He was furious with Buddy for the way he treated the replacement players and how he failed to coach them. He was furious that Ryan had sided with the players, and therefore against management, during the strike. And now he was furious about this "scab ring" incident. This was not the NFL Braman envisioned when he bought the team from Leonard Tose. He knew he would have opponents. He never thought one of them would be his own coach. Braman was ready to fire Ryan right then and there. He had enough.

Harry told Braman to wait. He told him he believed, despite his antics, that Ryan had made the Eagles a better team and was on the right track. Gamble pleaded with Braman to give Ryan another year and that if the team did not win, he could fire both of them. Harry meant it. He also believed this team would succeed under Ryan. And he was right.

In 1988, the Eagles returned to the playoffs for the first time since the wild-card playoff loss to the Giants in 1981, and had their first division title since the Super Bowl season of 1980. It all came down to the final game of the season. The Eagles were in Dallas and went into the game with a chance to either miss the playoffs entirely, qualify as a wild-card team, or win the division. And little of it had to do with the outcome of their game.

Here's the way it went down. The Eagles won easily, but for a moment were out of the playoffs. Then Atlanta knocked off New Orleans, and Jim Mora, on a last-second field goal by Morten Andersen, and the Eagles had clinched at least a wild-card berth. Then the Jets, with offensive coordinator Rich Kotite, upset the Giants on a touchdown pass to Al Toon in the final seconds and the Eagles were division champs. It was a wild finish to the day.

In the broadcast booth, I talked about the final plays of the Eagles win while Stan watched the Giants game on a monitor and let everyone know what had happened there. I've said before, and I've told people that you really can't tell the difference between a win and a loss on the plane ride home after a game. This one was different. This was like New Year's Eve. There was a constant celebration; you would have thought they won the Super Bowl.

The Eagles had to wait to learn their first-round opponent in the playoffs. The Minnesota Vikings played the Los Angeles Rams in the wild-card game, and the outcome determined the next round's parings. Minnesota won, and that meant the Eagles would go to Chicago to take on Mike Ditka and the Bears.

Ryan's and Ditka's rivalry was legendary. Ditka was forced to keep Ryan on his staff when he was hired as head coach. And while the two helped the Bears to the Super Bowl in 1985, they did not share a friendship. And Ditka was not so thrilled when the Bears defensive players carried Ryan off the field after the Super Bowl win. Now the two would meet in a playoff game at Soldier Field.

When the playoff field was determined, Buddy said then, "We're not going to sneak into town. We're going to go in with our horns blowing and our lights blaring. They'll know the Eagles are in town."

Most thought he was speaking figuratively. We didn't know he was serious. When we landed in Chicago we got off the plane and on to the team bus and headed, we thought, to the hotel. I sat next to Wade Phillips, the defensive coordinator at the time, and all of a sudden we saw Soldier Field. Wade shook his head and said, "Oh no, he can't be serious." Just then, all four buses turned on their lights and we circled the field and the horns began to blow. We circled the field three times before we headed to the Marriott.

The next day the Eagles lost in the fog to the Bears, and lost playoff games the next two years to the Rams and to the Redskins. In between, Ryan continued to have his share of controversies and headline grabbers.

In 1989, during a nightly coach's dinner, Buddy choked on a pork chop and was saved by his offensive coordinator Ted Plumb, who performed the Heimlich maneuver. Defensive coordinator Jeff Fisher said he walked in and saw Plumb's arms around Ryan in what looked like a stranglehold and thought Buddy had criticized his play-calling once too often. Ditka, Ryan's nemesis, capitalized on Buddy's misfortune. He did a commercial for his Chicago-based restaurant in which he said, "Buddy Ryan would have never choked on one of our pork chops, they're too tender."

Again in 1989, against Dallas on Thanksgiving Day, another controversy erupted. Kicker Luis Zendejas, who the Eagles had released midway through the season, signed with the Cowboys. Jesse Small, an Eagles linebacker who never quite lived up to his potential, took Zendejas out on a vicious hit during a kickoff. The Cowboys cried foul and head coach Jimmy Johnson accused Ryan of having put a bounty on Zendejas. Ryan laughed and said Johnson tried to take attention away from his poor team. He also asked why he would want to hurt a "kicker who can't kick."

Most of the 1990 season was spent on the speculation as to whether Buddy would be back the next season and what he had to do to come back. His contract expired at the end of the season and his feuds with Braman had become public. Some felt another playoff appearance wouldn't be enough. The feeling was the Eagles had to make it at least to the NFC Championship Game, if not the Super Bowl, for Ryan to continue as Braman's coach.

Tight end Keith Jackson, Buddy's first-round pick in 1988 and already a two-time All-Pro, held out of training camp. Jackson, and his agent Gary Wichard, felt he had outplayed his contract with the two Pro Bowl appearances and wanted a new deal. Braman had a firm stance on renegotiating a contract and refused. Even though they had given Randall Cunningham a new contract a year earlier.

Jackson had also asked me if I would take part in a rap video that he taped the day before training camp opened. I did it, and as I left I told him I would see him later that night at camp. He said, "No, you won't. Merrill, I'm not going to be there. I'm not coming until I get a new contract." He gave me the exclusive interview with the promise I would not use it until after the rest of the players reported. Jackson missed the entire training camp and the first two games of the regular season. The Eagles lost both games he missed and were 0-2 as they prepared to play the Rams in Los Angeles.

That Tuesday I was out playing tennis, and when I got home Cindy was on the phone in what looked like a deep conversation. I asked her who was on the phone, and she said, "Keith Jackson." They talked for about 45 minutes and she commiserated with him over the whole ordeal. I talked to him after she was done and he told me he really wanted to come back, but didn't know what to do, or how to do it. The next day he was back. Buddy sent a limousine to the airport for him and he arrived in style. Buddy also orchestrated the press conference, which was held on the first floor in the coaches meeting rooms and was devoid of any front office people, or even the public relations staff. During the press conference, Jackson talked about a conspiracy that Braman and Gamble had to get rid of Buddy. He felt he had to come back to help the team win and save Buddy's job.

The Eagles won Jackson's first game back against Los Angeles and on the plane back home, Buddy looked at me and said loud enough for everyone to hear, "Hey Merrill, guess who I gave a game ball?" I said, "Who?" He said, "No. 88 (Jackson), just to shove it up the owner's ass." If Buddy wasn't in enough trouble already, that just dug his grave deeper. The Eagles, at that point might have needed to win the Super Bowl for Buddy to come back.

They didn't, of course, and when they lost to Washington in the first round, Ryan was fired. Braman was asked much later what would have happened if the Eagles did get to the Super Bowl, and he said, "It just would have made it tougher."

CHAPTER TWELVE

Jerome Brown and Co.

It was a hot summer night, one of those hazy, sticky late June nights when you needed the air conditioner on and a cold drink constantly refilled in your hand. I got a call from a radio station in Los Angeles and I couldn't believe what I was told. There was an unconfirmed report that Jerome Brown was killed in an auto accident in his hometown of Brooksville, Florida. And they wanted my comments and anything I knew.

I didn't know anything, and I was stunned when I heard. It was like a boulder crashed through the ceiling of my house. I spent the next two hours on the phone, getting and giving more information about what had supposedly happened. Finally, the Eagles verified that Jerome, and his young nephew, Gus, were killed when his car slid off a wet road and crashed into a tree. I drove down to the stadium where, as it turned out, Evangelist Billy Graham was speaking, and one of his guests was Reggie White. I saw Reggie in the tunnel when I got there and tears streamed down his face. He went out and gave an emotional speech that had everyone in tears before he was finished. I still couldn't believe it.

For Jerome to get killed in a car crash was not hard to fathom. We all thought that the way he lived, fast and hard, he would one day come to a screeching halt. But on the other hand, this hulk of a man, this half-man half-child, seemed invincible. Jerome once played in a playoff game after he took 12 shots of cortisone in his shoulder the night before. But he played—he always played. He might have missed as many practices as any player I've ever covered, but he never missed the game. Jerome Brown was there on Sundays. But now at the age of 27, and at the peak of an All-Pro career, he was gone and it seemed unreal.

Jerome was more than a great player and one of the best defensive tackles in the game, he was the all-time character. He was funny. He was tough. He was profane to the point that it would drive Reggie, an ordained minister, crazy. He never seemed to care what he said, or who was around when he said it. And he was honest, maybe to a fault. When he made the Pro Bowl after the 1990 season, he was asked what this meant. And he replied without hesitation, "More money, more money, more money, more money."

There are usually four buses that go from the hotel to the stadium the morning of a game. And I generally take the last one. Jerome always took the last one. You get to see the players in a different light just hours before a game. Some of the guys who are usually very vocal can be very quiet and intense. Others will have a Walkman over their ears and will stare straight ahead focused on the game plan in their mind. Jerome was Jerome; it didn't matter if it was minutes before a game, or minutes after a game—he was the same. He bounced onto the bus and he would be laughing and telling off-color jokes and just trying to get everyone loose. When we would get to a visiting stadium, opposing fans would often already be in the parking lot and they would yell at the Eagles. Most players would ignore it. Not Jerome, he would yell back. Every Sunday to Jerome was a family picnic. And the Eagles were his family.

Training camp at West Chester did not officially start until Jerome pulled up in his black Ford Bronco with the speakers blaring loud enough that you could hear the music back in Philadelphia. Players always reported the night before camp began, usually around 6 p.m. And right around 5:55 you would hear the thunder. It was the Bronco, and it was Jerome. He drove up Rosedale Avenue to the West Chester campus and pulled right up on the lawn to the players entrance. There would be several fans around to get autographs and lots of children to see their heroes up close. And Jerome would get out of the Bronco, stretch, and at the top of his lungs scream, "F— West Chester!" The fans would be in shock. The mothers, or fathers, would cover their children's ears. Jerome would look at us and laugh, and training camp could start.

I did a show in the late 80s from the Broadway Restaurant Bar and Grill with a different player every Monday night. I never bothered Jerome to do it, because I didn't figure he would be interested. While he was a good guy and a fun guy to be around, he was not the kind of player who would get into a deep discussion about the game. And we didn't pay the players to do the show. All they got was dinner at the restaurant. They did it, because I asked.

One day I was in the locker room and Jerome nearly accosted me. "When you going to put me on your show? When you going to put me on your show?" he continued to badger me. I was surprised. And I said, "How about next week?" Later that week I asked if we were set, and he said, "I can't, that's my bowling night." He saw the look on my face, and he said, "Merrill, you know I love you. I'll miss bowling to do your show." And he came and he was terrific. But there was a price involved. He went home with three of the biggest corned beef sandwiches you ever saw, and I didn't think he had two friends waiting for him.

Another memory I have of Jerome occurred during his second year. Before a preseason game, on what must have been a 100-degree day, we sat on the plane and waited. The plane was supposed to take off at 2 o'clock and it was 2 o'clock and Jerome was not there. Buddy was furious. He looked at his watch one more time and decided to take off without him. Just then, you heard the thunder. The black Bronco roared up Island Avenue about a million miles per hour. The players park in a lot that is attached to where the chartered flight takes off, and they can just walk about 25 yards to the plane. They don't have to go through the terminal.

Jerome turned into the parking lot on two wheels and came to a halt—I don't know if he even turned the engine off. He ran full speed to the plane. Buddy also had a rule about travel. He felt a road game was a business trip and you dressed for business. He demanded that every player wear a tie and jacket. Jerome ran onto the plane and he had a tie and a jacket and no shirt. The sweat poured off him and under each arm he had a bucket of Kentucky Fried Chicken.

Which leads to another Jerome story. The season before he died he sat at his locker one day and told the media—he loved to talk to the media about anything—about his plans for the future. "I want to play a few more years," he said. "I want to make the big money. Then I'm going to go out and buy some KFC franchises. And all I'm going to do is ride around in my Cadillac, smoke cigars, I'll probably weigh about 400 pounds, and check on my chickens." Unfortunately, he never got the chance.

Another time a writer from the *Philadelphia Tribune* went around the locker room and asked every player if he could meet anyone living, or dead, who would they want to meet, and why. A lot of the players said Dr. Martin Luther King, others said Malcolm X. Reggie, of course, said Jesus Christ. Jerome told the writer, "Janet Jackson. Why? Why do you think?"

The season after Jerome died, the Eagles honored him before a game, and retired his No. 99. Except the Eagles did not exactly plan to retire the number. Reggie White, and Seth Joyner decided to retire Jerome's number. They took it upon themselves, while they were on the field for the pregame ceremony to announce that No. 99 would never be worn again by an Eagles player. The front office staff heard the announcement the same time everyone else did, and at that point what could they do?

Also that year, the Eagles never touched Jerome's locker. They left it as it was. It was kind of eerie. They even took it with them to their playoff game in New Orleans that season, and recreated it in the visiting locker room of the Superdome. The Eagles played that entire 1992 season, their only playoff season under Rich Kotite, as a tribute to Jerome.

I first came to know about Jerome Brown when he was at the University of Miami. The Hurricanes played Penn State that year in the Fiesta Bowl. Brown was the guy who led his team, all dressed in Army fatigues, out of the formal dinner the night before the game. He stood up and announced, "The Americans didn't have dinner with the Japanese the night before Pearl Harbor." And out the Hurricanes stormed. I thought to myself then, this guy is something else. Little did I know then I would learn to love this same guy.

If Jerome was the central character of the Buddy Ryan years, he had plenty of supporting actors who shared in his glory.

One was Seth Joyner, the low-round draft pick from Texas-El Paso, who was actually released his rookie year, resigned, and developed into an All-Pro linebacker.

While Seth and Jerome were the best of friends, they were completely different in personality. Jerome was fun-loving, happy-go-lucky, say anything, do anything. Seth was sullen, intense, always focused, and always with that famous scowl on his face. Once you got to know Seth, you could see he was an intelligent, articulate man who liked to have fun. But it wasn't the same as Jerome. If

Jerome was slapstick, Seth was sarcasm. Jerome was boisterous. Seth was understated. Jerome could say anything about anyone and it would draw laughter. Seth would criticize and it would draw concerned looks. And Seth did criticize, especially after Buddy Ryan was fired.

In a *New York Times* article, Seth called Rich Kotite, the head coach at the time, a puppet. After a loss to Washington, Seth went off about the play of the entire team. He said, "while the defense didn't do anything, the offense was worse. You just mention the words 'Washington Redskins' and they fall apart. And our special teams were garbage." After a loss to Tampa Bay, he tore Kotite from limb to limb. "Sometimes you have to have guts," he said to the media among other things. On the plane, everyone was down. It was hot and we just wanted to get home. Seth looked right at me, our eyes met and he said loud enough for the entire plane to hear, "Merrill, was that the dumbest coaching you have ever seen?"

That was Seth. He hated to lose, and he took every loss personally. He had worked so hard to go from that low-round draft choice to the Pro Bowl, and he expected everyone else to work just as hard and when they didn't, he let them know. And he loved Buddy Ryan. He, along with Clyde Simmons, followed Buddy to Phoenix. When Ryan was fired and replaced by Kotite, who Seth did not respect, he became the angry young man. He would never mention the firing, but in the years that passed he would just call it, "The Change."

Defensive end Clyde Simmons was the third member of the Brown-Joyner trilogy, and while his career path paralleled Joyner's, they too were nothing alike personality wise. Simmons was a ninth-round draft pick out of Western Carolina, the same year Joyner was selected in the eighth round by UTEP. They both worked their way into the Eagles' lineup and eventually into the Pro Bowl. They also had the same agent, Jim Solano, and became the first non-quarterbacks to earn a $1 million salary before they went to their first Pro Bowl. They also left the Eagles together to rejoin Buddy Ryan in Arizona in 1994. On the field, Simmons played with the same tenacity as Joyner and Brown, from his right end spot. Off the field, however, he was totally different than both.

Simmons was a quiet man who let his actions on the field speak for him. There were actually times, during his career, when he would completely hide from the media. Although as his career progressed and he became a veteran on a young Jacksonville Jaguars team he emerged as the team spokesman on several occasions. Where Clyde and I had a mutual love was for dogs. He owned a Rottweiler, and we would talk about it all the time. Dogs were my second love, and any time I could get into a conversation about them I would, and that was one subject Clyde enjoyed talking about as well.

When you look back on that great Eagles defense with Jerome, Seth, Clyde, and Reggie, there were so many different personalities.

Reggie was the Reverend, an ordained minister, who was a coach's dream, and an opposing player's nightmare. Jerome was the classic bad boy. The kid who should have had to stay after school. He ran wild and created havoc everywhere he went. Clyde was the quiet guy, who did his job and went home afterwards. Then there was the rotation of Mike Pitts and Mike Golic.

Pitts was a first-round pick by Atlanta, who Buddy acquired in a trade with Atlanta for defensive end Greg Brown in 1987. While he never lived up to his first-round status, Pitts was a solid, consistent lineman who blended in well with the stars around him. Golic, a free agent out of Notre Dame who Buddy claimed on waivers from Houston, was almost as much the class clown as Jerome was. And the two of them would have great locker room battles every year before Notre Dame played Miami. One year Buddy even let it get to the point where he started Golic over Brown one game, because Notre Dame beat Miami the day before. Golic did not have the physical talent of the other players, but worked so hard and became an integral part of this defense.

Byron Evans was the middle linebacker and one of the lesser known players on a national scale, but a very good player who was cheated out of a big paycheck because of injury. Evans, who Buddy called BNE (his full name was Byron Nelson Evans, and although he was born in Arizona was not named after the famous golfer), was a fourth-round pick in 1987. It took him time to break into the lineup, but once he did, he was a force. He was one of the hardest hitters I had ever seen, and like the rest of that defense, intimidated the heck out of the opposition. By 1993 he had risen to near stardom and was offered a multi-million dollar contract before the 1994 season started. He turned it down, with hopes of getting even more after the season, but in week 10 of the 1994 season he suffered a terrible knee and leg injury in a loss to Cleveland, and never played again. Off the field, Byron might have been the most modest of the gang. I did a show on Monday nights at the Boathouse Row Bar at the Rittenhouse Hotel and Byron was my guest one night. I introduced him as one of the outstanding young linebackers in the NFL, a guy who personified the physical play that helps you win in this league. And Byron walked up and leaned over to me and said, "Man, Merrill I'm not that good."

The leader of the secondary was cornerback Eric Allen, a second-round pick of Ryan's in 1988. And actually a part of one of the best trades Ryan engineered. Before that draft, it was clear the Eagles needed a cornerback, and the top two were Allen and Terry McDaniel. Ironically, 10 years later, Allen has been traded to the Raiders and they are now looking to trade McDaniel. But the Eagles took tight end Keith Jackson in the first round, because he was just too talented not to take. Buddy still wanted a corner, and when Allen slipped, he traded a second-round and a fourth-round pick to Tampa Bay to get the Bucs' second-round pick, and he took Allen.

Eric was an intelligent player who rarely made a mental mistake. If a receiver beat Eric, he just flat out beat him. It wasn't because he was out of position or made the wrong decision. Off the field, Eric and I became friends. He invited us to his wedding reception. Some people feel you should not get too close to a player, or become too much of a friend, that it could color your analysis of him. But in my job I've always felt it helped me to get close. The players would feel comfortable with me, and know they could trust me, and it has helped me throughout my career.

People often ask me who is my favorite Eagles player of all-time. It's an impossible question for me to answer, there have been so many. There are guys who have become close personal friends of mine. There are guys who I watched in awe. There are guys who I thought the world of as individuals, but they were not great players.

Among my favorite Eagles players of all time was a guy who came out of tiny Cheyney State without any hype or any billing. He was as unheralded a free agent as the team had ever signed. And when he got to camp back in 1984 it was almost impossible to have a conversation with him. He was so shy and lacked the confidence in his articulation abilities.

Andre Waters grew up in Pahokee, Florida, where he would chase rabbits, sometimes for dinner. He somehow found his way to

Cheyney State and then as an undrafted free agent with the Eagles, who most thought had no chance of making the team. Every year there are players who show up at camp just to fill out the roster. They are called "campers", and some even come back year after year. They have no chance in the world to ever make the team.

That was what it appeared Waters was in 1984, but every day he did something that made you take notice. Most of the time he was getting into fights, because of a hit he made on a veteran player. But he made some big hits on defense, and he returned some kick-offs that were impressive, and he made the final roster.

In 1984, Waters was the Eagles' kickoff return man and he took one back 93 yards for a touchdown that helped them beat Washington, 16-10. That was his claim to NFL fame until Buddy Ryan came on in 1986. Ryan loved Andre and loved the way he fought every day in training camp. It took less than a handful of practices before Buddy promoted Waters ahead of veteran Ray Ellis as his starting strong safety.

Off the field, he worked on his speech, and became one of the team's better quotes because everything he said was heartfelt. He certainly did not have a vocabulary like fellow safety Terry Hoage, but he was passionate in his words and rarely, if ever, turned down an interview request.

Waters got himself in trouble on the field with what some felt were dirty hits. He was nicknamed Dirty Waters, and it became a big deal when ABC's Dan Dierdorf on a Monday Night Football telecast singled Waters out as the dirtiest player in the league. The Eagles, more specifically Buddy Ryan, refused to talk to Dierdorf or the MNF broadcast team the next time the Eagles were on Monday Night Football.

My read on Andre was he had to play hard and had to intimidate if he was going to stay in the league. That was how he made the roster in the first place, and that was what was going to keep him on it. He didn't have great size or speed. He had heart, and he had intensity, and he used them both the best he knew how. There were times when his play cost the Eagles with 15-yard penalties for late hits or unnecessary roughness. But after a few of those hits, he didn't need to take any more, receivers and backs stayed away.

Waters' style fit perfectly on a defense filled with big hitters and even bigger characters. It was a group I'll never forget.

Without Question

Rich Kotite never seemed to feel real comfortable in Philadelphia. He was a New Yorker who had been taken out of his city, and shipped south. It always seemed he wanted to get back to the Big Apple, although when he did it turned into even a worse disaster for him than his four years with the Eagles.

Those four years, from 1991-94, seemed to be one major blowup after another. Even when the team won under Kotite it wasn't under the best of circumstances. The major players on the team, especially the defensive players, still resented him because he wasn't the man he replaced, Buddy Ryan. It was a tumultuous four years to say the least.

I found out just how much Kotite disliked his surroundings during his final season, 1994, when he called me into his office and let all of his anger and frustration out. It was just before a road game at Washington. The team was 5-2 at the time, on their way to a 7-2 start before the NFL's all-time collapse.

Rich saw me outside, as I waited for the bus that would take us down to Washington. It was early, and he told me to come inside and wait with him. We went downstairs to his office, and when we got there he started, and he didn't stop.

"Let me tell you something," he said. "When this ends. When I'm out of here, and I am out of here, I'm out of here for good. I will leave this city so fast. And I'm never coming back here. You know what this town is, it's a town of losers. These people don't deserve a winner. They don't know football. This town is nothing but losers,

I tell you. They love that 1980 team, right? That's all I hear about is that 1980 team. They think that was the greatest team of all-time. Well, let me tell you something, that team lost the Super Bowl. They were losers."

It was unbelievable. He went on and on, and he took shots at all the Eagles icons. "They want to raise statues of guys from 1980," he said. "Those guys never won anything." I guess he was under pressure. Jeffrey Lurie had bought the team from Norman Braman before the season began, and everyone knew a coaching change could occur at the end of the year.   Rich had just had enough, and wanted to vent all that frustration. For some reason, once again, I was the guy who was picked to listen.

That was not how the Rich Kotite Era began. It was 1991, just after the playoff loss to Washington, and we were all called down to the stadium for a press conference. Buddy Ryan, whose contract expired, was not going to be rehired was the way the announcement went. It was a kinder way of saying Ryan was fired.

Buddy talked that morning, and despite what had happened appeared in good spirits. He even joked that this was the first time a coach had ever been "fired for winning", and later named one of his thoroughbred horses, Fired for Winning. He was so unemotional, when you considered he had just lost his job.

We stayed around, because we were told by the Eagles public relations department that there would be another press conference later that afternoon. We figured Braman and Harry Gamble would speak and give us their reasons for the decision, and answer questions about who a possible replacement might be.

Again the name Howard Schnellenberger was being bantered about. Braman knew the former University of Miami head coach, and Stan told me he had heard there had actually been discussions between the two.

Around 4 o'clock we were told the press conference was about to start. I remember Bill Conlin, the Daily News columnist, told me just before it started, "Rich Kotite is the new head coach. Trust me. It's done." Sure enough a few minutes later, Braman and Harry Gamble walked into the room with Rich Kotite, and announced him as the new head coach.

The decision had come down to either Kotite, the offensive coordinator, or Jeff Fisher, the defensive coordinator. I got along very well with Fisher, and would not have been upset if they hired Jeff. But I wasn't upset with the choice of Kotite, either. Jeff was still very young, and I was sure his day would come, and it eventually did with the Oilers. Rich had been around for a while, and had paid his dues as an assistant and a coordinator.

It didn't start to go bad for Kotite until his first draft. And again, you didn't realize at the time just how bad. The Eagles made a bold move on draft day 1991. They traded their No. 1 pick, the 19th overall, and their No. 1 pick the following year to Green Bay for the Packers' No. 1 pick, the eighth pick overall. With that pick they just acquired, the Eagles selected Antone Davis, a huge tackle from Tennessee, considered by many to be the best offensive lineman in the draft. Davis, and Charles McRae another Tennessee tackle, were both "can't miss" players according to the draft experts. McRae had gone the pick just ahead of the Eagles to Tampa Bay.

How bad did this turn out? Davis was never the player he was supposed to be, and Green Bay used the pick they acquired from the Eagles in a trade with Atlanta for quarterback Brett Favre. That was the way it began for Rich Kotite.

What first bothered me about the Davis pick was at the end of minicamp, just a week after the draft, the team had decided that Davis was not a left tackle, but a right tackle. When you invest a first-round draft pick, and another pick the following year, when you do that you expect to get a left tackle. It took only a week, and they told us he was a right tackle.

Davis then held out of training camp—in Braman's nine years as owner he never had his No. 1 pick in training camp on time—and it hurt him and the team.

During that training camp another facet emerged under Kotite that I had never encountered before. After one of the morning practices I approached one of the assistant coaches, offensive coordinator Zeke Bratkowski for an interview. For years I had always enjoyed interviewing the assistants, and getting their ideas and views on the team. As I approached Zeke, one of the public relations people stopped me, and said all requests for interviews of assistant coaches had to go through their department and be approved by Rich. I had never heard of such a thing.

Later I learned that it was done to protect defensive coordinator Bud Carson, who had been fired as the head coach of the Cleveland Browns but had agreed to a "gag" clause in his contract that prevented him from saying anything derogatory about the Browns.

But couldn't Bud Carson have taken care of that on his own? Did every other assistant coach have to be restricted, or put off limits? It was strange. It didn't make any sense. Rich, himself, was still fine with me, and I believe with everyone else. He was very accessible, and talked every day after practice for as long as you needed him.

Next came a preseason game in Cincinnati.Antone Davis had finally signed, and played his first game that night. During the broadcast, Stan turned to me and said, "Watch this, it's a pass." Sure thing, Randall dropped back and threw a pass. Next play, same thing. Stan said, "Watch this, it's another pass." And it was. And he called run, or pass, on every Eagles play and was right every time. Now Stan was never the kind of broadcaster who predicted every play. That wasn't his style. What was happening was that Antone Davis tipped off every play by his stance. Stan said this on the air.

Word got out to the newspapers that Stan could tell what the play was going to be, because of Davis' stance. Stan was asked about it after the game, and told the writers the same things he had already said on the air. It was big news, and when we got back home, the Eagles were not happy. They were very upset. Rarely, if ever, in all my years had the team ever commented on any broadcast, either positively, or negatively. They have never told us what to say, or what not to say. Ron Howard, the Eagles public relations director, actually asked Stan if he would come to camp and talk to Antone about exactly what he had done. And he did, and it worked. It was then I realized that Stan would have made a great offensive line coach, and I told him that numerous times, and he always told me I was crazy.

The next episode also involved Davis. We were back at JFK Stadium for practice just before the start of the regular season. The team did its laps around the field, and as Antone ran, he tripped on one of the supports of a portable goal post that was stationed in the end zone. He went down, and had to be helped from the field. He left that day on crutches, and went to get a MRI. As it turned out he was fine, but the next day the back page of the *Daily News* had a picture of Antone falling down with the big, bold headline "Ka-Boom."

If that didn't make Kotite crazy, what happened the next day certainly did. The Eagles had their walk-through in Veterans Stadium, and the Phillies happened to be home that same night. Andre Waters picked up a baseball bat, and started to swing it and was playing around with a couple of other players. An *Inquirer* photographer started to snap some pictures, and in the process Kotite snapped as well. He threatened the photographer that if those pictures were in the paper he was going to close practice to the media. Well, the picture ran.

The next day we were all back at the stadium, and we were informed the press would not be allowed at practice for the rest of the season. I could not believe this had happened. I had gone to practice every day since I had become the play-by-play man. It was part of my pregame regimen. First of all I liked to watch the plays they ran, so I would have a better feel for describing them. And if they put a gimmick play in that week I wanted to see it so I wouldn't be surprised by it. I could not believe that Rich Kotite had closed practice, and I could not believe the front office would allow him to close practice. I talked to Harry Gamble about it, and he said it was the head coach's domain and he did not want to interfere. He said he did not agree with the decision. He thought it was wrong, and voiced that opinion to Rich. But he refused to overrule his coach.

I thought that was the day Rich Kotite lost whatever benefit of the doubt he may have had with the media. And since then the Eagles' practices have never been opened again. What I believe, is that while a coach should have control of his team, this is something that should come from the top. I don't believe an owner should allow his coach to close practices to the media, and beyond that I feel the commissioner should not allow a team to close practice to the media.

There probably isn't a coach in the world who would open his practice if he had a choice. Well maybe Buddy Ryan would have, because his practices were not just opened to the media, but to fans. And they would be packed with people on a daily basis. But most coaches would want their practices closed, and it should not be their choice. The owners and the commissioner should step in, and demand that practices remain open.

Football has become a big business, and as it has grown, so has the media coverage. I remember back to when all you really got was a story about the game every week. Now there are stories every day in the newspapers, analysis of the games, profiles of the players, opinions, columns, notebooks, every day.

What people don't realize is that the media is the link between the team and its fans. When you take something away from the media you also take it away from the fans. The media can report more accurately, more insightfully, if it is allowed to watch practice.

But Kotite closed that door, and the media went after him. The next day he was called Coach Uptight. He was described as paranoid. The newspapers began a war with him and, for some, it lasted all four years he was there.

I have always put coaches in three different categories. There are coaches who can come in and turn a franchise around; take a losing program and make it a winner. Both Dick Vermeil and Buddy Ryan did that with the Eagles. There are coaches who are in that vast middle ground. They know their x's and o's and they don't hurt a team, but they don't do anything special, either. And there are coaches who are below the cut, they actually do nothing to help the team and some times can hurt the team with poor decisions. I thought Kotite, at least in his four years with the Eagles, was in that vast middle area.

But the thing was, Rich never helped himself, at least as far as the media was concerned. I mean I didn't expect him to buy us presents, but he never used the media properly. Vermeil was a master at it. Buddy loved to play with the media, and as it turned out 50 percent of them loved him and 50 percent hated him. But Richie, even more than closing practice, just never knew how to deal with the media.

There was a game against Dallas in 1991, a great game, a 24-0 win in which the Eagles sacked Troy Aikman 11 times. We raved about the game on the air and about how well they played on both offense and defense. We raved about how well prepared they were and gave credit to Rich, and his staff as well.

The next day, however, I noticed as I looked at the game statistics, the Eagles did not run the ball very well, actually they had struggled. So I asked Rich at his press conference, "Yesterday was an outstanding performance, but when you look at the various aspects of your offense you're not getting much from your running game. Does that concern you?"

He could have answered that any number of ways. He could have said he wasn't concerned, because we wanted to throw the ball more yesterday. Or, he could have said yes I am concerned and that's something we have to work on more. There were a lot of different routes he could have taken. Instead, he looked at me and yelled, "No." He snapped. I went up to him after the press conference to explain what I wanted, and he just walked away from me. I don't think he talked to me for the next two weeks. And then, a few weeks later, it was as if nothing had ever happened.

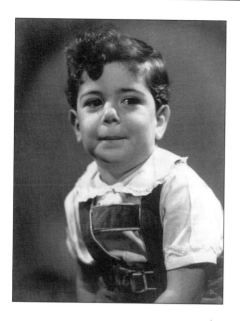

Here I am at two years old...

and at eight years old when my TV commercial career hit its peak.

My Dad, Mom, sister Carole (7) and I (10) pose outside our Overbrook Park home.

I needed the help of a chair to tape an interview with Temple star Jim Williams. The interview would later air on WRTI-FM, Temple's student station.

My first official bit of publicity–Temple University News.

Follow the Owl's on WRTI-FM

with
MERRILL REESE

BASKETBALL on 90.1

Best College Sports Coverage

Cindy and I on our wedding day.

Bill Cosby returns to a Temple alumni day and plays some tennis with Cindy and me.

Here I am with (L to R) former *Philadelphia Inquirer* columnist, Frank Dolson; legendary Temple basketball coach, Harry Litwack; former Eagles president, Harry Gamble, and Temple sports information director, Al Shrier.

Lt. Reese, USNR, driving a ship. Actually, as a public affairs officer, this was hardly one of my duties.

The morning crew at Philadelphia's WWDB-FM, (L to R) Jack O'Reilly, Wynn Moore and me. These were the culprits who arranged our "tribute to burlesque."

What a thrill it was for me to join the staff of WIP—then the number 1 station in the city.

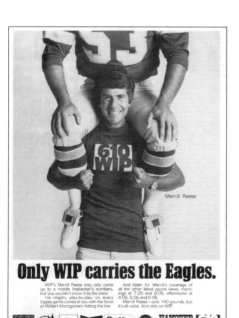

An award-winning ad and my personal favorite. Do you think I was carrying the player? I was actually kneeling down in front of the stool holding the model.

Promotions were a common occurrence. Here I am in a rodeo. What will they think of next?

My original Eagles broadcast crew at WIP. (L to R) Statistician Jack Edelstein; color analyst Jim Barniak; Bill Bergey (still in his playing days); me; producer Jerry Rosset, and spotter Bill Werndl.

An annual event was breaking down in the helmet during the Philadelphia Thanksgiving Day Parade.

Here I am with Eagles president Harry Gamble (left), and quarterback Ron Jaworski as we broadcast the weekly "Celebrity Sports Talk" from Ron's golf club.

A favorite moment at the Vet meeting my long-time hero, Arnold Palmer. Pictured here on my left are Cindy, and color analyst Bill Bergey.

One of my favorite weekly shows—live from the famous Old Original Bookbinders. (L to R) Reggie White, me, Randall Cunningham, and Mike Quick.

A charity event with Herman Edwards (left, "Miracle of the Meadowlands"), me, and wide receiver Harold Carmichael.

Quarterback coach (L) Doug Scovil played an important role in Randall Cunningham's early development. He's pictured here with me and Ron Jaworski.

A lighter moment at the studio as I overpower big Stan Walters at arm wrestling. Do you think he let me win?

Here I am with three of tennis' all-time greats...

Billie Jean King

Jack Kramer

Arthur Ashe

My son Nolan grows up with the Eagles...

Nolan gets a lift from linebacker Jerry Robinson.

Nolan meets Marian Campbell.

Nolan with Rich Kotite (without question) during a rare moment of tranquility.

Nolan with
defensive back
Eric Allen.

Nolan with one of
Buddy's favorites,
number 88—Keith
Jackson.

A more recent picture of Nolan, now a booth assistant, with me at the Vet.

Last year's crew (L to R) engineer Lane Massey; statistician Jack Edelstein; producer Joe McPeak, me, Nolan, and Big Stan.

It took a while, but Buddy Ryan and I became friends.

Former wide receiver Harold Carmichael—a player I have always looked up to!!

Former Eagle and current TV sports anchor Vai Sikahema and I watch practice.

Paul McFadden, former Eagles kicker, me and Ron Jaworski.

Former NFL star, defensive back and a current pregame host, Johnny Sample.

(L to R) WYSP pre and postgame host Tom Cardella; longtime Philadelphia sportscaster Bill Campbell; me; Dan Baker, Eagles and Phillies public address announcer; and veteran broadcaster Bill Bransome.

Me and former Eagles defensive back and CBS analyst Irv Cross.

Former Miami Dolphins kicker, Garo Yepremian, and I play golf for charity.

Ray Rhodes and I tape an interview at practice.

Here I am at mini camp with Eagles owner Jeffrey Lurie (left), and Eagles vice president Joe Banner.

The Eagles' 1998 number-one draft pick, offensive lineman, Tra Thomas—a huge acquisition.

Eagles quarterback Bobby Hoying and I talk golf on a spring day at Veterans Stadium.

It was a pleasure receiving the 1997 Pennsylvania Sportscaster of the Year Award from NBC's Bob Costas at a national convention in Salisbury, NC.

Here I am with my
daughter, Ida.

The Reese family today: (L to R) Cindy, Nolan, Ida, me and "Coach"
(our Bouvier des Flandres).

Kotite made his share of mistakes that first year. The team did well when you consider it lost Randall Cunningham the first game of the season and still won 10 games. But it had the league's best defense, ranked No. 1 across the board in every category, and failed to make the playoffs. The biggest mistake he made was when Cunningham got hurt, and he signed former Jets quarterback Pat Ryan to take his place. Ryan could not play any longer, and it showed. When McMahon got hurt, it forced the rookie Brad Goebel into the lineup, and he wasn't ready. The team signed Jeff Kemp later in the season and he helped, but it was too late.

During that offseason between the 1991 and 1992 seasons a major move occurred as far as the Eagles broadcasts were concerned. After 23 years on WIP, the new flagship station of the Eagles radio network would be WYSP, an FM station.

A few years before that, WIP had been sold to Spectacor, and the decision was made to make the station an all-sports station. Format styles get old, and the adult contemporary music that WIP played had lost its appeal. Other than Ken Garland's morning show, WIP's ratings were not very good. Initially I was happy with the idea of being the sports director of an all-sports station. I still did the morning show, although Ken Garland left to go to WPEN. They had brought in sports talk hosts like Bill Campbell and Howard Eskin. They started a show with different sportswriters and Angelo Cataldi, who still worked at the *Inquirer*, hosted what was called the Morning Sports Page. I never asked and never wanted to do a call-in show. My passion is play-by-play. That's why I got into this business. To me a sports talk host has to be an all-out sports junkie who loves to debate. That's not me. If I'm at a party and somebody comes up to me and says, "The Eagles stink." I usually say, "You're entitled to your opinion", and I walk away. I'm not an argumentative type. There were times when I was forced to fill in if one of the guys was sick, or something. But I never wanted to do it on a full-time basis. I just wasn't controversial enough.

What happened to me was my hours were spread over the course of the day with sports updates. They didn't want any interviews, or any opinions, from me. They just wanted me to read sports updates throughout the day. This was not what I wanted to do. So I left the station and reworked my contract so that I would only do the Eagles games. I took a paycut, but I couldn't have been happier. I made up for the loss of money by broadcasting Big Five college basketball games with Dan Baker, who was the executive director of the Big Five. Dan worked so hard to preserve that Philadelphia tradition, and I was honored to work with him that season.

I wondered how Dick Vermeil would have handled all-sports radio if he had come back to coach the Eagles in 1995. There was no wonder with Kotite. He hated WIP and the feeling was mutual. He refused to go on the air, and they in turn chastised him unmercifully. It was an all-out war, and a battle a coach could never win. Rich became his own worst enemy with this stance. I often thought he could have made it a lot easier on himself, like Ray Rhodes does now, if he would have just cooperated a little bit more.

In any event, I came home one day from a tennis match, and Harry Gamble called to tell me that the team had decided to change radio stations. He said he wanted me to hear it from him, and he also said that the new station was very receptive about keeping Stan and me. Later that night it was announced that WYSP was the new station. There was still no word about the broadcasters, but I remained confident. Concerned, but confident. By the end of the week I met with Ken Stevens and Tim Sabean from WYSP and my contract was in the works.

So after 15 years I was now on the same radio station as Howard Stern. At one time I would have told you it was crazy to think of football on a FM rock music station, but this was a sign of the times. More and more FM stations were getting involved in sports, and Infinity Broadcasting, which owned WYSP and an ever growing list of other stations was a forerunner in the business. Mel Karmazin is a broadcast visionary, who as head of Infinity and the parent company, CBS, pursues NFL rights aggressively and almost always hits his target.

Our first year with WYSP turned out to be Kotite's best year as head coach. The Eagles made the playoffs, and won their first playoff game since the 1980 NFC Championship Game against Dallas when they beat New Orleans in a wild-card game, 36-20. Even that season, as successful as it was, did not go without controversy from the head coach. He benched Randall Cunningham for one game in the middle of the season, and lambasted a couple of beat writers for what he felt was unfair criticism of him and his staff. He returned Randall to the lineup a week later. He never returned to the good graces of the media.

After the 1992 season ended, the Eagles' exodus began. Reggie White, the team's best defensive player and a future Hall of Famer left as a free agent. White's departure was the beginning of the end. It had actually begun a year before when Keith Jackson left.

But White was the big one who got away. Eleven players left that season as free agents. Included among them were Jim McMahon, Mike Golic, Ron Heller, Keith Byars and Mike Pitts. The Eagles tried to replace the lost players with free agent signings of their own, but just as they failed in the draft they did the same in free agency. Players like Tim Harris, Keith Millard, Mark Bavaro and Michael Carter were long past their prime when they arrived in Philadelphia.

When Reggie left, the Eagles did get two No. 1 draft picks as compensation. I have to admit I thought that was fair at the time. One of the problems I had with Dick Vermeil was how he kept his players too long. I remembered back to when the team could have traded Bill Bergey to the Baltimore Colts for a No. 1 pick. The Eagles turned it down and Bergey played just one more year. That No. 1 pick would have been there a lot longer.

With two No. 1 draft picks in place of already over-30 Reggie White, maybe it wasn't so bad. Little did I know that they would again waste the two No. 1 picks. In the 1993 draft, armed with two first-round picks, the team selected guard Lester Holmes, with the compensation pick, and defensive tackle Leonard Renfro with their regular pick. Holmes was a decent player who hurt his knee, and was never the same again. Renfro was a flat-out bust who played two seasons, never recorded a sack, and was eventually released.

The following draft, again armed with two No. 1 picks, the Eagles tried again. This time they selected Bernard Williams, a left tackle from Georgia, with the first pick, and traded down with the compensation pick and took defensive tackle Bruce Walker of UCLA. Williams started his entire rookie season and played pretty well for a rookie. Stan really liked Bernard, and thought he would be the Eagles' left tackle for the next decade. He was close. He lasted 16 games. Williams tested positive for marijuana in the offseason, was suspended for the 1995 season, and has never played again. Walker was even worse than Renfro. He was so bad he was released after his first training camp.

Kotite's drafts are what killed him. He did get two good players in his first draft, linebacker William Thomas in the fourth round, and defensive tackle Andy Harmon in the sixth round, and that was it. In 1992 he drafted running backs Siran Stacy and Tony Brooks and quarterback Casey Weldon, and none of them panned out. They were all released by the following season. The only player he got out of that entire draft was 10th-round pick Mark McMillian. In 1993, Holmes played a little before he got hurt, and that was it.

It had gotten ridiculous. The Eagles continued to lose good players through free agency, and they couldn't draft anyone to replace them. The team missed the playoffs in 1993, and needed a win in a meaningless final game of the season in San Francisco just to finish 8-8.

Kotite's 1994 draft day came just after Jeffrey Lurie had bought the team from Norman Braman. Actually the deal was not totally completed yet, and both men were around at the same time.

John Wooten, a long-time football man who was an All-Pro guard for the Jimmy Brown-led Cleveland Browns and a scout for the Dallas Cowboys, was brought in before that 1994 draft to give some assistance. Braman made it clear before a Monday Night Game in 1993 that he was not pleased with the team's draft performance and a change might be made. Enter Wooten.

It didn't take long for Kotite and Wooten to get on different sides, and on each other's nerves. After the first day of that draft, in which the Eagles selected Williams, Walker, and running back Charlie Garner, rumors circulated that the team had tried to trade Cunningham to the Los Angeles Rams. The trade would have been made so the Eagles could move up in the draft, and select quarterback Trent Dilfer, of Fresno State.

Wooten addressed the media early the second day of the draft, just after the team selected offensive lineman Joe Panos, of Wisconsin, and as he always did, told the truth. Wooten may have been too honest. He talked openly about the trade scenarios that involved Cunningham. He also said that Panos would be the team's starting center by October, which sent the beat writers off to make phone calls to starting center David Alexander.

Later that day, after the draft had ended, Kotite met the press and was ballistic. He was obviously informed by his public relations staff of what Wooten had said, and he denied it all. He said Cunningham was never mentioned in any trade talk. He said Alexander was, and would be, his center, and if any moves were going to be made they would be made by him. He was out of control. He ranted. He raved. And through it all Joe Banner, the new owner's top assistant, stood in the corner of the room and listened.

Kotite's final year seemed doomed from the start. Just as Norman Braman wanted his own coach after he bought the team in 1985, Lurie would eventually want his own coach as well. Some thought Kotite might even be fired before the season began, but the deal between Braman and Lurie dragged out so long that by the time Lurie had full ownership, it was too late for him to do anything.

And the Eagles began that '94 season like a new team. They won four of their first five games, and after a loss at Dallas, won three more to get to 7-2. Along the way they won one of the most impressive games I had ever seen, a 40-8 rout of the eventual Super Bowl champion San Francisco 49ers. That game was also the debut of Garner at running back and he ran wild. The rookie back from Tennessee ran for over 100 yards and came back with another 100-yard effort the following week in a win over Washington in which he carried the ball 28 times.

The day after that Washington game, and again in the midst of good times, Kotite lost it. Tom Cardella, whose manner was nonconfrontational, asked Rich during his press conference if he felt Garner had gotten the ball too much. Garner had just come off a serious rib injury that kept him out of the lineup most of the preseason and the first three games of the regular season. And he left the San Francisco game early with a shoulder injury. Plus, Garner was only 175 pounds at the time. It was not an unfair or unrealistic question.

But Kotite turned blue. He roared, "This is bizarre," and he went on a tirade. The assembled press corp just sat there amazed at how he went out of control over an innocent question about his use of an injured running back. Again he had several different ways to answer the question. He could have said it was a one-game deal, and we don't plan to use him that often every week. Or, he could have said that Charlie felt great that day, and could have gotten even more carries; whatever. But he went crazy, and kept screaming the word "bizarre."

Rich had a way with words. In his first season he often answered reporter's questions with the phrase, "There are no cookbook answers." When that became a popular joke, he stopped. But his favorite phrase, what he became known for and is ridiculed still about, was the phrase, "Without question." He used it before his answers, after his answers, he probably said it in his sleep.

During that 1994 season the team was 7-2 after nine games, and looked like not only a playoff-bound team, but a possible division champ, and maybe even had a chance to get home-field advantage throughout the playoffs. Throughout the run, Lurie was asked again and again about Kotite's future, and he always answered the same way, "That it would be evaluated at the end of the season." He added that he felt Rich was doing a good job, and he was thrilled with the way the team was playing.

Well Kotite had enough. After that seventh win over Arizona and Buddy Ryan, he told two writers who he felt close with, the *Inquirer*'s Frank Dolson and *USA Today*'s Gordon Forbes that he "would keep his options open at the end of the season as well." He mentioned something else, that his record spoke for itself. Well, the Eagles never won another game that season. They lost their final seven games and finished 7-9, out of the playoffs. It was the greatest collapse in NFL history. No team had ever been 7-2 and failed to finish at least .500 on the season. Never.

Kotite was fired after that final loss, and two days later was hired by the New York Jets. He had gotten his wish. He had returned to the Big Apple. And two years later, he was fired again after his Jets team finished 1-15.

Opposites Attract . . . Sometimes

Jim McMahon was always somebody I admired as a player. I've said before how much the quarterback position means to me, and how important it is to a football team. I felt Jim McMahon epitomized the way the position should be played.

I knew a lot about McMahon before I ever met him, because of Doug Scovil. Doug knew Jim from their days together at Brigham Young University where Doug was the offensive coordinator when Jim played, and again in Chicago. He loved him.

Doug told me what an amazing athlete McMahon was. How he could throw the ball left-handed 40-50 yards and hit his target. How he was an All-America punter. How he was a great baseball player. How he was a great golfer, which I later learned first hand. What he was most was a great competitor. Jim McMahon hated to lose at anything. And you could ask anyone who played dominoes with him in the locker room before practice.

Scovil also told me a story about this one charity golf tournament McMahon played in where there was a pond right in front of the green. Jim took his shot, and splash, right into the pond. He took out another ball, hit again, and again, splash into the pond. One more time he went to his golf bag, and one more time he pulled out another ball. And one more time it went right into that pond. He became so furious he walked over to the pond, threw his entire bag into the water, and stomped off the course. Five minutes later he was back. It turned out he had left his car keys in the bag. So he jumped in the pond after the bag, fished it out, got his keys, and then threw the bag back in the water, and left. That was Jim McMahon.

When McMahon became available as a free agent just before the 1990 season, there were rumors the Eagles might be interested. Buddy knew him, of course, from their days together in Chicago and loved him. Normally, I don't get too excited about who the team may sign. But this was one deal that I wanted to see get done. I thought McMahon would be the perfect veteran backup they needed behind Randall Cunningham, and I thought maybe just by osmosis Randall could learn from Jim, and pick up some of his leadership qualities and his toughness.

The Eagles did sign McMahon, and on his first day of practice during a voluntary camp, he came onto the field with a question mark on his back. The Eagles practiced at JFK Stadium and that relic was packed with fans. They were everywhere; they lined the field. Of course that was back when the fans, and the media, were allowed to watch practices. Everyone wondered which number McMahon would wear. He always wore No. 9, but the Eagles' third-string quarterback, Don McPherson, had that number. So he came out with this question mark taped to the back of his uniform jersey.

That was also the first day I met Jim. I had my back to the field, and was in a conversation with this woman who always brought her dog to practice. We were talking about dogs. All of a sudden I felt this hand on my shoulder. I turned around, and it was McMahon. He said, "Merrill, I've heard a lot of nice things about you, and I just wanted to say hello." I was shocked. This was a guy who I admired long before he became an Eagle, a guy who I desperately wanted to become an Eagle, and he wanted to meet me?

From that first day on we became good friends. Jim wasn't deluged by the media on a daily basis, mainly because he wasn't playing, and secondly because even when he did play he had limited press conferences. He had felt he had been burned by the media in his final days in Chicago, and decided then he would choose when he would talk. But I could always go up to him, and we would just talk football, or talk golf, and I learned a lot about both from him. We also talked about his injuries, because I couldn't believe all he had been through. He had to have set an NFL record for most MRIs in a season, and in a career. He told me once that the pain he felt was like a toothache throughout his entire body. But he never complained about his injuries. And he always tried to play through them. I mean, if there was anyway Jim McMahon could play, he played. That was one of the reasons why his coaches and his teammates loved him so much.

Well almost all of his teammates. Randall never exactly hit it off with Jim. I don't know if he felt threatened by him, but my hope that Randall would learn from him, or pick things up from him, did not happen. Instead, it went the other way. Then again, McMahon didn't help the situation, either.

When veteran journeyman David Archer made the Eagles roster as the third quarterback in 1992, he and McMahon almost drove Randall crazy. Archer and McMahon were old friends from their days together in San Diego and their lockers were next to each other in the near corner of the Veterans Stadium locker room. Randall's locker was situated one spot over from McMahon's. Every time Randall walked past them, they would whisper, and then suddenly stop. It was right out of junior high, but it bothered Randall to no end. And when he walked away, McMahon and Archer would just laugh like a couple of kids who had just pulled another prank on the school nerd.

But other than that, I thought McMahon was a great team leader. He was a player the team could rally around, and they did when Randall was injured in 1991. If McMahon could have just stayed healthy that season, with that great defense the Eagles had, it could have been like Chicago in 1995 again. He could have taken them a long way. I felt the offensive linemen, especially, loved him. He was almost like one of them, instead of a quarterback. And Richard Dent, the MVP of that Bears' Super Bowl win, told me last year how much the defensive players in Chicago loved McMahon. How they felt he was one of them.

And I have to admit, in spite of his sometimes unpleasantness toward the media, Jim McMahon was one of my favorite players. He was before he became an Eagle, and he certainly was after he became an Eagle. I was happy that he was able to get another Super Bowl ring with Green Bay in 1996, even though he rarely played that year as Brett Favre's backup. But I was also convinced that if the Packers needed him he would have been able to do the job for them.

Jim retired after that season, and I'm sure he just works on his golf game now, which is probably ready for the PGA Tour. But if he ever wanted to get into coaching, he would be a great quarterbacks coach, and a great offensive coordinator. I was just thrilled that after seeing him on television for so long that I got the chance to get to know him, even if it was just for a few years.

That's one of the funny things about this business. One day I'm watching Jim McMahon in the Super Bowl, and the next thing you know I'm sitting next to him on an airplane and we're talking about golf.

Unfortunately it does not always work out that way.

Ricky Watters was another player who I had admired from afar. I had watched him on television when he played his college football for Notre Dame, and of course I saw him often enough when he played for the San Francisco 49ers. When the Eagles signed him to an offer sheet before the 1995 season, I was excited. Deep down I thought the 49ers would probably match the offer and keep him, but they didn't.

Watters, I thought and hoped, would be the great running back the Eagles lacked since Wilbert Montgomery left 10 years earlier. Earnest Jackson, Keith Byars, Heath Sherman, and Herschel Walker all had their moments and all were decent running backs, but none of them made you forget Wilbert. Ricky Watters, I thought, just might.

Just as I remember my first meeting with McMahon, I remember my first meeting with Watters, but not as fondly. It was about an hour before his introductory press conference and I was down in the locker room. He had just come off the field with the coaches and a couple of front office people. He stood by himself near what would become his locker, and I walked over to introduce myself. This guy looked even better than I thought he would. He was sculpted; his muscles were well defined. He was a physical specimen.

I approached him and said, "Hi Ricky, my name is Merrill Reese. I do the Eagles' radio play by play. I just want to welcome you here. I've watched you play for Notre Dame and the 49ers, and I've always admired you as player. I just wanted to say hi, and wish you the best." With that I extended my hand. He looked at me and walked away. That was it. I felt empty, but I thought, well maybe he's preoccupied with the press conference, and just getting here and all of that.

Minutes later at his press conference I saw a different person. This Ricky Watters was warm, charming, funny, and entertaining. Most players are better with a one-on-one interview, or with a small group of media, and get a little nervous, or quiet in front of a large group. Ricky was the opposite. He loved the big press conferences, the bright lights, the television cameras. He played up to them like no other player I've ever seen.

Throughout his first training camp I tried a few other times to get to know him, and it was always to no avail. One day after practice he held court with an average-sized group of media, and was wonderful. He talked about how much he liked it here, and how the Eagles could accomplish as much as the 49ers. He was the master of positive propaganda. I thought I would give it another try. He appeared to be in a great mood, so maybe this was the right time to get to know him better. The group of media broke up, and I started to walk off the field with Ricky. I said to him, "It's been fun watching you practice, you really go at it hard." And he looked at me, and walked away. There I was again.

But Ricky really did practice like no other player I've been around. If you didn't know who he was, you would think he was a kid off the street just trying to make the team, not the best player on the team. He gave it everything he had on every play. He ran out every carry, whether it was supposed to be a five-yard gain, or whatever, he took it 40 yards. He went the distance with everything.

Which is why I was so surprised at what happened after his first regular season game against Tampa Bay. The Eagles played poorly in what was also Ray Rhodes' first game as head coach, and lost, 20-6. In the fourth quarter of the game, Ricky did not go all out for a pass over the middle. On the air, Stan said, "He had alligator arms, and that is something players hate to see."

After the game, Ricky compounded the problem when after he was asked about the play, responded with his infamous, "For Who? For What?" comment. He basically said he was not going to put himself on the line to make a catch in a game that had already been decided. That was not exactly the best way to start his career in Philadelphia. Two days later he held a press conference to explain what he said, and apologized. Again, he turned on the charm, and I didn't believe him for a minute.

I remember I said something about it to Dave Spadaro, the editor of *Eagles Digest,* and he asked me why I was so cynical. Me? Cynical? I've never been cynical. I'm less cynical than anyone I know. I get teased by writers who have told me that I never see past certain players. How I think every Eagle is a great guy. And that if they signed Charles Manson, I would figure out a way that he could help the team. Now, I was being called cynical.

Later that season I got a call from Mike Missanelli, who co-hosted Ricky's television show at the Eighth Floor every Monday night. Mike wanted to know if I could come on the show as a guest that Monday from 8 to 9 o'clock. I did the "Ray Rhodes Show" every Monday from the Engine 46 Steakhouse from 6 to 7 o'clock, so it would work out rather well. My first thought actually was, "Why should I do his show? Ricky has been so cold toward me." But I decided I would do it, and maybe this would help break the ice. Maybe this would be the perfect breakthrough I needed.

So I finished with Ray's show, and headed down Delaware Avenue to the Eighth Floor. The producer met me at the door, and told me I would be on the second half of the show. I sat in the back room, and I never saw Ricky because he was on the set. Finally around 8:55 I got called to go out. Mike welcomed me, and I joked that, "I had hoped to come on for the 9:05 segment." At which point Ricky turned to me, and said, "Well we have the golden voice with us. And boy, you do a great job describing the plays and the games..." We talked for a few minutes. He asked me a few questions, and the show was over. I thought to myself, this wasn't the end of the world. I waited a long time, but it might have been worth it. At least now I finally have a relationship with the star of the team.

As the show ended, everyone walked off the set, and I went up to Ricky and I said, "It was a lot of fun being on the show." And he looked at me, and he turned and walked away. And that was it. When the red light was on, Ricky was fine. I have to say in all of my years he was the one key player who I never got to know. And that was the way he wanted it. I don't think he ever knew my name, or wanted to know my name. We never even had a two-way conversation.

But as much as I never got along, or didn't get a chance to get along, with Ricky Watters, I tried to never let it cloud my judgment of him as a player. He was a great player. He had his problems with the coaching staff and he had his sideline antics, and I have to agree with people who felt he cared more about Ricky Watters than he did the Philadelphia Eagles.

But his leadership was something else; he led by example. And like I said, nobody ever worked harder, or practiced harder. I will remember Ricky as a person I didn't particularly like, but you can't take away what he did on the field.

I've had my share of experiences with different players through the years. One came during the 1989 season after I had done Dream Season for ESPN with Steve Sabol. The Eagles had lost punter John Teltschik for the season and continued to look for his replacement. They brought in a player who most of us had never heard of, and I thought somebody said his name was "Ron" Tuten. Of course it was Rick Tuten, who later became an All-Pro with Seattle.

I walked up to him, as I would any new player and greeted him with a handshake and, "Hi, Ron." He looked at me, smiled and said, "My name's Rick, but aren't you Merrill Reese? I've seen you on the Dream Season."

A crazy coincidence just happened in 1997 with fullback Kevin Turner. It was a Friday late in the season, and Kevin ended our conversation rather abruptly, and said, "Sorry, but I have to run. My wife is being induced into labor this afternoon." I wished him luck, and asked him if they knew if it was a boy, or a girl. He told me it was going to be a boy. I asked if they had picked out a name, and he said it was Nolan.

I told him that was my son's name, and all of a sudden he got this look on his face, and said, "You're kidding, this is unbelievable. The middle name we picked out is Reese. That will make his name, Nolan Reese Turner." They announced the baby's birth at the game on Sunday, and a lot of the writers made it a note in their stories for Monday. When my son, Nolan, went to school that day, everyone thought Kevin Turner named his son after him. And he just shrugged his shoulders.

One time my friendship with players almost got me into trouble. It was during the 1996 season, and on a Tuesday I scheduled some golf with Bobby Hoying and Tom Hutton. We asked kicker Gary Anderson, who was probably the best golfer on the team, if he wanted to join us, but he said he never golfed once the season started. Gary went fishing that day instead.

The next day, everyone was back in the locker room except Anderson. He had pulled a muscle in his back, and was now doubtful for Sunday's game. Somehow word got out that he had hurt his back golfing with me.

First I heard it from Joe Banner, the team's vice president. He said, "Hey Merrill you have to leave our kickers alone." I didn't know what he was talking about. Next was Ray Rhodes, "Hey man, I gotta team to run, you can't mess with my kickers," he said to me. Finally I said, "Ray, what are you talking about?" He said, "You took my kicker out golfing, and now he can't kick." I told him Anderson wasn't with me. It was Hutton and Hoying.

Later I saw Anderson, and he wanted to know why I told everyone he was out golfing, when he was fishing. Actually, he probably would have been better off golfing than out on the water with a cool breeze on his back. But fortunately the story got straightened out, and so did Anderson's back. He did not miss the game.

Another kicker almost got me in trouble once, too, except we didn't get caught.

Tennis, as you know by now, is one of my loves. It was one of Eagles punter Max Runager's as well. Every day during training camp one season, Max and I would play in between the two practices. Somehow he avoided going to the dining hall for lunch, which was required, and instead met me behind the building and we sped off to this place he knew of that had private tennis courts. We would play for an hour and a half until he had to report back. Vermeil would have killed us if he ever knew.

Of course for a punter it was a much better way to stay in shape than standing around most of practice inventing ways to look busy.

Tight end Keith Jackson and I were always friends. One Wednesday I came into the locker room and had a lot of work to do. That was the day I needed to tape my interviews for the pregame shows.

Keith saw me, gave me that look he gave, and said, "Merrill, you've been working too hard. Give me that tape recorder and I'll get your interviews for you."

And he went around the locker room and interviewed everyone I needed and more. He came back with 14 different players on tape for me, and the interviews were good. There was no doubt in my mind that Keith Jackson had a future in the media, and I was not surprised at how well he did on TNT during the 1997 season.

We always wanted to have a player join the post-game show, and two of the best were Eric Allen, the Eagles' All-Pro cornerback during the Buddy Ryan years, and Rich Miano, a safety during the Rich Kotite years. Both players were very intelligent and very honest and could analyze the game for us in a manner in which a lot of players could not.

The big difference between the two was that Eric could say just about anything and not offend anyone. His status with the team, and the fact that he was an All-Pro player gave him that privilege. Rich, on the other hand, was just as honest, but because he was considered a journeyman player, his opinion wasn't valued as much by the other players or the coaches. And he was constantly getting yelled at by the staff for things he would say on the post-game show.

I found it interesting that while Eric's comments were much more blistering than Rich's ever were, he never had a word said to him, and Rich would always be in trouble.

Another player who did the post-game show was free safety Greg Jackson. His agent called us before the season and said Greg wanted to get into communications when he was finished playing. Was there a chance for him to get a jump? Eric was gone by then and we had the opening, so Greg joined the show.

This was during the 1994 season, and Jackson was fine at the beginning when the team jumped out to a 7-2 start, but at the end when the team lost its last seven games, he stopped showing up altogether. This was the classic example of a player not quite understanding the business aspect of what we do, and what needs to be done.

CHAPTER FIFTEEN

Hollywood Hero

If I had all the money in the world and nothing to do with it, the last thing I would do is buy an NFL franchise. As much as I love football and love the Eagles, I would never want to be an owner.

You can't win. Even if you do win, the coach and the players get all the credit. And when you don't win, it's because the owner didn't spend enough money.

Take a look at the last two Eagles owners. Norman Braman was chastised for never being around, for being an absentee owner, as he was called. Jeffrey Lurie is criticized for being around too much, for being a hands-on owner.

Who needs it?

And it's not just in Philadelphia. The Maras have had their problems with the Giants. The McCaskeys have been embroiled in controversy in Chicago. And the Browns, after Paul Brown, have had their trouble in Cincinnati. The words popular and owner are seldom used in the same sentence.

Leonard Tose was popular among Eagles fans as the team rose from the depths of the league to the Super Bowl, but it wasn't long after that the same people who praised him wanted to run him out of town.

Again, like I said about Dick Vermeil being here in a different environment, it's the same way for an owner. He also has to deal with controversy in the age of this evolved journalism that includes talk radio, ESPN, and all those cable sports channels with discussion shows. Every step you take is magnified, and debated, and pontificated to the nth degree. And panels for these shows are picked because Mr. A and Mr. B are on one side of an issue, and Mr. X and Mr. Z are on the other side of the issue and it makes for good television, or radio. And it makes for nothing but headaches for an owner.

Norman Braman began his ownership in Philadelphia as a popular figure because he bought the team from Tose, and saved it from being moved to Phoenix. By that point Tose was Public Enemy No. 1, and anyone would have looked like a hero compared to him. For Braman it did not last long.

Trouble began during his first training camp as owner when half the team, or at least it seemed like half the team, held out over contract issues. So Braman's honeymoon lasted all of about four months.

He was ripped from the start for not caring about winning; that all he wanted to do was make money. Well, Norman Braman was a businessman, and a very astute businessman to say the least. He turned a profit on the Eagles every year he owned them, and sold them to Jeffrey Lurie for $190 million—almost triple the $65 million he paid Tose. That was good business. But I thought he wanted to win as well. The Norman Braman I knew wanted to succeed in everything he did. Sure he wanted to make money, that was part of his success, but he wanted that same kind of success on the football field. It killed him when the Eagles lost. I was around Norman Braman after tough losses and he would be devastated. He was pained by losing. This man wanted to win at everything, and he especially wanted his largest investment to be a winner. I never believed the people who thought that Braman didn't care if the team won or lost, as long as he made money. I knew better.

I felt Norman Braman's biggest problem was his approach to public relations. That was what he didn't care about. Norman Braman couldn't care less what the fans thought about him, or what some newspaper writers, or columnists, thought about him. Or at times even what his players or coaches thought about him. He was way beyond worrying about things like that. Sure he was nicer to me than he was to a lot of people, especially others in the media, but he was also very nice to his Eagles employees. Every year when the season ended, he took the entire office staff—everyone employed by the team and his or her spouse—on a vacation. One year it was a cruise to the Bahamas, another time it was a long weekend in Miami Beach. For a guy who supposedly didn't care and was an Ebeneezer Scrooge in the eyes of many, that was a pretty nice bonus at the end of the season.

Braman's popularity declined as free agency began and the Eagles started to lose key players. Braman was the villain when Reggie White left for Green Bay. But he never got any credit when he signed Reggie and got him out of his USFL contract. Braman paid the USFL $1 million to get Reggie, because Marion Campbell, the head coach at the time, and Harry Gamble, the general manager, told him Reggie would be worth it. One thing Braman did was listen to his people. He liked football, and thought he knew the game, but he never professed to be an expert on it. And he never got involved in any of the football decisions. He left all of that to his head coach, be it Marion, Buddy Ryan, or Rich Kotite, and of course his top man, Harry Gamble.

I did not agree with his decision to fire, or not rehire as the case was, Buddy Ryan. But again he was the one who hired Buddy back in 1986. Braman was the one who gave him his first chance to be a head coach after a long career as an assistant. Very few owners were willing to take a chance on a volatile coach like Buddy. Braman did. And I truly believe he hired Rich Kotite to replace Buddy because he felt the team was so close to the top, and he did not want to go outside and bring in a new coach who would have to start over again. Obviously, it didn't work out. But I thought too much of the blame was placed on Braman for why it didn't.

I never thought Braman would sell the Eagles, either. But I learned that everything has its price. I remember him telling me once how he looked forward to the day when his daughter, Susan, would take over control of the team. She had worked in the front office, and was elevated to a vice president's role by the time he did sell. And not long before that I had a private meeting with him.

We met on a Thursday afternoon, and discussed the possibility of my leaving the radio station and joining the Eagles on a full-time basis. I would still be the play-by-play man, but I would also do special appearances and host various televisions shows for the team. He had been looking into a deal where the Eagles would still sell the broadcast rights to a radio station, but the club would hire the announcers. This is a practice more common to baseball, basketball, and hockey—sports with many more games. That deal, however, never materialized.

Susan, Norman's daughter, had also gone to Dallas and investigated the way Jerry Jones had turned the Cowboys into a marketing giant, and looked into all the television and radio shows they produced. Norman wanted to do the same kinds of things with the Eagles, and I was going to be very involved.

So I was as shocked as anyone when I heard the Eagles could be sold, or were about to be sold. And I was also stuck in the snow when I found out.

I went out on that snowy February morning to drive up to WBCB, the station I used to work at in Levittown, of which I was now a part owner with Pat T. Deon. As I backed my car out of the driveway, I went right into a snowdrift. And I was stuck. I tried to drive out of it, and it only got worse. I went back into the house to call AAA, and the phone rang. It was Tim Sabean, our operations manager of WYSP, and he said to me, "Merrill, do you know the Eagles are being sold?" I said, "Tim, listen I have a lot going on right now. My car is stuck in the driveway. I can't get out. What do you mean the Eagles are being sold?" He said, "The Eagles are being sold. It's all over the radio. It's all over the news." I couldn't believe it. But I switched my plans, and once AAA came and got me out of my driveway, I went to the stadium instead of up to Bucks County.

Craig Carton, who worked as a talk-show host at WIP, had gone on the air with the story that not only was Norman Braman selling the team, but he named the new owner, a movie producer from Hollywood named Jeffrey Lurie. They reported it as a done deal. Well everyone was down at the stadium—except Norman Braman— he was on a cruise to Vietnam at the time. All the Eagles did was hand out a press release that said that throughout the years the club has often gotten offers from people interested in buying the team. It would not confirm, nor deny, anything about this particular offer, and if this Jeffrey Lurie was involved. To me, the fact they did not deny it was all I needed. As far as I was concerned, the team was being sold, and I never saw it coming.

Channel 6 actually tracked Braman down on his cruise, and he went on the air and again refused to deny the report. One thing this Eagles administration did over the years was deny false reports, and there were no denials being made about this one.

The next thing I knew we were learning everything about Jeffrey Lurie—his family, the history of General Cinema, where his family's money came from, what he liked for breakfast, everything. The story broke on a Thursday, and by Sunday I felt as though I had known Jeffrey Lurie for years, and I had yet to meet him. All I knew was he produced three movies, "Sweet Hearts Dance", "I Love You to Death" and "V.I. Warshawski." None of them won an Oscar, but I thought to myself if this guy could convince Kathleen Turner to play in V.I. Warshawski, he should do well in attracting free agents to come play for the Eagles.

And the general public was excited. They didn't care who Jeffrey Lurie was, or what movies he produced, or what he ate for breakfast. He wasn't Norman Braman, and he was going to save the Eagles. The fans had their Hollywood Hero.

It seemed as if it took longer than it had to for the deal to become official, but when you're talking about a deal that involves almost $200 million, it's probably good to take your time. While we waited for the approval of the sale from the league, Lurie was not allowed to talk about it. But one Friday I got a call that Lurie would be in town to look over the stadium, and while there would not be a formal press conference, he would meet the media in the locker room area. Of course I went down to the stadium, and when I got there, Ron Howard, the public relations director, came over to me and said, "You know what, Jeffrey's right-hand man said that he used to be a friend of yours." And I thought to myself who did I know who could possibly know a Hollywood producer?

Jimmy Stewart? Peter Boyle? Would they remember me? No way. Bill Cosby? No, if he were involved I would have heard by now. You couldn't keep that a secret.

Then Ron said, "The guy's name is Joe Banner." I hadn't heard that name in ages. Then it hit me—Joe Banner used to be a reporter at WCAU radio and he used to help Al Meltzer at Channel 10. He also assisted Ralph Lawler, the sports director at WCAU radio, and I would see Joe at different basketball games, or other events, when I was doing work for WWDB. We would run into each other all the time. All I remembered about Joe was that he was a real hard worker, real industrious, and very serious about his work. I didn't know much about him personally, and I had no idea where, or how, he knew Jeffrey Lurie. As it turned out the two grew up together in New England and had remained friends.

I saw Joe in the locker room that day, and we talked about the old times. He told me what a great guy Lurie was, and how excited they both were to be getting into all of this. Just then, Lurie came in. He seemed like "one of the guys." He certainly did not have a Hollywood look about him, and he made a point early on to let people know he thought of himself as more of a New Englander than a Californian. He was a diehard Boston Celtics fan and loved to talk about his frequent trips to the Boston Garden as a kid. He actually tried to buy the New England Patriots a few years before he purchased the Eagles, but the deal fell through.

The media, especially WIP (which just hated Braman) literally sang Lurie's praises. They did parodies of the "Battle Hymn of the Republic", and inserted the words "Lurie, Lurie, Hallelujah." Jeffrey Lurie's popularity hit a high before he was even officially the owner of the team. He was adored by the public before he did a thing, and it was all because he wasn't Norman Braman. His press conference, in May, when everything became official, was huge. I almost expected to hear "Hail to the Chief" when he arrived. And he handled the press conference wonderfully. He answered every question. He had a grip on what this town wanted to hear, and he gave all the perfect answers. It was too good to be true.

There was also this tremendous reception at the City Hall Courtyard after the press conference. Every newspaper ran pictures the next day of Lurie throwing footballs into the audience. It was a gala event, and the city had fallen in love with the Eagles' new owner. One thing Lurie did, and he did it right away, was get the old Eagles' players back involved with the team. That night in the Courtyard I saw more former players—Bill Bergey, Mike Quick, Harold Carmichael, Ron Jaworski, Wilbert Montgomery, Reggie Wilkes—than I had the entire time Braman owned the team.

I had a great time that night; it would have been hard not to have a great time. But I thought to myself, "Jeffrey you better enjoy this, because it's not going to last." No matter what he did, no matter how sincere his intentions were, it was impossible in a city like Philadelphia that has a passion for the Eagles the way it does to make this popularity last. I just hoped he knew that. He could make some popular moves and have some exhilarating moments, but there would be heartaches and disappointments, and at those times he would wonder why he ever got involved in this. I really believe being an owner of a professional football team is one of the most difficult positions in the world.

Today another problem an owner faces is being pitted against his head coach. And Jeffrey Lurie has had it happen to him. Lurie has been accused of not allowing Ray Rhodes to sign the players he wants. He has been accused of not allowing Rhodes to keep the players he wants. He's been accused of meddling in the football affairs of the team, especially around the draft. And while Braman was accused of being too cheap to spend money, Lurie gets accused of not having enough money to spend.

Now for some facts. Since Lurie bought the team, every draft pick, every one of them, has been signed in time for training camp. Sure, there's a rookie salary pool now, and that makes it easier. But tell that to Dick Vermeil who waited weeks and weeks for his No. 1 pick, Orlando Pace, to report to the Rams' training camp in 1997. Lurie and Banner have never had a rookie miss even one day of camp. That's big. One of Buddy Ryan's biggest complaints about Norman Braman, and where the moniker "The Guy in France" started, was because the Eagles never had their picks in camp. The rookies would miss time, fall behind, and would never catch up.

Also, since Lurie bought the team, the Eagles have been right up against the salary cap every season, which means they have spent every dollar they are allowed to spend. When there has been money left over, it was spent on a player's contract extension. An example of that was at the end of the 1997 season, the team decided to extend Rodney Peete's contract and did so the final day of the season. They have also extended the contracts of at least one starter in the middle of the season each year.

So Lurie's money problems, and the Eagles money problems, have been grossly exaggerated. Has every decision he made been the right one? Of course not, nobody in any business can say that. But Lurie has tried his best. Lurie loves football, and he wants to win. Even his harshest critics can't argue with that.

But football fans, especially Eagles fans, are demanding. Eagles fans have been through a lot over the years, I know I'm one of them. And fans get very frustrated. But at the same time, fans can just go out and scream, and bleed green, and let their emotions run the gamut, and they don't have to deal with the consequences. I've always felt that Eagles fans are phenomenal fans. They have a passion like no other fans I've seen. They come out in terrible weather. They've supported bad teams; but they feel this is their team. And one of the best things Jeffrey Lurie did was when he said early in his ownership, "This is not Jeffrey Lurie's team. This is Philadelphia's team." I think he meant that. Because Jeffrey Lurie is also a fan, and he knows how a fan feels.

You hear all the time that Jeffrey is just waiting for the right deal, and the Eagles are going to move to Los Angeles. I don't buy it. Lurie wants a new stadium, the same way a lot of owners want a new stadium. But I'll be shocked if the team moves out of the area. I would not be surprised in the least if the team moved out of the city and into a suburb. Keep in mind the Cowboys play in Irving, not Dallas, and the Cardinals play in Tempe, not Phoenix. For that matter, the Eagles are the only team in the NFC East that actually plays in the city that carries its name.

I think Jeffrey Lurie has found out how tough it is to own a football team. He hasn't been as visible as he was in his first few years as owner, and maybe that's good. Maybe he needed to step back a bit. But the problem is when you're an owner there is no middle ground. You're either too involved, or not involved enough.

And that's why I'll just stay in the play-by-play business. The view is much better.

A Ray of Hope

I was very excited about the possible return of Dick Vermeil and, like most Philadelphians, rooted for the team to hire Dick Vermeil. I had seen him in the past take a team that was battered and torn, and he picked them up and eventually took them to the Super Bowl. I thought he could do it again.

When the Vermeil talks broke off that Saturday I admit I was upset. I didn't know where the Eagles would turn for their next choice. There were so many names being bantered about. One name that surfaced was Barry Alvarez, the head coach of the University of Wisconsin and a former Notre Dame assistant under Lou Holtz. One story even had him in town to meet with Jeffrey Lurie. Actually it was later learned he was here on a recruiting trip.

I even called Jim Irwin, the play-by-play man in Green Bay who I knew also did some Wisconsin games, and asked him about Alvarez. As we talked about Alvarez and the Eagles' coaching search, Ray Rhodes' name came up in the conversation. Irwin knew Rhodes from when he was on the Packers' staff for two years as defensive coordinator under Mike Holmgren. Irwin told me Rhodes was a great guy who would make a good NFL head coach. He was more flattering about Rhodes than he was Alvarez. Still it appeared Rhodes was a longshot for the job. His name had been mentioned, but it was always as an afterthought.

Other names that had been in the news as Kotite's successor included University of Miami head coach Dennis Erickson, who took the Seattle Seahawks job instead; Butch Davis, the former Dallas assistant who took the University of Miami job after Erickson left; and Gary Stevens, the Miami Dolphins' offensive coordinator. The *Daily News* ran with a story that Stevens was the next head coach with a back page headline blared in big, bold type "It's Even Stevens."

It got to the point where I wondered if they would ever hire a coach; it seemed as if it dragged on and on forever. Actually it wasn't as long as it appeared, but because of the Vermeil situation and the daily coverage of that ordeal, it seemed like the wait was longer than it was.

Ironically, the same day of that Stevens headline in the *Daily News*, February 2, 1995, the Eagles announced that Ray Rhodes was their new coach. Joe Banner told me that when they interviewed Rhodes, he just blew them away. "We knew right then and there he was our guy," Banner said.

Rhodes' reputation from his days in San Francisco was that he was not very good at dealing with the media. He was supposedly a very quiet man who kept to himself, and worked diligently at his defensive sets. There was a story that when he was in Green Bay, his wife, Carmen, convinced him to take a cruise with her after the season. He agreed, but only if he could take his playbook with him. At his initial press conference he came across just fine. He answered all the questions and gave good answers. One I remember was when he was asked if he felt he was "the politically correct choice" as the first-ever African American head coach of the Eagles. Rhodes' answer was, "I just hope I'm the correct choice."

I thought Rhodes was an interesting choice in that we really didn't know much about him. He had played for the Giants and 49ers and coached the 49ers, first as an assistant and later as the defensive coordinator. But he remained pretty much in obscurity. He was mentioned a few times before as a possible head coaching candidate, but it had never become that serious. This certainly wasn't the big name coach that Vermeil would have been. For that matter, most of the other names mentioned carried more popularity and notoriety than Rhodes.

After that first press conference, my next dealing with Rhodes was at his pre-draft briefing. I thought then that this guy was as prepared for a draft as anyone I had ever been around. After the four Kotite drafts produced very little, I was convinced the Eagles had a guy who knew how to draft. He appeared to be ready for anything. And then on draft day he traded up with Tampa Bay, and selected Mike Mamula, a pass rusher from Boston College, who had put on an incredible display of speed and strength at the scouting combine. Ray has never called Mamula a bust, but he has made it clear that it's time for him to start playing like the seventh pick of the draft.

One player the Eagles passed to take Mamula was Warren Sapp, the defensive tackle from the University of Miami who had tested positive for marijuana, and had been labeled a risk by some teams. The Eagles, who had drafted Bernard Williams the year before, could not afford another risk. The whole character issue of a draft pick has become much more prevalent today than it was back in the Vermeil years. In the 1998 draft, the player who fell because of off-the-field problems was Randy Moss, the talented wide receiver from Marshall. He was another player the Eagles may have been able to use, but were scared away from for various, and I assume legitimate, reasons.

I don't know if the character of the players has really changed that much from back when I started, or if the athletes are just under the microscope a lot more today than they were 20 years ago. In the earlier days, a drunken driving charge was looked at as "boys will be boys." That was before groups like MADD and others came into existence, and the crime is perceived more severely and the offender pays more dearly. But I think there were a lot of things going on back then that just weren't reported. Players got away with more, and the public knew less about them. Basically, we knew who the player was and how he played. We knew how fast he could run, and if he had good hands. We didn't know as much about his personal life. Today, a team has to weigh all of those risks before they determine whether it is going to make a guy a millionaire. There is so much information available about every player and so much to sort through that you have tough decisions to make. Through the years, the Eagles have been burned. I already talked about Buddy Ryan's pick of Alonzo Johnson and, of course, Bernard Williams. Sometimes you just can't take a chance.

Rhodes is the first coach I've had the chance to do a live radio show with since I did one with Ed Khyat back before I was even the play-by-play man. I did the Marion Campbell Show, but that was recorded earlier in the day, and the questions were left on an answering machine. Ray and I do his show every Monday night during the season from a local restaurant. During training camp we do the show from the WYSP trailer, and believe it or not, those are the ones I really enjoy. In the trailer we just kick back on those big comfortable chairs, take the calls, and relax. Afterwards, Ray will stay around and just talk about the team.

Ray is also much more at ease during training camp than he is during the season. He isn't under the same kind of pressure and isn't coming off either a tough win, or worse, a tough loss. The training camp shows, despite the fact that there isn't a live audience present, are really a lot of fun to do. Actually though, very few coaches enjoy the crowds as much as Ray does. I'm sure if you ask him, he would tell you he does the show because it's part of his deal and it's something he has to do. But in reality he has a good time. And he couldn't be nicer to the fans. He signs every autograph, every one. We announce that Ray has to leave when the show is over, but he stays around and makes sure everyone who wants an autograph gets one.

Mondays are long enough days for head coaches in the NFL as it is. A guy like Ray Rhodes gets a few hours sleep after the Sunday game and is back in his office at the crack of dawn. He'll watch film of the game all morning, meet with the players, go to his weekly press conference, and then go back and meet with his coaching staff. By the time he gets to the radio show at 6 o'clock, he's exhausted. I mean he's really tired. I'm not exactly raring to go myself, especially after a road game, but at least I usually get a full night's sleep, so I'm not nearly as tired as Ray.

I remember one show back in 1996. The Eagles beat the Miami Dolphins the day before, which happened to be Ray's birthday. He had a million things on his mind that day, and none of them had to do with him turning 46. Steve Geltman, one of WYSP's sports marketing managers, came to me before the show, and before Ray got there, and told me that they had made arrangements with the restaurant. He said that around the middle of the show all the waitresses were going to come out, and sing Happy Birthday and bring Ray a cake. I said, "I don't think he's going to like this." Steve said, "It will be great."

We did the show. We just got finished with a caller, and all of a sudden six waitresses came out with this huge cake that was loaded with sparklers, and they started to sing, and Ray turned to me, off mike, and said, "I don't want that bleeping cake." I turned back to him and said, "Just eat the bleeping cake."

Ray has run hot and cold with most of the writers who cover the team on a daily basis. There have been times when he has been better than anyone, and has entertained the media with what he calls "When-I" stories. Then there are times when he glares and scowls at the media over the most innocent of questions. And one thing that Ray often has to watch is his language. He has even joked about how his mother and his mother-in-law have told him to watch it. But, I have to say, we do his show live, and we've never had a close call with him saying something that should not be heard over the air.

I thought Ray's first year was a great season. He had come in and cleaned up the mess from the year before, the seven-game losing streak, and returned the Eagles to the playoffs. The win over Detroit, an incredible 58-37 game that wasn't even that close, was the absolute zenith. But Ray wasn't happy because the season ended with a playoff loss to Dallas, 30-11. And for Ray Rhodes, it wasn't good enough. He has been spoiled by the success he enjoyed with the 49ers, and anything short of the Super Bowl is not going to be enough. The Eagles were beaten badly in that playoff game at Texas Stadium, and that left an awful taste in his mouth.

Ray's second season was also a playoff year, but also ended with a bad loss, a 14-0 shutout to San Francisco at a messy Candlestick Park. The weather conditions were just brutal that day. It had rained most of the week, and again during the game, and the field was a quagmire. Ray really thought the Eagles were going to win that game; he told me that the week before. He was very confident. He thought his knowledge of the 49ers would be a great asset. But Ty Detmer picked that day to have his worst game of the season. He threw two end-zone interceptions, and never got the team on the scoreboard.

Detmer, who the Eagles signed as a free agent from Green Bay, challenged Rodney Peete for the starting job in training camp, but eventually lost. When Peete went down with a season-ending knee injury in the fifth game of the season, the Eagles had a big decision to make. They could have gone with Detmer, or they could have gone out and acquired Jeff George, who had just been released by the Atlanta Falcons after a blowup with head coach June Jones. There were several columns in the various newspapers that wanted the Eagles to sign George, the former No. 1 overall pick. Fans called WIP and wanted George signed on almost a two-to-one basis.

Rhodes and the Eagles decided they would stick with Detmer, and for a month it looked like they were geniuses. Detmer had the month of his life. He won his first four games as the starter. He threw four touchdown passes in a win over Miami. He threw for 342 yards in a win over Carolina. He beat the Cowboys in Dallas, with some help from an end-zone interception by middle linebacker James Willis. Detmer looked like the guy he backed up in Green Bay, Brett Favre, for that month. But by the end of the season he was just average. And in the playoff loss, he was below average.

Ray lost confidence in Detmer that day as well. He learned then that he would not be the quarterback who would eventually get him to the Super Bowl. And that bothered him, because he knew he needed a big-time quarterback if he were to attain his goal. And Detmer wasn't the guy. Would George have been the answer? We'll never know.

The quarterback Rhodes really wanted when he came to Philadelphia was Mark Brunell, whom he and offensive coordinator Jon Gruden both knew from their days in Green Bay. Brunell, like Detmer, was a backup to Favre for the Packers. But the left-hander from the University of Washington was more like Steve Young, who Rhodes also admired from his time in San Francisco.

Green Bay put Brunell on the market before the 1995 draft, because he would have become a free agent the following season. With Favre firmly entrenched as the Packers' starter, Brunell surely would have gone the free agent route and Green Bay wanted to get something for him, while it could. The Eagles were the first team in line, and actually completed a trade with the Packers that would have sent a second- and fifth-round draft pick to Green Bay for Brunell.

The problem was the Eagles could not get the deal done. There are hundreds of stories as to what exactly happened and who was to blame. Some said it was Bob Wallace, the Eagles' former negotiator who eventually left to join the Rams. Others blamed Jeffrey Lurie and Joe Banner. The bottom line was Brunell and his agent wanted a three-year deal, and the Eagles wanted a five-year deal. And there was never a compromise. He was traded instead to Jacksonville and has enjoyed great success, including a win over the Eagles in 1997. When Rhodes is asked about Brunell, he bites his lip, rolls his eyes and just wonders what if.

After two playoffs season, Rhodes expected a lot from his team in 1997. He called it his best team ever and the media played on that all season. It was something he probably wished he had never said. But Ray had good reason to think the '97 team would be improved. The team had spent big money, $11.5 million, on center

Steve Everitt from Baltimore to improve the offensive line. They signed linebacker Darrin Smith away from Dallas to improve the team speed on defense. They added placekicker Chris Boniol, also from Dallas, who some thought might be the best kicker in the game.

There were good, young players like cornerback Bobby Taylor and defensive tackle Hollis Thomas on defense, and the expected return of defensive tackle Andy Harmon, who was ready to come back from a serious knee injury.

None of the reasons for his optimism materialized. From an opening-day loss to the Giants at the Meadowlands to the disaster in Dallas on Monday night two weeks later, the Eagles started slowly and finished poorly. The brightspot of the season was a brief run near the end of the season under second-year quarterback Bobby Hoying that brought the Eagles even at 6-6-1 with three games left. But another loss to the eventual division champion Giants, followed by losses at Atlanta and Washington, left the team with a 6-9-1 record, their worst since 1986.

Rhodes faced another difficult personnel decision during that season as well. Matt Stevens, a safety claimed on waivers from Buffalo, had been suspended for steroid use. The suspension was up after the fourth game of the season, and the team received a one-week roster exemption. By the sixth game, Stevens was ready and the roster move had to be made.

Harmon, one of the team's most popular players and before his injury one of their best players, had not come back as expected. He was used on a part-time basis, but by the fourth game had been on the field for just a handful of plays per game. Rhodes announced on our radio show the night after that fifth game that he had released Harmon. It drew criticism from the press and from the fans. Here was a guy who was injured playing football, who tried to come back and play again. Later in the season, Harmon and the club came to a settlement over what could have turned into an ugly grievance against the team. But it was a sad situation. There were very few players who have come through this town who were as nice and as dedicated as Andy. He was the kind of guy who would do anything for you, and often he had helped me with charity events and the like. And he never asked for anything in return. The cruel bottom line is that football is a business and the decision the Eagles made was that he could no longer help them because of a bad knee, and so they released him.

It was just another plan that went awry in 1997. Everitt got hurt in training camp and never lived up to his expectations of a potential All-Pro. Mike Zandofsky, a guard signed as a free agent, was released midway through the season. Smith was bothered by injuries all season, wasn't anything close to the player he was in Dallas, and finally landed on injured reserve. Boniol had his problems and did not kick as well as he did in Dallas.

Ray changed quarterbacks almost every other week, at times it appeared every other quarter, and it didn't work. Rodney Peete didn't have the success he had in 1995 when he led the Eagles to the playoffs and the wild-card win over Detroit. Ty Detmer didn't have the success he had in 1996 when he led the team to the playoffs.

As the team floundered in 1997, speculation that Rhodes had problems with the front office began to surface. I've never been told by Ray that he wanted out, or that he could not wait to get out. And I have never heard anything from Jeffrey Lurie, or Joe Banner, that they are not happy with Ray. Sure, when a team has a bad season, the owner is disappointed. And so is the coach. There isn't a coach anywhere who hasn't wanted more than his owner could deliver. Every coach wants to keep all of his potential free agents and sign a bunch more. In a salary-capped NFL, that is not going to happen. Lurie and Banner feel they have given Ray all the support he has needed for the most part.

Does Ray Rhodes have to win in 1998 to keep his job? I don't know. I know Rhodes wants to win, and I think he wants to stay here. And I know Lurie and Banner certainly want him to win, and want him to continue to win here.

I don't think this is the same situation as Norman Braman and Buddy Ryan had where Braman could not wait to get rid of Ryan. And I don't think it's even like Jeffrey Lurie and Rich Kotite, where Lurie wanted to bring in his own coach. Rhodes is Lurie's coach. How much longer will that be the case? We'll just have to wait and see.

My Guy, My Pick

In all my years as the Eagles play-by-play man, I've never been asked my opinion about a college player, and I've never given it. That's not what my job is all about.

With that said, I was also never as excited or felt as gratified as on the night of the 1996 draft when at the end of the third round, the Eagles selected quarterback Bobby Hoying out of Ohio State.

We were in the Grand Slam room, tucked away on the 200 level of Veterans Stadium for that draft. By the time the third round began, the television cameras were gone, and there was no longer an introduction of each player to his team. What you had to do was watch the tracker on the bottom of ESPN2. And that was where I saw it. Philadelphia Eagles was on the bottom of the screen and then the words "current selection" flashed, and the name Bobby Hoying, Ohio State appeared. I was thrilled; I let out a scream. I felt at that point the Eagles had a successful draft. I felt better about that pick than any pick I had seen the Eagles make in all of my years. This was my guy.

You have to understand, from the start of the season I had done nothing but talk about Hoying to anyone who would listen. I annoyed all of the writers who were sick of hearing about this kid from Ohio State and were all over me when he did not get selected in the first round, as I predicted he would, or even the second round, which to me was mind boggling. I had badgered everyone in the Eagles' front office I found who would give me the time to talk, and even head coach Ray Rhodes.

It all started because of my younger cousin, Heidi Kaye, who was an outstanding gymnast, and a member of the junior national team. During her senior year of high school she was recruited by colleges from all over the country. I got involved, and helped her and her parents sort through all of the possible choices. I had been to a lot of the campuses that she was going to visit and I just gave them my opinion. When it all came down to the end, I voted for Ohio State, and they agreed. So Heidi went to Ohio State, and all of a sudden I became an Ohio State fan.

I watched Hoying play as a junior on that great team that included Eddie George at running back, Terry Glenn and Joey Galloway at wide receivers, Ricky Dudley at tight end, and Korey Stringer and Orlando Pace at the tackles. But like I've said before, I've always geared myself toward the quarterback. And I saw this kid who was 6-3, with a strong arm who could move really well. I saw a kid who I thought had a real chance. I thought for sure he would only get better and better.

His senior year I watched every Ohio State game. If I was on the road and missed the game, I would have the game taped and watched it later that week. When I saw him during his senior year I knew this was a guy who could play. He was the prototypical NFL quarterback, I thought. And people who I trusted, like Dick Vermeil, who broadcast a lot of the Ohio State games, agreed with me. Ron Jaworski, who does a lot of work for ESPN and NFL Films, told me he liked Hoying. And that was when I got on my campaign. God, did I want the Eagles to draft this kid. And my worse fears were, what if they didn't and Dallas did?

I talked to John Wooten, and I talked to Chuck Banker, who was more involved with the Eagles' pro personnel, but Banker told me I was right. I would see Ray all through the season, and I would ask him if he had seen Hoying yet. I had Hoyinged him to death. I remember I saw Art McNally, the supervisor of officials, a day after Hoying and Ohio State had beaten Penn State at Happy Valley, and I asked Art what he thought. And he told me, "He's terrific."

One negative I heard about Hoying was he wasn't a good practice player, that he wasn't very accurate at practice. I really didn't care what he did in practice; I had seen what he could do in a game. The only other negative was that he had so much talent around him at Ohio State that it made him look better than he was. Well, Troy Aikman has a lot of talent around him with the Dallas Cowboys. To me, that doesn't take away from Aikman's greatness.

What I've learned about quarterbacks is that the most important pass they have to throw is the 18-yard out pattern. Most every quarterback can throw the bomb, and in reality, how often do you really need to throw it? When you judge a quarterback, the 18-yard out was the pass you judged him by. This is where a quarterback must be able to deliver the ball with enough velocity to avoid getting picked off. I saw Bobby Hoying throw that pass on a laser time and time again. I just felt this was a very special quarterback, and I was set on trying to do whatever I could to get him to the Eagles. What I couldn't understand was why he wasn't higher on more lists. The draft guides had him as the top quarterback prospect in the draft, but they also had him as a second-round pick. I couldn't understand why he wasn't considered a first-rounder.

The season ended and the coaches went to the Senior Bowl. I watched the Senior Bowl on television, and in the middle of the game I called friends and told them they had to watch the game. Hoying was unbelievable. He threw every pass, and he threw every pass perfectly. He didn't show any flaws in his game. He won the MVP of the Senior Bowl, and now I was sure this guy was going to go high in the draft.

Ray came back from Mobile, and when I saw him the first thing he said to me was, "I saw your boy Hoying, OK. He can play. I saw him. He can play." I said, "Are you going to take him?" He said, "I'm not going to say anything about that, but he can play. He's the most equipped quarterback in the draft."

I was confused. If he was that good, why the hesitancy? Just take him, take him in the first round. The Eagles had the 25th pick of the draft that year, and I was worried he might be gone before they picked. He was there, and they passed on him to take Jermane Mayberry, an offensive lineman from Texas A&M-Kingsville. He was still there in the second round, thanks to the Rams' selection of Tony Banks, the quarterback from Michigan State. You would never get Dick Vermeil to say it, but if he had been the coach of the Rams a year earlier, I am quite certain that Hoying would be in St. Louis today. But the Eagles passed him with both of their second-round picks, and instead opted for Jason Dunn, a tight end from Eastern Kentucky, and Brian Dawkins, a safety from Clemson. At that point I had all but given up hope that the Eagles were going to select Hoying.

And then they did. I still can't explain how, or why Hoying lasted until the third round, the 85th player chosen overall. I was just thrilled that he did.

People kid me all the time that I picked Hoying for the Eagles. I can't tell you that the Eagles picked him because of me. Although I do call him "My pick." But maybe my words perked up a couple of ears, maybe made the Eagles looked at him a little more. Maybe the fact that I was so overbearing and never stopped talking about him made them look a little harder. It's like a television commercial that you see so often. When you actually see the product you're at least familiar with it, and maybe you give it a try. I don't know.

We had Bobby on our WYSP postdraft special by phone the following night, but I didn't meet him until a week later at minicamp. I walked over to him, and as I did, Joe Banner was there and introduced us and told Bobby, "Merrill is our play-by-play guy, but he should be your agent." Bobby didn't disappoint me in that minicamp, either; in fact he impressed me even more. Sometimes you watch a guy on television, and then when you see him in person and he's not as big, or he doesn't look as good. But Bobby was the same guy in person I saw in all of those Ohio State games I watched. The talent was there, and I saw it from Day One.

Now the Eagles had drafted quarterbacks through the years, and had failed on most of them. Not since Randall Cunningham in 1985 had they drafted a quarterback who had ever thrown a pass for them. They had swung and missed on the likes of Don McPherson, Craig Erickson, who they drafted and never signed, Casey Weldon, and Dave Barr. I knew this time they had gotten it right.

But there were detractors even within the organization. Ray has told me, without naming names of course, but that there was a definite split in the organization over Hoying. Some people even thought as late as last year that Koy Detmer, who was drafted in the seventh round of the 1997 draft, was better than Bobby, and would beat him out last season. Obviously, they were wrong.

Hoying took just one snap his rookie year. It was the final play of a loss on Monday Night Football to Dallas, and he was sacked on the play and fumbled. But I felt the learning process was good for him. The Eagles had two veterans in Rodney Peete and Ty Detmer and then brought in another good veteran in Mark Rypien when Peete was injured. I felt Bobby would learn from all of them. I felt that was a good trio of quarterbacks for a young quarterback to be around. Detmer knew the west coast offense as well as anyone, and would make a great teacher of the intricacies of the system. Rypien was a Super Bowl MVP, and had been through the NFL gamut from star to backup. He would also be a good teacher for Hoying. And I was very pleased when Peete resigned with the Eagles at the end of the 1997 season to be Bobby's backup and mentor. Rodney Peete has the perfect temperament to be the veteran backup to the emerging young star.

By his second year, 1997, I felt Bobby should have been the Eagles' starting quarterback from the beginning of the season. The same people who called me crazy when I wanted the Eagles to draft him in the first round, thought I was even crazier this time. But my reasoning was that the Eagles were not going to get to the Super Bowl that season no matter who the quarterback was. With that in mind, why not get busy with the quarterback who someday might take you there? And that was Hoying. To me it was time to make the move, why prolong the inevitable? It was Bobby's time.

I guess some people thought that the NFC East was not very strong last year, and they were right, and that if the pieces fell into place the Eagles could win the division. So they should have stayed with the veteran quarterback, either Peete or Detmer. I did not agree.

Hoying played a lot of the preseason and played pretty well. However, he played mostly with backups and against backups. I thought he should have had a chance to play with the starters and against the opponents' starters and see what he could do. Instead, the Eagles had the Detmer/Peete II battle all through preseason and split the starts between the two veterans.

What I noticed in that preseason was not just how strong his arm was, I knew that, but that he could run even better that I thought he could. He was really mobile. The fans started to jump on Bobby's bandwagon early in the season and some of the media began to come around as well. All of a sudden there were columns saying what I had said before, basically, "Stop the Toying, Go With Hoying." During a Monday Night Football loss to San Francisco, Detmer was benched for the third, and final, time. And unlike the first two when the ball was handed to Peete, this time it was Hoying's turn. The loss to the 49ers dropped the Eagles to 4-6 on the season, and finally Ray Rhodes decided the future was now.

Hoying's first start was a road game at Baltimore and I have to say I was probably as nervous as he was. I joked before the game that now I knew how Bob Griese felt before he broadcast a Michigan game when Brian played. Not that Bobby was my son, but here was the guy I campaigned for, the guy I had staked my reputation on with the other members of the media and with some people in the organization, getting his chance to start. Right before the game, Mike Lombardi and Bryan Broaddus, the Eagles' two former personnel men, stopped by the booth, and patted me on the back and said, "Let's see how your guy does today." And as we left the stadium that day both of them shook my hand, and said he really came through.

The Eagles settled for a 10-10 tie when Chris Boniol was wide on a 40-yard field goal attempt as the overtime came to an end. But Hoying played well. In his first NFL start, he completed 26 of 38 passes for 276 yards, and drove the Eagles to the tying touchdown late in the fourth quarter. He also had four passes dropped on him, and withstood nine Baltimore sacks. The following two weeks he was even better, and the Eagles beat a good Pittsburgh team and Cincinnati to get even at 6-6-1 on the season. Against Pittsburgh he threw for 246 yards and two touchdowns, and outperformed the Steelers' bright young quarterback Kordell Stewart. But the Cincinnati game was my favorite.

What I liked so much about that game was the poise Bobby showed. Sure it was the Bengals, and they didn't have the greatest defense in the world, but still he brought them back in the final seconds. Bobby marched the Eagles from their 26 to the Bengals' 13 with five seconds left, and Boniol made the 31-yarder to give the Eagles a 44-42 win. On the day, Bobby completed 26 of 42 passes for 313 yards and four touchdowns. He also beat his boyhood idol, Boomer Esiason, who he watched as he grew up just outside of Cincinnati.

Bobby became the city's darling. His picture was everywhere. The front page of the paper, the back page of the paper. The *Daily News* ran a headline "Hoy to the World." The city could not get enough of Bobby Hoying. He was the new hope. He was what this city needed and wanted. Even after a subpar performance in a loss to the Giants, and slow starts against Atlanta and Washington, the fans stayed behind him. He did not play as well as in those losses as he did in his first three games, but in the Atlanta game he drove them back and gave them a chance to win. Against Washington he played a great second half. That showed me something about him that I hadn't seen before. Bobby Hoying does not get down on himself. He does not let a poor series, or a poor quarter get him down. To me that is a sign of a good quarterback.

I was probably happier than anyone because of Bobby's success. More than just because I can say I was right, but because the

Eagles finally have their cornerstone for the future. There are other areas that certainly need to be filled before the Eagles can legitimately talk about the Super Bowl. And no quarterback, Bobby Hoying, or anyone else, can do it by himself. But at least the Eagles know, or should know, that they have the most important piece to the puzzle in place.

I knew it the night they drafted him.

The Boys in the Booth

Maybe it's the quarterback wannabe in me. But you know how after a big game, the quarterback always thanks his offensive linemen and the people around him? Well I have people who have made it easier for me as well.

Over 21 years of being the Eagles' play-by-play man, you need a lot of good people behind the scenes, and I've been fortunate to have some of the best. In this business, you rely so much on your producer, your spotter, your statistician, and your technical crew. Without those guys I would have been lost. Then again, there have been times when I wish they would have gotten lost.

My first color analyst was the late Jim Barniak, who before he came to the booth was a columnist for the *Philadelphia Bulletin* and later the sports director at Prism, Philadelphia's first cable sports channel. Jim and I had a rather unique experience back in 1978 when the Eagles played New Orleans in Mexico City.

We flew to Mexico City with the team, of course, and in flight Otho Davis, the Eagles' long-time trainer and practical joker, gave everyone a pill to take that he said would fight off Montezuma's Revenge. Instead, the pill he gave us turned everyone's urine Eagle green, and players were astounded and scared to death when they went to the bathroom. That was how the trip began.

The game was scheduled for 4:30 Saturday afternoon. And we weren't sure what to expect in a different locale and on strange soil. I always went to the game on the team bus, but because we didn't know what to expect, Jim and I decided to go a little earlier just in case. We had heard the conditions were on the primitive side. We got a cab outside of the hotel and the driver spoke little, if any, English, but we pointed to our game credentials and that, we hoped, let him know where we wanted to go.

He drove and drove for what seemed like an hour, or an hour-and-half and pulled up to this desolate stadium. There was nobody around, no cars in the parking lot. We tried to explain to him that this could not be right. He called someone and found out that since the tickets were printed, the site of the game had been changed to a bull ring on the other side of town. Now, I was worried.

But this guy drove about 100 miles per hour over these dirt roads, and now I was even more worried, as my life flashed before my eyes and I was back in Pottstown reading my own death notice. We got there, and the field had no grass. They just painted the dirt green, and painted the yardlines, which were anything but straight. It was the first time I felt like I should have said, "first down and 10-and-a-half." We sat in the middle of the stands, surrounded by the Mexican spectators and in the 100-degree heat. In the middle of the game, some fan wandered by, picked up my binoculars and just kept walking. After the game, Ron Jaworski was very critical of the whole situation. Ron was vilified in the Mexican newspapers, and we still joke that he's not allowed back in the country.

So that was Mexico City.

I have been fortunate to have two good producers in my 21 years. Jerry Rosset, my college friend, was my first producer and stayed until 1985 when he decided to go to law school and become an attorney, or as he said, "get a real job." Joe McPeak began in 1986 and came with us from WIP to WYSP in 1992. Jerry had a terrible experience at the Meadowlands in a game against the Giants. Keep in mind the producer never sits during a game. He is always up on his feet, pacing behind the air people and the engineers, getting the commercials ready, watching the "redcap" on the field who signals television time outs. There is just a lot for him to do.

Well as the Giants game started, Jerry turned to me during a break and said, "My hemorrhoids are killing me." I nodded, and thought, What could I do? As the game progressed, so did his pain, and every time I looked at him he appeared to be in worse shape. He made it through the game. We had 90 seconds between the time I gave the final score and when we came back for a post-game wrap. At this point, Jerry could take no more. He screamed, "My hemorrhoids are killing me and I'm bleeding profusely." And with that he took off for the men's room. Except he did not take off his headphones.

As I saw him turn and run, I tried to stop him, but it was too late. Jerry reached the end of the booth and everything, all the equipment, about 35 pounds of it, just crashed to the floor. I never saw anything like it. And I never saw everyone put it back together so quickly. We had it all back and ready to go with three seconds to spare before we went back on the air.

Joe McPeak took over for Jerry in 1986, the same year as Buddy Ryan. He was just out of college and still had a little fan in him. He was a little awestruck at first to be part of the NFL and part of the Eagles broadcast team. But all in all, Joe was a rather quiet person who did his job very well and never had much to say.

We spent the week in Anaheim prior to the Raiders game that season, and decided it might be worth our while to attend Raiders coach Tom Flores' midweek press conference in Manhattan Beach. So we did. We sat in the back of the room and listened to Flores answer questions about his team and the game. All of a sudden, Joe stood up and out of nowhere blurted out, "Coach, is it true that Harry Long is a cheap-shot artist?" Stan turned to me. I turned to Stan. We couldn't believe it. Harry Long? Of course he meant Howie Long, the Raiders' All-Pro defensive end. Flores turned purple. "What was that question?" He asked. Joe, by this point, had ducked away from embarrassment. And I just said "Sorry, coach, he didn't mean anything."

On broadcasts, you would like to cover the national anthem before the game. By that I mean try to time it out perfectly so that your commercials cover the playing of the anthem. Most times it works, sometimes it doesn't. When it doesn't, I like to know the name of the singers, or the band who performed the anthem to acknowledge them on the air. There were two instances when I wished we would have covered the anthem completely.

One time in Arizona we came back too soon, and I signaled to Joe to get me the name of the anthem singers. He handed me a piece of paper with the name, and I said on the air, "That was Fly By that just performed the National Anthem." Joe looked one line too far down on the rundown sheet. Fly by was what some airplanes did after the anthem, not the name of the group.

The other time was in Pittsburgh. Again we came back from the break before the choral group was finished, and I asked for their name. This time it was our statistician Jack Edelstein, and as you'll soon see, I should have known better. But he handed me a card, and I read on the air, "The National Anthem at Three Rivers Stadium performed by The Pennsylvania Home for the Criminally Insane Glee Club." I had no idea what I said until about 15 seconds later and then it hit me. I could have killed Jack.

One of my worst moments in the booth came during a home game against the Giants, with Bill Bergey as my color man. It was a cold day late in the season and both teams struggled. I turned to Bill as I looked at the clock, and I read, "2:02, 2:01, 2;00, 1:59, how come we're not getting a two-minute warning?" Bill turned to me and said, "I don't get it." I didn't know what was happening. I started to make a big deal of it. Jerry was behind me and tried to get my attention, but to no avail. Now, people in the stands who had brought radios with them, had turned around and were yelling at us. I had no idea what was wrong. Finally, Jerry handed me a note that read, "IT'S THE FIRST QUARTER." I never felt so dumb. It was just such a bad game, and such a cold day, that it felt as if it had been too long to be just one quarter.

That was on me. And it was one of the two most embarrassing moments I've had in the booth. The other came in Dallas in 1996.

This one nobody noticed, except me, but it bothered me for a long time. When Eagles linebacker James Willis intercepted Troy Aikman's pass in the end zone at the end of the game, I never saw it. I mean I knew the pass was intercepted, but I did not know by whom. I was completely screened. That was when I looked for my spotter, the Eagles public relations assistant Derek Boyko, who normally does a good job. I yelled, "It's intercepted, it's intercepted." I looked over toward Derek, and Joe McPeak had tackled Derek and now he could not get to the board to point to James Willis. I looked back to the field and by this time Troy Vincent had the ball after a lateral from Willis. I said, "Vincent has the football, he's down to the 40, 35, 30, 25, 20, 15 ,10, the Eagles win, the Eagles win."

The next day people stopped me and said what a great call it was. It was a terrible call; it was my worst call ever. The only criticism I got was from a *Daily News* writer who wrote that I never called it a touchdown. But I never said Willis' name. On the plane ride home, Joe could not apologize enough.

Another embarrassing moment for me, which was not my fault, came after the 1980 NFC Championship Game. We were in the booth after the game, and we interviewed players who were still in the locker room.

I started to talk about linebacker John Bunting and what a great game he had, and what a big hit he had put on Tony Dorsett early in the game, and how that play had set the tone for the game. And I thought we had John in the locker room, and I said, "John, tell us about that hit on Dorsett." There was a brief pause, and then the voice at the other end said, "Merrill, this is Max." They had gotten me punter Max Runager instead of Bunting and never told me.

Another funny story involved George Hickman, who was one of my spotters during the Buddy Ryan years. George had the biggest crush on one of the Eagles' cheerleaders named Wendy. For some reason, and completely on his own, he decided one game to hang a banner out over the booth, that read "Hello, Wendy." Except that he covered the WIP billboard. Mikel Herrington, our program director went wild.

All Herrington cared about was how much exposure the station got and he could not have his permanent sign covered by a "Hello, Wendy" banner. I felt for sure George was going to be fired. He was finished. And I knew if I tried anything to save him I would just make it worse. Nothing I ever said to Herrington got through. Whatever I wanted, he did the opposite. So the next morning I went into Herrington's office and said, "If I were you I'd fire George Hickman today. How can a guy be so stupid to do what he did?" And I went on and on.

Herrington looked at me and said, "Don't get so upset. George is a young guy. I'll talk to him." And we saved his job.

There are millions of stories about Stan. Some of which we have already mentioned. The thing about Stan is that he loves the game. He is what you might call a football purist. And he has theo-

ries; boy does he have theories. One of them is that time of possession is not an important statistic, despite what coaches tell you.
Stan thinks a more telling stat is points scored per 100 yards and
points allowed per 100 yards and the difference between the two.

But Stan is a character. He loves to eat and he would eat
through a broadcast. One time during a game he had this sandwich
with hot peppers and I turned to him after a play for a comment,
and he couldn't talk. His eyes were red and he pointed to the sandwich. The peppers had gotten to him.

Stan is also very honest. In all of his 14 years he was not a
homer. If a bad call went the Eagles' way, he would say they got
away with one. He was very down the middle on things like that.
The Eagles played Dallas one day at the Vet and it seemed like the
Cowboys had gotten the best of the calls. Stan was furious. He was
raging. And he started to scream about Tex Schram, the Cowboys'
general manager. He said "Tex Schram has those officials in his
pocket."

Schram, who was in the booth next to ours and was scheduled to be our halftime guest, found out what Stan had said. Schram
knocked on our booth window and had his pockets pulled out to
show there was nothing in his pockets. He also refused to come on
at halftime and had Stan taken off the Cowboys' mailing list.

Stan hated the preseason games, and if it were up to him, they
would have been done away with long ago. And he would moan
and groan about them all through the preseason. One time, during
a preseason game, he left the booth to get a sandwich. When he
came back, Joe told him that the station called and said our ratings
were never higher. Stan said, "Oh yeah, great. Let's see how high
they can go." And he left for the rest of the quarter.

Stan got his when we went to Tokyo for a preseason game
against New Orleans in 1994. Cindy was supposed to make the trip
with me, but Nolan got sick and she had to stay home. At the hotel
in Japan, she was still registered with me. The next morning when
we went to breakfast it was Stan and I. The Japanese host met me
at the entrance, and said, "Welcome, Mr. Reese. I hope you enjoy
your breakfast." Then he turned to Stan and said, "Welcome, Cindy."

Bill Werndl, who worked as my spotter through the years and
now has his own highly rated radio show in San Diego, can be
summed up in one word, wacky.

Stan used to say that Bill thought they played the season just so they could figure out the draft order. He was a draftnik to the worst degree.

And Bill would debate you on any topic, and he drove the players crazy.

When he first started with us, he wasn't on the air. But he would be on the bus, and as the players boarded the bus, Bill would go into a Howard Cosell impersonation. "Now getting on the bus, the big tackle from Texas, Jerry Sizemore..." And the players hated it.

Once on a flight to a game, I thought a player was going to kill him. The Eagles had just acquired a defensive linemen from Oakland named Art Thoms. He hadn't even been with the team a week. From behind he looked a lot like Dennis Franks, one of the team's offensive linemen who Billy knew pretty well. So Bill came up behind Thoms, who he thought was Franks, and whacked him on the head with a rolled-up newspaper. Thoms turned around and nobody was there. Bill had hid behind a seat. This happened again, and again Thoms looked around and nobody was there. Bill was about to do it a third time, and just as he was about to hit him again, Thoms turned around and I thought Bill was going to pass out, or get killed.

Jack Edelstein probably deserves an entire book. I've never met anyone quite like him. His family owned Pioneer belts, and the joke was that he was paid a lot of money to stay out of the family business. But he knew everyone ever connected with the Eagles and knew everyone everywhere. He dated Marilyn Monroe. He was nearly engaged to Gloria DeHaven. He was best friends with Councilman Jack Kelly and had known Jack's sister, Princess Grace Kelly, since they were kids. He was the best man at Red Buttons' wedding and his date that night was Tina Louise, who played Ginger on Gilligan's Island. His roommate at one time was Sonny Jurgensen, and another of his close friends was Mike Ditka. When Jerry Lewis was in town a couple of years ago to do "Damn Yankees", he asked how he could find Jack Edelstein. The guy has lived an incredible life.

And in his spare time he found ways to keep our lives interesting.

Jack has the knack for a double-talk routine that is just hilarious. He's been asked to do all kinds of speeches. Once Dick Vermeil asked him to address the team as a chairman of the rules committee. And he told the players they should take notes. A lot of the veterans knew Jack and knew what was about to happen. The rookies, and new players, did not. Every third word, or so, is mumbo jumbo. And by the end he was not making any sense at all, and the players didn't know what to do.

Another time he brought Prince Albert, Princess Grace's son, to an Eagles practice and then into the locker room to meet some of the players. Because Jack was rarely taken seriously, as he introduced Prince Albert nobody believed him. Bill Bergey and a couple of others players yelled, as Jack said this was Prince Albert, "let him out of his can."

One of Jack's favorite pranks was perpetrated when he drove over a bridge, whether it was the Ben Franklin, or the Walt Whitman. He had an arm that was a cadaver from one of his medical friends, and he put a jacket over the arm with a quarter in the hand. And he reached it out of the window, and as the toll taker took the money, the arm stayed, and Jack pulled away.

Another time on a road trip to Detroit for a game with the Lions, we stayed at the Pontiac Hilton and a local high school had its prom there the same night. There was a large painting of Abe Lincoln that hung in the lobby over a sofa. As the night went on, you could hear the music from the prom, and all of a sudden I saw Jack up on the sofa, and he spread his arms as wide as they would go and he reached up and took down the Lincoln painting. I asked him what he was doing, and he said, "Just watch." He walked through the ballroom, got up on the stage, motioned to the band and asked the drummer to give him a drum roll. Jack took the mike, and said, "Good evening, I'm Jack Edelstein from the Mayor's office. I'd like the senior class president to please come to the stage. This kid walked up to the stage, and Jack presented him with painting as a gift from the Mayor's office.

Then there was the time before a game with Washington. We had breakfast together at the Crystal City Marriott. Stan and I came down together and Jack had already gotten a table. A few minutes later two players, Reggie White and Clyde Simmons, joined us. We had already ordered and Jack asked for a honeydew melon. When they brought the melon it came with a slice of lime. Jack proceeded to cut the lime into six small slices, and then picked up the honeydew and squeezed it on the lime. I thought Reggie and Clyde would die. And all Jack said was, "I really like a little honeydew on my lime."

Those are the people I've dealt with through my 21 years and I've loved just about every minute of it.

Merrill's Top 10

You try to put together a list of the top games, or plays over 21 years and it's pretty tough. Some games pop into your mind immediately, and then you think of a few others, and before you know it, your top 10 list has about 27 entries.

Well, I managed to trim the list to my 10 most memorable games, and 10 most memorable plays of my career. Of course, I added some honorable mentions to the list, because I just couldn't leave some of those memories out.

*1.   January 11, 1981, Philadelphia
        Eagles 20, Dallas 7*

Number one has no equal. Hopefully, one day I'll be able to top this with a Super Bowl win, but until then, this is the best.

The whole build up for the game, the week in Tampa, Dick Vermeil downplaying the team's chances, the excitement that surrounded the game was memorable.

It was a very cold day at Veterans Stadium, one of the coldest home games I can remember. But the weather didn't keep the fans away. There were 70,696 jammed into the Vet that day, and by the end, none of them felt the cold. They were too happy.

The play everyone remembers was Wilbert Montgomery's 42-yard touchdown run that put the Eagles ahead, 7-0, and I do too, as you'll see later. But another play that doesn't get as much recognition was a hit by linebacker John Bunting on Dallas running back

Tony Dorsett, who tried to go wide and was just leveled at the line of scrimmage, early in the game.

Friday before the game, Brad Sham, the Cowboys's long-time play-by-play man, and I did a simulcast sports talk show that was called a "Tale of Two Cities." We alternated calls between Dallas and Philadelphia, and it was broadcast on both WIP and KRLD in Dallas. It was a great hour of radio, one of the best shows I've ever done.

I wasn't sure what to expect. I mean the Eagles were home, which was a big advantage. But this was Dallas, and I had my heart broken too many times. I figured the game would go down to the wire.

It didn't. It was tied, 7-7, at halftime, but the Eagles dominated the second half. Tony Franklin's 26-yard field goal put the Eagles ahead to stay, and Leroy Harris' one-yard touchdown run gave them a 10-point lead in the fourth quarter.

Montgomery ran for 194 yards, and the Eagles defense held Dorsett to 41 yards. It is, as Rich Kotite would say, without question the biggest win in my 21 years.

2.   *September 17, 1989, Washington D.C.*
      Eagles 42, Washington 37

The big story happened before the game began when quarterback Randall Cunningham signed a $21 million contract extension.

The Eagles, who always struggled at RFK Stadium, started poorly. Twice in the first half they trailed by 20 points. Washington scored touchdowns on its first two offensive plays of the game.

The Eagles fought back, and trailed 37-35 with 1:16 left. But Gerald Riggs, who ran for over 200 yards on the day, broke a long run that appeared to seal the win for the Redskins.

Except that linebacker Al Harris stripped the ball from Riggs and handed it to safety Wes Hopkins who went 77 yards to the Washington four yard line.

Some plays you see, and some you need help on—this one I had dead. I saw the whole thing, and made an accurate call.

Cunningham, who was 34-for-46 for 447 yards, threw his fifth touchdown pass of the day, and his third to tight end Keith Jackson for the win.

It was an incredible day, and an incredible ending. For this team to win a game like that at RFK, and for Randall to have that kind of day was just unbelievable.

3.   *November 10, 1991, Cleveland, Ohio*
       Eagles 32, Cleveland 30

That morning in the hotel as we ate breakfast, Joe McPeak overheard a conversation Eagles executive George Azar was having about Jim McMahon. McPeak came back and told me, "I just heard George say McMahon can't lift his arm high enough to brush his teeth. He's not going to be able to play."

McMahon had been injured on and off the entire season and now was bothered by a sore elbow and a sore knee. What made it worse was he had taken a shot Saturday night to be able to play, but had an allergic reaction and now was in worse shape. His roommate Ron Heller had to help him get dressed that morning, and he barely made it up the steps at old Cleveland Memorial Stadium.

I got to the game even earlier than normal, and during the pregame show I had to make a decision whether to say anything about McMahon. It's always been my policy that anything I see on the plane, or in the hotel, I leave there. But this was big news. I tried to get to Jim, because he would have told me, but he wasn't around. So I asked some questions, and decided to go on the air with it.

As it turned out, McMahon played, but the Eagles were terrible. They trailed, 23-0. The only bright spot in the first half was cornerback Ben Smith's interception which ended Bernie Kosar's NFL record streak of 308 passes without an interception. Later in the game, Smith suffered a knee injury that ruined what could have been a brilliant career.

I still don't know how he did it, but McMahon brought the Eagles back, and back, and back. He threw for 341 yards and three touchdowns. The final touchdown, a five-yarder to Calvin Williams, who was about nine yards deep in the end zone, gave the Eagles the win. I can still see that pass. McMahon got all he could on the ball, and Williams shielded the defender and actually caught the ball with his chest.

The play was set up when Cleveland's Webster Slaughter tried to field a punt inside the five yard line. Ken Rose hit him, and forced the fumble, and Britt Hager recovered.

All through that 1991 season the defense carried the Eagles, but in their best win that season it was Jim McMahon, and the special teams, that did it for them.

4.   *November 3, 1996, Dallas, Texas*
       Eagles 31, Dallas 21

The Eagles had lost to the Cowboys at home earlier in the season on Monday Night Football when they blew a 10-point lead, and in the process lost quarterback Rodney Peete for the season.

In this one it looked like they might blow another double-digit lead, and lose again. Ty Detmer, who ran for one touchdown and passed for another, had played a great game, and had helped the Eagles to a 24-13 fourth-quarter lead.

Dallas came back on a touchdown run by Emmitt Smith and a two-point conversion and cut the lead to 24-21. The Cowboys got the ball back and Troy Aikman drove them downfield. It was first and goal at the Eagles' three yardline. There was no doubt in my mind the Cowboys were going to win, and it was going to be another terrible flight home from Dallas.

On first down Smith swept left, and cornerback Troy Vincent actually threw him out of bounds at the two. That was a play that Smith had run so often for a touchdown, and usually over the cornerback. Vincent made a great play. On second down, Smith went up the middle, and backup linebacker Sylvester Wright came up and stuck him for a one-yard loss. On third down, Aikman dropped back to pass. I thought the Cowboys might draw, but he passed. Why Aikman would make such a bad read, I'll never know. But his pass for Eric Bjornson was intercepted in the end zone by James Willis. Vincent took the lateral from Willis and went in for the touchdown.

5.   *November 2, 1979, Dallas, Texas*
       Eagles 31, Dallas 21

Ironically, numbers 4 and 5 had the same final score against the same team. The Eagles had lost nine straight games to the Cowboys, and had not won in Dallas since 1965 until this Monday Night game.

Early in the game on a third-and-one call, Jaworski faked a handoff to Montgomery and went deep to Harold Carmichael for a long gain.

But the biggest play of the game came after Harvey Martin knocked Jaworski out of the game, and John Walton came off the bench and threw a 29-yard touchdown pass to Charlie Smith to put the Eagles ahead to stay.

Also in that game Tony Franklin kicked a 59-yard field goal, the longest in Eagles history and still the fourth longest in NFL history. And it would have been good from 69 yards out. It was a monster kick.

That was huge for the Eagles to beat Dallas in Dallas on a Monday Night. In my opinion that game set the tone for everything that followed. That game told the team they were good enough. That was the major brick in the foundation that took them to the Super Bowl.

6.   *December 2, 1991, Houston, Texas*
**   *Eagles 13, Houston 6***

There was not a lot of spectacular offensive plays in this one. But the Eagles defense was so good that night in the Astrodome, that this game must be included. I had never seen so many bone-jarring hits in one game.

What I also remember about this game is I saw Bum Phillips, the former Oilers head coach in the pressbox before the game. His son Wade, the former Eagles assistant was then head coach in Denver and won a crucial game the day before that might have saved his job. I said to Bum, "That was a nice win for Wade." And Bum said, "Yeah, that's one more week I don't have to feed him."

Jim McMahon got knocked out of the game with an elbow injury, and Jeff Kemp came off the bench and threw the winning touchdown pass, a 21-yarder to tight end Keith Jackson for the only touchdown of the game.

Kemp was a gritty quarterback, who the Eagles could have used earlier in the season during the Pat Ryan/Brad Goebel debacle.

This game belonged to the Eagles defense, however, which forced five Oilers turnovers, sacked Warren Moon four times, harassed him all night, and held the high-powered Houston offense to a total of 247 yards.

Linebacker Seth Joyner had two sacks, forced two fumbles, and recovered two fumbles. Safeties Wes Hopkins and Andre Waters terrorized the small Houston receivers in their run-and-shoot attack, and by the middle of the game they were scared to come across the middle. Hopkins was even fined for a vicious hit he put on Earnest Givens. This was the kind of game Waters and Hopkins lived for. You could hear the hits, and almost feel them up in the booth. I wanted to scream a couple of times.

And backup cornerback Otis Smith made a huge play when he put a big hit on Houston receiver Drew Hill, forced a fumble, and recovered it deep in Eagles territory late in the fourth quarter.

Houston drove to the Eagles' 23 yard line on its final drive, but Moon's last pass of the game in the end zone for Haywood Jeffires was batted away by Joyner.

The Oilers called the Astrodome the House of Pain that season, but as Eagles defensive tackle Jerome Brown proclaimed after the win, "They brought the house. We brought the pain."

7.   *December 20, 1992, Philadelphia Eagles 17, Washington 13*

The Eagles needed the game to make the playoffs. Actually the winner was in, and the loser had to win the next week and get some help.

Randall Cunningham threw a 28-yard touchdown pass to Calvin Williams, and Heath Sherman, the team's offensive MVP that season, scored on a two-yard run. Vai Sikahema also had a long punt return (47 yards) that set up a field goal.

But the key to the game was Washington's last drive. The Redskins started at their own five with 3:35 left and drove all the way to the Eagles' five. Three times the Redskins converted on third downs, and once on fourth down.

It appeared time had run out and the game was over when Washington failed on a third-down play. But the referees stopped the clock, because an Eagle had picked up the loose ball, and the Redskins were given one last play.

Mark Rypien dropped back and spotted Gary Clark just over the goal line in the middle of the end zone. But Reggie White forced Rypien to roll, and he had to let it go about a second late. The ball still was headed right to Clark, but in that instant, Eric Allen dove fully extended, reached out with his right arm, and knocked the ball away.

That win clinched a wild-card spot for the Eagles, and put them in the playoffs for the only time in Rich Kotite's four years as head coach.

8.   *December 3, 1989, East Rutherford, New Jersey*
        Eagles 24, Giants 17

This was a cold, windy day at the Meadowlands. It's always windy at the Meadowlands, but this day was more blustery than ever.

What will be remembered most about this one was Randall Cunningham's 91-yard punt, the longest in Eagles history, and the third longest in NFL history.

Backed up near their end zone, in a 17-17 tie, Buddy Ryan sent Cunningham into punt. John Teltschik, the regular punter, was injured earlier in the game. If Cunningham shanked it, the Giants would have been in great shape. Instead, with the wind at his back, he got off a high, deep kick that went 65 yards in the air, and bounced inside the Giants' 10 where Dave Meggett finally retrieved it, and returned it a few yards.

On the Giants' next play, Mike Golic, not known as a sackmaster, got to Phil Simms, sacked him, and forced a fumble. Mike Pitts recovered, and the Eagles had a first-and-goal. Keith Byars scored from two yards out, and the Eagles had a win that put them in first place.

The Eagles defense, which led the league with 51 take-aways that year, scored two of the team's three touchdowns, and set up the other touchdown and field goal.

Andre Waters scored on a three-yard run after a lateral from William Frizzell, who recovered a Phil Simms fumble caused by Reggie White. Clyde Simmons took a Simms interception back 60 yards for a touchdown. The big defensive end scored three touchdowns in his career at the Meadowlands.

Eric Allen's interception set up a field goal, and Allen had an 87-yard interception return for a touchdown brought back on an offsides call.

Byars and Anthony Toney combined for 36 carries and 134 yards rushing on the windy day.

9.   *October 2, 1994, San Francisco, California*
        Eagles 40, San Francisco 8

The Eagles went out to Candlestick Park as a big underdog, and instead blew the 49ers away in just an amazing game.

It marked the debut of rookie running back Charlie Garner, who was unstoppable. Garner ran for 111 yards on just 16 carries and scored the first two touchdowns of the game on runs of one yard and 28 yards. It was 14-0 after the first quarter, and 30-8 at halftime.

The Eagles rolled up 437 yards of offense against the San Francisco defense, which was coached by Ray Rhodes, and the Eagles defense held the 49ers vaunted west-coast offense to 189 yards and 11 first downs.

I kept saying on the air, "I'm not going to believe this until we are on the plane flying home."

In the middle of the game, San Francisco coach George Seifert pulled quarterback Steve Young, and the two had words on the sidelines.

There are two sidelights that make this game even more incredible.

Who would have possibly thought that after this game the 49ers would go on to win the Super Bowl, and the Eagles would not even make the playoffs?

And even more amazing, who would have thought the offensive-minded coach whose team scored 40 points that day would be fired, and be replaced by the defensive coordinator whose team allowed those 40 points?

That's just one of the oddities of the NFL.

**10.   *November 30, 1997, Philadelphia
         Eagles 42, Cincinnati 40***

Maybe I rate this one so highly because it was recent. Maybe it was because Bobby Hoying came up so big. But this was such a dramatic shootout, and we hadn't seen one of these in such a long time.

The Eagles had gone into the game as the only team in the league that hadn't scored at least 25 points in a game all season, and this was week 14.

Hoying led the Eagles to a 24-14 halftime lead, and it grew to 34-21 after three quarters. But Boomer Esiason, who a year earlier had beaten the Eagles in Arizona, looked like he was going to do it again. Esiason took the Bengals to 21 fourth-quarter points and a 42-41 lead with a minute to play.

I remember I said, "Now the Eagles trail the Bengals, and there is less than a minute left. This will tell us what Bobby Hoying is all about. Let's see what the young quarterback can do."

And darn if he didn't do it. He took the team 61 yards on a drive that began at the 26 yardline, and ended with Chris Boniol's 31-yard field goal as time expired.

Hoying connected twice with Irving Fryar for gains of 28, and 18 yards. The 18-yarder came on third-and-11 from the 31 yardline and made Boniol's field goal a chip shot. The poise that Bobby showed on that drive is the kind of poise a big-time quarterback has. And this came in only his third NFL start.

Honorable Mention

Other games which at one time or another would have made the top 10 list include:

- The 58-37 wild-card game win over Detroit in the 1995 play-offs.
- The 20-17 win over Dallas, also in 1995, when the Eagles defense stopped Emmitt Smith twice on fourth-and-inches.
- The 35-30 win over the Jets in 1993 when Randall Cunningham and Fred Barnett both got hurt, and Bubby Brister came off the bench to lead the win.
- The 17-14 win over the two-time defending Super Bowl Champions Pittsburgh Steelers in 1979.
- The 24-21 win over Cleveland in 1982 just before the NFL players strike.
- And the 36-20 win over New Orleans in the 1992 NFC wild-card game.

If you think about 21 years and 339 games, there were an awful lot of plays that I've called from the Eagles broadcast booth.

The number-one play was easy, after that it got tough, but here are the top 10 Eagles plays I've broadcast, plus an all-time series of plays.

1.   *January 11, 1981, vs. Dallas*
Montgomery's 42-yard TD Run

It might not have been the most spectacular play I've ever seen. And it certainly wasn't anything unusual. It was just a running back off right tackle, but it was the biggest play of the biggest game.

I knew, and I think everyone in the Delaware Valley knew, after that play that the Eagles were going to the Super Bowl.

Early in the first quarter, Montgomery took the handoff from Jaworski, and went behind the blocks of Jerry Sizemore and Woody Peoples and broke free for the touchdown.

Here's the way I described it that day.

> *"Second down and 10 for the Eagles, the Cowboys have six defensive backs in the game. Jaworski hands off to Montgomery, up the right side, 25, 20, 15, 10, touchdown! Montgomery exploded up the right side, and the Eagles have scored first. Wilbert rambled 42 yards. The blocks, Sizemore and Peoples, and the Eagles have struck..."*

That play gave me a feeling I had never had before, or since. I knew the Eagles were going to the Super Bowl.

2.   *November 19, 1978, vs. Giants*
       The Miracle of the Meadowlands

I was numb. I didn't realize what I had seen until the next day. If someone told me I was describing a play that would be replayed thousands of times, that I would have kids come up to me and say, "Pisarcik fumbles the football..." These are kids who weren't born yet when it happened. But that play has been shown so many times on HBO, and ESPN, and every highlight film, that everyone has seen it, and heard it by now.

That play was not only the strangest play in Eagles history, but one of the strangest in NFL history. There has never been another play like it. Here's the way I described it.

> *"Under 30 seconds left in the game, and Pisarcik fumbles the football. It's picked up by Herman Edwards. He's at the 15, 10, 5, touchdown Eagles! I don't believe it! I don't believe it! I do not believe what has just occurred here ladies and gentlemen! As Pisarcik came forward he fumbled the football, Charlie Johnson hit him and Herman Edwards picked it up and ran it in for a touchdown!"*

3.   *November 10, 1985, vs. Atlanta*
       A Quick 99 yarder

The game was a good game, nothing great. And it went overtime. The Eagles were backed at up their one yardline, and I was concerned the Falcons might get a safety and win the game. If there was holding in the end zone, even, that would be a safety, and the game would be over.

The Eagles had been in five overtime games before this one, and had lost four and tied one. So I wasn't that confident they would pull this one out, either. And with the ball at the one yardline...

Well, here's what happened.

"Here it is second down and 10 for the Eagles, Jaworski on second-down retreats, he's looking, he fires the football over the middle complete to Quick. He's going to go, 25, 30, 35, 40, midfield, 45, 40, 35, 30, 25, 20, Mike Quick touchdown! The Eagles win! The Eagles win! Forget the extra point, Jaworski to Quick, 99 yards, and the game is over!"

4.   *December 2, 1990, vs. Buffalo*
       Amazing Randall

It was a cold, bitter cold, day in Buffalo.

All day Randall Cunningham looked like a bullfighter against the Bills defense, and on this play he was incredible.

Randall dropped back into the end zone, Bruce Smith, the Bills' great defensive end, seemed to have him sacked. It looked like Smith wasn't just going to sack him, but he was going to take his head off in the process.

Somehow Cunningham miraculously escaped and fired the ball to midfield where Fred Barnett made a leaping reception and ran away from the defense for the touchdown. The play covered 95 yards and is the second longest touchdown pass in Eagles history.

After the game Randall was asked by one of the writers, Reuben Frank, if he sometimes amazes himself with what he can do, and Randall said, "Yeah sometimes I even amaze myself."

Of course that quote got him in trouble, because the Eagles lost the game, but all he did was answer the question.

5.   *October 3, 1993 vs. Jets*
       Allen's Interception

The Eagles have made a ton of great defensive plays over the past 21 years, but this one might be the best.

For a sheer play this was as great a play as I've ever seen, and for excitement, this was as exciting a play as I've ever seen.

The Eagles had fought back all game, after falling behind 21-0, and losing Randall Cunningham and Fred Barnett to season-ending injuries.

With the Jets ahead, 30-28, in the fourth quarter, Boomer Esiason moved his team into Eagles territory again. But Eric Allen intercepted an Esiason pass at the six yard line and weaved and danced and avoided just about every Jet player for a 94-yard return for a touchdown that put the Eagles ahead to stay, 35-30. He must have run about 150 yards on the play, and made at least seven Jets miss him. He showed the most remarkable agility I have ever seen.

It was also Allen's third interception in four games and the second time in as many games he returned one for a touchdown. After he scored, he handed the ball to Cunningham, who had just come back on to the field after having his leg placed in a cast.

This is how I described it.

> *"The ball has taken a lot of strange bounces in this game. Nine seventeen, 9:16, left in the fourth quarter, Jets lead by two, and in a position to get more. Second down and nine they're at the 20 yard line of the Eagles. Thorton, the tight end, goes into motion. Esiason, play action, he's back, he's firing, and it's intercepted again on the far side of the field. Intercepted by Allen, spinning at the 10, out to the 15, the 20, cutting to his left at the 25, 30, Allen to the 40, Allen to the 45, 50, 45, 40, Eric Allen down the far sidelines, steps over a man, he's going to gooooo! Eric Allen! Eric Allen with a miraculous return of an interception! And the Eagles take the lead. Eric Allen with an absolutely miraculous return, getting help from a block by Ben Smith! Ninety-four yards, and the Eagles lead!"*

6.   *December 10, 1995 vs. Dallas*
        Groundhog Day

Another defensive play, this one against Emmitt Smith on fourth down and inches at the Dallas 29 yard line.

In a 17-17 tie, Dallas faced a big decision with just over two minutes left in the game. Barry Switzer, a rambling, gambling man, decided to go for it. Smith carried and was stopped for a loss by the Eagles defense.

But wait—the officials' whistle had blown, signaling the two-minute warning, and the play didn't count. Dallas had another chance.

Again Switzer decided to go for it, again Troy Aikman handed the ball to Smith, and again the Eagles defense stopped him for a loss.

This was how Stan and I saw, and described, the play.

> *Merrill:"The Eagles stopped them once. Can they stop them again? It will be fourth down and one, and Switzer's going to go for it again."*
>
> *Stan:"I think Switzer should be punting here."*
>
> *Merrill:"I wish he were punting here."*
>
> *Stan: "He's got a lot of confidence in his offensive line."*
>
> *Merrill:"Can they do it again? They could pass, too, to (Jay) Novacek, who's in motion. Here they go, fourth down, they go to Smith and they stop him again! They stop him again! And this time they can't take it away! The same play—it's Groundhog Day! It's Groundhog Day! They did it again!"*

I had just seen the Bill Murray movie with Nolan, where every time he wakes up it's the same day, and that's what came out of my mouth. People who saw the movie told me it was a great line. People who didn't see the movie had no idea what I was talking about.

7.   *October 10, 1988, vs. Giants*
        Randall vs. Carl Banks

The Eagles had not been on Monday Night Football for seven years before the ABC crew finally made it back for this NFC East rivalry.

And Randall Cunningham gave them reason to come back.

Cunningham was all but flattened by Giants linebacker Carl Banks as he rolled to his right. He was no more than three inches from the ground, and he somehow raised that mighty right arm and fired a touchdown pass to veteran tight end Jimmie Giles.

I believe Monday Night Football, for its 25th Anniversary, listed its greatest plays of all time, and this was one of them.

8.   *December 20, 1992, vs. Washington*
      End Zone Breakup

Eric Allen, one of my favorite players, made my favorite play list twice. This was his famous deflection against Washington that clinched the playoff spot for the Eagles.

It wasn't an unusual play, because you probably see a defensive back knock a pass away from a receiver 25 to 50 times during a season. What made that play memorable was because that was the season on the line. This play made it more for its significance than for the sheer play itself.

Here was the way I called it.

> *"Here we go, the last play of the game. Rypien under center, (Ricky) Sanders goes in motion. Rypien rolling, being chased by Reggie, firing, it's incomplete! The game is over! The Eagles win! Eric Allen breaks up the final pass—Eric Allen dove in there! They are going wild! They are going crazy! The Eagles are in the playoffs! It couldn't be more dramatic! The Eagles make the playoffs by beating the Washington Redskins, 17-13!"*

9.   *November 22, 1992, vs. Giants*
      "Rocky" Sikahema

Special teams have to be included somewhere on my list, and Vai Sikahema's 87-yard punt return for a touchdown against the Giants was the best I've seen. It was also the longest in Eagles history.

The Eagles had not had a punt returned for a touchdown since Gregg Garrity did it against the Raiders in 1986, and they haven't had once since. So in the span of 11 years, they have had just one punt return for a touchdown—Sikahema's.

I almost forgot how to describe a punt return. But Vai's was a classic. It put the game away, and then he did his Rocky rendition on the goalposts at Giants Stadium.

Here was the way I saw it, and the way you heard it.

> *"What a big you-know-what this would be. Here is the punt by (Sean) Landetta, no block on this time. He drives it. Sikahema backs up. He takes it at the 13. Starts right, across the 20, 25, 30, 35, 40, 45, midfield, 45, 40, 35, 30, Sikahema at the 20, the 10, touchdown Vai Sik-a-hem-a! It happened! He finally broke one! It was bound to happen—and Sikahema is punching the goalposts! The Eagles have broken this game apart! The Eagles have taken this game and ripped it apart at the seams!"*

10.   October 13, 1996
Irving's Catch of the Day

There have been a lot of great catches, but the greatest I've seen was Irving Fryar's catch against the Giants in Ty Detmer's first start.

The reason that was so incredible was because he came across the middle, he leaped for the football and somehow had to turn his hands backwards to catch the ball, and cradled it back to his chest. I never saw anyone contort his body the way Irving Fryar did to make that catch.

Fryar came across the middle and the ball was thrown high and a little off target. It was not routine the way a receiver would normally reach out with his palms facing him. The only way he could have caught it was with his right arm somehow twisted, and he cradled it in his wrist, and got it back to his body. Then he got hit, and held on to the ball. It was one of the greatest athletic displays I've ever seen, and the greatest catch.

Honorable Mention

- Wes Hopkins return of a fumble recovery off a lateral from Al Harris against Washington in 1989.
- Tony Franklin's 59-yard field goal against Dallas in 1979.
- Cunningham's 91-yard punt against the Giants in 1989.

- Mike Quick's finger-tip catch in the end zone against Atlanta in 1983.
- Reggie White's touchdown return against Washington when he stole the ball from quarterback Doug Williams in 1987.
- Clyde Simmons' touchdown on a recovery of a blocked Eagles field goal against the Giants, in what became known as Miracle II.
- And Fred Barnett's brilliant touchdown catch against New Orleans in the 1992 wild-card game.

All-Time Team

This is my All-Time Eagles team from 1977 through 1997. It's my dream team, the guys I would want to see together as Eagles, if just for one game.

The funny thing about trying to select this team was that it was tough for two reasons. At some positions, like linebacker and wide receiver, there were so many good players that I hated to leave some guys off the team. For instance, Irving Fryar and Seth Joyner missed the cut.

But at other positions—like guard and center—there were so few choices, it was hard to come up with a true All-Star.

Consider that the Eagles haven't had an All-Pro center since Jim Ringo in 1967, and haven't had an All-Pro guard since Buck Lansford in 1956, and you see what I mean.

With that said, here we go with a team that comprises parts of three different decades of Eagles football.

OFFENSE

Offensive Line

Tackles—This was easy. The Eagles' two standout linemen, and their last two Pro Bowl linemen, were the two tackles who played together in the Super Bowl.

The right tackle was Jerry Sisemore, the former No. 1 draft pick out of Texas, and the left tackle was Stan Walters, who the team acquired in a trade with Cincinnati.

Sisemore was just a great player. He was highly regarded coming out Texas, and was the third player selected in the 1973 draft. Defensive end John Matuzak went first to Houston, and quarterback Bert Jones went second to Baltimore.

The Eagles originally played him at guard, but he eventually moved outside to tackle and was a mainstay there until he retired after the 1984 season. At one point Sisemore played in 127 consecutive games for the Eagles. As a run blocker, Sisemore had no peer. He was just a tremendous drive blocker.

Stan and Jerry were very good friends and great tackles. But that's where the similarities ended. Jerry was the tall, strong Texan, and a man of very few words. He was a classic Texan, who called everyone partner. When Jerry walked by, you thought you were in an old cowboy movie. Stan loved to talk, and would hold court at his locker room on almost a daily basis. He did a radio show when he played, and, of course, became my color analyst for 14 years.

As a player, Stan was a great pass blocker. He went an entire season once during which he allowed just one sack. That's about 14 sacks less than the Eagles allowed last year from the left tackle spot. Stan played the game from a mental aspect as much as he did a physical one. He thought out every play and every game, which is probably why he became such a good analyst.

Guards—This was tough, but Ron Baker and Woody Peoples rated the edge over the rest.

Baker came to the Eagles from Baltimore in 1980, and became a starter almost immediately. He never made it to the Pro Bowl, but I never remember him having a bad game, either. His strength was his consistency. He played eight years for the Eagles, and was part of the last NFC East Championship team in 1988, his final season. He retired in 1989 after a freak foot injury suffered in the shower stall at training camp in West Chester.

He was also part of the 1986 Eagles offensive line that allowed an NFL record 104 sacks. His quote about that line will never be forgotten.

"Sure I'm embarrassed by it," Baker said the following year. "What am I supposed to tell my kids? I was hurt that season?"

Peoples only played three years for the Eagles. He was an All-Pro for San Francisco in 1972 and 1973 before he came to the Eagles in 1978. He helped solidify the line that eventually helped take the Eagles to the Super Bowl. As a matter of fact the rest of the linemen said then that Peoples was the player who brought the line together.

Like Sisemore, he was very quiet, and like Stan Walters, he could pass block in his sleep. I don't know where Woody Peoples is now, or what he is doing, but I'm sure you could put him out on the field and he would be able to pass block.

What's amazing is that Baker and Peoples both weighed between 250 and 260 pounds, that's 40 to 50 pounds less than the current Eagles guards weigh. But during their playing days they were not small, they were average-sized linemen. It just shows you one of the ways the game has changed. And we're not talking about the 1940s, or 1950s, Baker played up until 1988. That's only 10 years ago. Now tight ends and fullbacks are more than 250.

Center—Again it wasn't an easy choice, but Guy Morriss was the best I've seen in the middle of the line.

Morriss was part of an outstanding draft class the Eagles had in 1973. Sisemore was the first pick, and they also got tight end Charle Young, safety Randy Logan and Morris that year.

Another Texan, Morriss played at TCU. By today's standards he was also small, about 255 pounds, or so. He was solid, not outstanding, and he played for the Eagles for 10 seasons. He played the game intelligently, and later became an offensive line coach for both New England and Arizona.

The Eagles really haven't had a great center in the past 20 years. Dave Rimington played one good year, in 1988. Dave Alexander played a long time, and was also solid, but not spectacular.

I almost gave this to Raleigh McKenzie, who played well his two seasons here, and was as great a guy as you would want to be around. But Morriss because he was here so much longer was the choice.

Receivers

Tight End—There was some deliberation here, but not much. Keith Jackson was the best tight end I've seen with the Eagles.

To me Keith was a great tight end. Some people say he didn't block well, but he wasn't asked to block. If he was he would have been able to do that well, too.

Charle Young was also a gifted, gifted football player who would have been a strong choice.

I gave it to Jackson over Young, because I felt Jackson was more consistent week after week, game after game than Young was. Charle Young made the spectacular play more often, but he didn't have as good an Eagles career as Jackson did.

Jackson set an Eagles rookie record with 81 receptions in 1988, smashing Young's mark of 55 set in 1973. Those 81 receptions are also the third most in Eagles history, and were the most until Irving Fryar topped it the past two seasons.

Keith Jackson was a true producer. When Buddy Ryan drafted him in the first round of the 1988 draft out of Oklahoma, he told us this guy would make plays, and that's exactly what he did. And he continued to do it after he left, first for Miami, and then for Green Bay.

Of course Keith had his problems with management, and left the team on bad terms. He held out before the 1992 season, and never returned. He became one of the first unrestricted free agents, and signed what was then a blockbuster deal with Miami.

I think Keith Jackson could have become one of the best tight ends to ever play the game, but football didn't matter that much to him. He liked to play, and he made a lot of money. But he got out when he was still at the peak of his game. He had just won a Super Bowl in Green Bay when he decided to retire. There's no doubt in my mind he could still be playing, and playing well. Still he was my pick for the best tight end I've seen in Eagles green.

If you asked me who the best pure blocking tight end was, it would have to be Keith Krepfle. He's also the answer to a trivia question. Who's the only Eagle to score a touchdown in a Super Bowl?

Wide Receivers—There were many good receivers to choose from. But Harold Carmichael and Mike Quick were the two best the Eagles have had since I've been around.

Ironically both men were expected to rejoin the organization in 1998. Harold Carmichael was hired as the team's director of player relations, and it will be great to see him around the club again on a daily basis.

Mike Quick is expected to join me in the broadcast booth for WYSP as my new color analyst. As this book was being written, Mike's deal was being worked out with the station. I'm looking forward to working with Mike in the '98 season, and couldn't have hoped for a better replacement for Stan.

I still remember Howard Cosell calling Harold,"The tall, angular wide receiver from Southern University." And I'll never forget the first time I was sent out to do a pregame show. The Eagles were at Albright College in Reading for training camp, and it was Harold's rookie year of 1971. He was a seventh-round draft pick, and I went to interview him. It did not go very well.

I was nervous because it was my first time around the Eagles. I asked Harold a question, and he answered, "Yes." This was supposed to be a 10-minute interview, and I had nine minutes and 55 seconds left. I asked him another question, and he answered, "No." I started to panic. I asked my third question, and he just nodded. This was not good radio. I managed to get 10 minutes out of it, and I'm still not sure how.

He was just not ready to deal with the media at that point, but slowly, and surely, he came around, and actually became one of the better talkers on the team before he left.

I saw early in his career that Harold was going to be a great player, and I always told him that. There were some who thought he wasn't going to make it. But I thought he would. He was more than just tall, he had athletic ability, and great hands.

When Harold retired in 1984, he ranked sixth on the NFL's all-time reception list with 590. He's also the Eagles' all-time leader in receptions, yards (8,978) and touchdowns (79). I'll always remember his streak of consecutive games with a catch at 127, and I remember when he broke Danny Abramowicz's record of 107 consecutive games.

Mike Quick was the Eagles' first-round pick in 1982. Most people know the story of how Dick Vermeil wanted another wide receiver, Perry Tuttle, of Clemson instead.

And how Vermeil mentioned to his close friend, Chuck Knox, then the head coach of Buffalo, how much he liked Tuttle. On draft day, Knox and Buffalo traded up ahead of the Eagles and took Tuttle. That left Quick for the Eagles.

What a lot of people do not know is that one of Vermeil's assistants, Dick Coury, who is still his receivers coach in St. Louis, told me before the draft that he really liked Quick better than Tuttle.

So while the rest of the Eagles staff was disappointed when Tuttle was gone, Coury was thrilled. I'll never forget seeing Coury after the pick, and him giving me the thumbs up sign. He had gotten the guy he wanted. And he was right.

Tuttle lasted all of two years in Buffalo. Quick became a five-time All-Pro, and set Eagles records for most yards in a season (1,409), most touchdowns in a season (13), and most 100-yard games in a season (six).

Mike was probably the most fluid athlete I've ever seen on the football field, and you see that same fluidity now on the golf course. His golf swing belongs on the PGA tour.

Training camp was never one of Mike's favorite times of the year. Whenever his contract was up, and sometimes even when it wasn't, he would miss camp in a "contract holdout." In reality, he would tell his agent, Jim Solano, not to even get serious about a contract until the end of preseason. Then he would report, and it would be as if he were there from the start.

One of the all-time disappointments in my years in the broadcast booth was the way Quick's career ended. He was so great for so long, as the Eagles struggled, and as the team rose under Buddy Ryan in the late '80s, Quick's knee injuries began to rob him of that style and grace that made him such a great player.

Irving Fryar has also been a great receiver for the Eagles. He had made some of the greatest catches I've ever seen, and if I could go to a three wide receiver set I would include him on this team.

Backfield

Running Back—There have been two great running backs on the Eagles in my time as play-by-play man: Wilbert Montgomery and Ricky Watters.

Certainly I'm human, and sometimes it's difficult not to have a favorite because you like one guy better than the other. And that's the situation here, and why my choice is Wilbert Montgomery.

I remember Wilbert's rookie year, and how he used to be so worried that every time Dick Vermeil walked into the locker room, he would hide. He thought if Vermeil didn't see him, he couldn't cut him. So he thought he if stayed out of sight lines, he might be all right for a few more days.

But you could see from the start that this sixth-round draft pick out of Abilene Christian in 1977 was gifted. You could see that in his first training camp. The reason he wasn't drafted earlier was because of a knee injury he suffered his senior year of college.

Wilbert was dazzling as an Eagle. His moves were breathtaking. I've never seen a back with his cutback ability. Stan used to say some offensive lines make their running back look better, but with Wilbert he made their line look better. He never needed a great, huge hole. He just needed a sliver of daylight and he was gone.

There was a banquet one year where the Eagles MVPs on offense, defense, and special teams were honored. Wilbert was the team's offensive player, and did not show up for the award. Harold Carmichael had to accept the award for him, that showed you how far the shy Carmichael had come. Harold said, as he accepted the award, "Every Sunday me and my teammates try to keep Wilbert away from people. Wilbert took it one step further tonight."

Wilbert just didn't like big crowds, and he was very humble. He didn't like to talk about himself, and didn't like the glory that his stardom deserved.

Montgomery left the Eagles in 1985 as the team's all-time rusher with 6,538 yards. He also has the record for most yards gained in a season, 1,512, and is second to the great Steve Van Buren in most yards gained in a game, 197, and most rushing touchdowns in a career, 45.

Ricky, who loved the big crowds and the glory, was also a great back. He was bigger than Wilbert, and could power into a hole better than Wilbert could. But Wilbert was more of the home run hitter. He would need just a small opening and he would break into daylight.

That was another factor is selecting Montgomery over Watters in what was a tough decision.

Fullback—This was one of the positions where the Eagles haven't had many, if any, superstars.

I decided to pick Kevin Turner, the team's current fullback, because I think he plays the position as well as I've seen it played.

Turner, who the Eagles acquired from New England as a restricted free agent in 1995, is a solid all-around player with terrific hands. As a matter of fact, he made three outstanding touchdown catches in 1997 alone. I mean three catches where he just went up in a crowd, and came down with the ball surrounded by defenders.

He's also an excellent lead blocker, and can take on the blitzing linebacker as well as anyone the Eagles have had.

Turner has only gotten the chance to carry the ball a handful of times in his three years with the Eagles, but he caught 91 passes over two seasons (96-97).

Keith Byars, the Eagles' first-round pick in 1986, went on to become an excellent fullback in both Miami and New England, but his role with the Eagles was never defined.

He would line up as the halfback one play, the fullback another play, and at tight end on some plays. He would be my pick for versatility as a player, but he was never really the fullback.

Anthony Toney was a good fullback, but unfortunately his career was hampered with injuries throughout, and he never became as good as he could have been.

Quarterback

I chose Ron Jaworski over Randall Cunningham, because of his consistency, because of his leadership, and because he's the only quarterback to ever take the Eagles to the Super Bowl.

Ron came to the Eagles in a trade with the Rams for tight end Charle Young, and he came with the reputation for having the big arm. He was called the Polish Rifle in Los Angeles. So he was not limited in his physical skills, but he was also gritty.

Not many people realize what a great athlete Ron was. When Ron came out of high school he could have played minor league baseball, but opted for football instead.

Ron also worked as hard as any athlete I've ever seen. Ron was the guy who put in the extra work in the filmroom. He was the guy who took the film home and watched them all night. He looked for every edge, and always wanted to get better.

When he had time, Ron could pick apart a defense like no other quarterback in the league. And his numbers were pretty good, too. He left the Eagles in 1987 as the team's all-time leader in career attempts (3,918), completions (2,088), yards passing (26,963) and touchdown passes (175).

Ron always had the drive to succeed, and that same drive has made him very successful after football in his business endeavors.

Again it was a shame to see Ron leave the Eagles the way he did. He felt he never got a fair shake under Buddy Ryan. And Buddy just felt it was time to get younger, and go in a different direction with Randall as his quarterback.

Ron expressed interest in becoming the team's general manager before the 1998 season. I think Ron would make a good front office man for any team. He's a diligent worker, and does a great job for ESPN, and NFL Films, and know the game inside and out.

Randall was the most gifted quarterback the Eagles have ever had, and maybe the most gifted to ever play anywhere. If there was one negative about Randall it was that he lacked total dedication. But he still had some phenomenal seasons, especially 1988 and 1990. Still, Ron did what Randall did not do, he took the Eagles to the Super Bowl. And that was the deciding factor in my decision.

DEFENSE

Defensive Line

Defensive Ends—Two defensive ends jumped to mind immediately, and they were Reggie White, of course, and Carl Hairston.

There were some other good ones as well. Claude Humphrey, who came to the Eagles from the Atlanta Falcons, Dennis Harrison, and Clyde Simmons. All of those guys could play the position and play it well.

Reggie was the obvious choice. He may be the greatest defensive end of all time. The competition was for the number two spot, and I decided on Carl Hairston.

Hairston, another low-round draft choice—a seventh-rounder out of Maryland State in 1976—was all over the field. He was in constant motion, and would chase the quarterback from one side of the field to the other. He never stopped.

Dick Vermeil tried to nickname him Hurricane Hairston to give him a little more notoriety, and some Pro Bowl attention. But it didn't work. The nickname that did stick was Big Daddy. That was what the players called him, and what he is still referred to today as he coaches the Rams' defensive line under Vermeil.

I thought Hairston was a very underrated player who played hard every down, and got the most out of his ability. He led the league in sacks in 1979, and had five straight season of 100 tackles, or more.

One of the things I remember about Hairston was that it seemed as if he got hurt at least once a game. It was never anything serious, but he played with such tremendous drive that he would just wear himself out every game. He would be down on the field, and you would think he was never going to play again, and he would be back one, or two, plays later. It happened every game.

After he retired in 1990, he was with Arizona at that point, Hairston became a scout for the Cardinals and later scouted and coached with Kansas City.

Reggie is the single greatest defensive player I have ever seen. He could just dominate a game, and often did throughout his brilliant career. I've often heard Eagles players, and coaches, say when they played the Giants that they had to know where Lawrence Taylor was at all times, and in order for a play to work Taylor had to be blocked. I'm sure teams that played the Eagles had to do the same for Reggie.

One of the greatest seasons ever by a defensive player, or any player for that matter, had to be Reggie's 1987 season. That was the year of the strike, and he missed four games because of it. Still he recorded an Eagles' record 21 sacks, which was just one off Mark Gastineau's NFL record. And he missed four games!

When Reggie left after the 1992 season, a lot of people thought he was on the downside of his career. Earlier I said I thought the Eagles might have made the right decision to let him go, and get two No. 1 draft picks. But Reggie went on to Green Bay, and helped turn that franchise around. I was happy to see him finally get that Super Bowl ring he so richly deserved when the Packers won Super Bowl XXXI.

I know Reggie has been involved in a lot of controversy recently. All I can say is that the Reggie White I know is one of the nicest people around. The Reggie White I know was nice to everyone, of all races, and creeds, and nationalities. He helped all people. The Reggie White I know would not want to hurt anyone, and was certainly not a racist, or a bigot.

Defensive Tackles—This wasn't so tough. Jerome Brown and Charlie Johnson were two outstanding defensive tackles.

Bud Carson, the Eagles' defensive coordinator, told me that Jerome did as much to free up Reggie as Reggie did to help the rest of that defensive line.

The Eagles' first-round draft pick in 1987, Jerome emerged as one of the best young defensive tackles in the game, and was at his peak when he was killed in the summer of 1992.

Johnson, was a low draft pick. He was a seventh-rounder in 1977, one round after the team selected Wilbert Montgomery. He was a guy who spent two years after high school in the Army, and he served a tour of duty in Vietnam. He then went to the University of Colorado and became a football star.

I can remember the coaching staff used to scream at Charlie Johnson almost every day in his first training camp. They saw that this guy could become a great player, and he did. Johnson went to the Pro Bowl three straight years between 1979-81, and was the game's best nose tackle back when the Eagles played a 3-4 defense.

Johnson, like a lot of the Eagles great players, left the team on bad terms. He demanded to be traded after the 1981 season, and he was traded to Minnesota where he finished his career.

Linebackers

Middle Linebacker—The middle linebacker was an easy choice. It had to be Bill Bergey. He cost the Eagles a ton of draft picks when they acquired him from the Cincinnati Bengals, but he also helped them get to the Super Bowl.

The story about Bergey that has to be told, involved his wife, Micky. Prior to the 1979 season, there was a televised preseason game between Dallas, and the Los Angeles Rams. Cliff Harris, a defensive back for the Cowboys, was injured during the game. He was stretched out on the field, and he didn't move. The medical staff came out, and they carried him off the field. And there was never another mention of the injury before the game ended.

I wondered myself how badly he was hurt. Then, the phone rang, and it was Micky Bergey. I had gotten to know the Bergeys pretty well, because I did a segment with Bill as part of the pre-game show. So Micky called, and asked me if I watched the Dallas game? She then made a surprising and unusual request. She said, "I saw what happened to Cliff Harris. If that was Bill I would be going absolutely crazy. Bill's played football his entire life, high school, college, the NFL, and he's never been hurt. He's had some bumps and bruises, but nothing that I ever had to worry about. But you know, he's running out of luck. I just have a bad feeling. I want you to do me a favor. If he gets hurt in a game—and it's on the road—at the first chance you get, please call me and let me know how bad it is." I said, "Sure, if that ever happens I'll call."

I never thought much more about it until a few weeks into the regular season. It was the third week of the season, and we were in New Orleans. Bergey went down early in the game, and ripped up his knee. He came off the field, and it didn't look that bad at first. But he tried to run on the sideline, and just went down again, as if he were shot. Word came up to the booth that he would be operated on the next day in Philadelphia. The first time we broke for a commercial, I reached for the phone and called Micky.

She answered the phone, and said, "Merrill, how bad is it?" Later that week, after the operation, I saw Micky and she thanked me again for the call. She also told me an interesting story. She said, "Do you know what Teresa LeMaster said to me?" She was the wife of Frank LeMaster, the Eagles' other linebacker. "She came to the hospital to see Bill, and she said 'Bill will be OK, and now Frank will get the credit he deserves.'"

Of course Bill came back the following season and helped the Eagles to the Super Bowl. Although all four of his Pro Bowl selections came before the injury.

Outside Linebackers—This was the hardest position to pick. I went with John Bunting, from the Super Bowl team, and William Thomas, from the current Eagles.

Bunting, a 10th-round pick out of North Carolina in 1972, was far from the most gifted linebacker I've ever been around. But he made a tremendous impact by being so smart. I don't think John Bunting ever made a mental mistake. He had talent, but he wasn't the great physical specimen that some linebackers were. John was the Eagles' defensive captain, and he had a great sense of anticipation. He made great plays by being in the right place at the right time, all the time.

I believe John Bunting, if he ever gets the chance to be an NFL head coach, will be the same type of coach Bill Cowher is in Pittsburgh. John has been a successful head coach on the Division III college level, and has been a highly-regarded assistant coach for both Kansas City and St. Louis. I knew Cowher when he played for the Eagles, and I see a lot of the same characteristics that I saw in Bunting. That same fiery nature and that same leadership quality. I think Bunting will be an absolutely outstanding head coach in the NFL.

The other spot came down between Seth Joyner and Thomas. I chose Thomas because of all he can do. He can blitz when asked. He's an excellent cover man, and I still think he has a lot of outstanding years ahead of him.

William Thomas, a fourth-round pick in 1991 out of Texas A&M by Rich Kotite, was another favorite of Bud Carson's. He's been to the Pro Bowl twice already in his career, and I'm sure he's going to get there again.

Seth was a ferocious linebacker who could also do it all, and I feel bad leaving him off this team. But you can only pick three linebackers, and Thomas rated the slight edge here.

Another good outside linebacker, and an All-Pro, was Jerry Robinson, the Eagles first-round pick in 1979. But again in a crowded field, he just missed.

Secondary

Free Safety—This was the easiest pick of all to make, and it was Wes Hopkins.

Wes was a tremendous player, and just an incredible hitter. He was a second-round draft pick out of SMU in 1983, and played like a first-round pick should.

It's funny Wes didn't impress a lot of people in his first training camp. He was bothered by a nagging groin injury, and just didn't do much at all. But when it came time to play, boy could he play.

Wes was very businesslike, on and off the field. He studied the game, and was ready to play every Sunday. He made his presence felt on the field, and dared receivers to come across the middle against him. Not many made that decision twice.

In 1986 Wes suffered a terrible knee injury that would have ended the career of many players. It took him almost two years to come back, but when he did he was still a very good player.

Strong Safety—Andre Waters was one of my favorite players, but the Eagles' best strong safety was the Wolfman, Randy Logan.

This guy played strong safety like a linebacker, and went to the Pro Bowl twice in his brilliant career. Logan was a third-round pick out of Michigan in 1973, and the Eagles got their money's worth from him.

Andre worked harder than any player, and made himself into a good football player. But Randy was just a natural athlete with so much talent. He was a big-time hitter who just separated the ball from the receiver so many times.

Randy was very quiet off the field. He was a warm, caring person and was very soft spoken. You would see him on the field and picture a much different person than the one you met in the locker room.

One time Randy bailed me out of a bad situation. We used to interview the players after practice, and it was around 5 o'clock on

Thursday night, and I asked Randy if he would tape an interview for my Friday part of the pregame show. It was a half hour interview. We finished it, I thanked him, and as I looked down I saw the tape spewing out of my recorder in tiny knots. We both knew the interview was ruined.

I didn't know what to do. Randy said, "I'll do it again, no problem." The problem was I didn't have another tape recorder. And it would take at least a half hour to get back to the station, and another half hour to come back here. Randy, instead, went with me to WIP and we taped it there. And he didn't receive anything for it. It wasn't like we paid him for the interview, or gave him any kind of gift certificate. He just did it.

After he retired, Randy started his own ministry, and is very involved with youth programs in the Philadelphia area. He is a very special person.

Cornerbacks—The two best corners I've seen with the Eagles were "The Silent Storm", Roynell Young, and Eric Allen, who I've talked about on numerous occasions already.

Roynell, the Eagles' first-round pick in 1980, was another quiet man, hence his nickname. He was tall for a corner, and very powerful. He struggled a little bit early in his career, had an especially poor game against the Giants his rookie year, but was able to put it behind him, and became just a great cornerback.

What impressed me so much about Roynell Young was his ability to start and stop on a dime. And his backpedal was as good as I've ever seen from a defensive back. He was probably the fastest cornerback the Eagles have ever had.

Eric was the Eagles' second-round pick in 1988. Buddy Ryan traded up with Tampa Bay to get a high second-round pick, and Allen made it pay off.

I also remember him having a rough time as a rookie. This was against Washington, and he was very upset about it after the game. I went down to his locker after the game, and we had a little talk. I told him I was close with Herb Adderly, and how Herb always told me that a cornerback has to have a short memory and a gunfighter's mentality. You have to go out there and feel you can't lose.

Later that season—after he established himself as a great, young player—he was quoted in an article in *Eagles Digest,* and said that his talk with me after the Redskins game really helped him.

Very rarely have I ever influenced a player to that extent, but since he felt that way I found it very rewarding.

SPECIALISTS

Kicker—I chose Paul McFadden over Tony Franklin in a battle of two barefooted placekickers.

Franklin was the more talented kicker, but McFadden was more consistent for a longer time.

McFadden was the classic boy next door. He looked like the kid who delivered the newspaper. He was a 12th-round draft pick out of Youngstown State in 1994, and the Eagles actually took another kicker, Manny Matsakis, in the eighth round of that same draft.

In 1984, McFadden set an Eagles record for most points in a season with 116, and most field goals in a season with 91. And while he was a slender man, McFadden got a lot of leg into his kicks, and was a good kickoff man as well.

Paul also did a great impression of me, and he and punter John Teltschik would imitate me and Stan doing a broadcast at the preseason show the team used to have every year.

Punter—I had to go with John Teltschik, mainly because he was so much more than just a punter. Buddy Ryan used to say Teltschik enjoyed making a tackle after a punt more than he did punting the ball.

Sadly, he was injured on a fake punt, which he would do more than any other punter I've ever seen, and was forced to retire much sooner than he should have.

The Eagles have had their share of good punters through the years, like Mike Horan, Jeff Feagles, and Max Runager, but Teltschik added that extra dimension.

Teltschik, who Buddy Ryan claimed on waivers from the Bears in 1986, set an Eagles record for most punts in a season with 108 in 1986, and also set a team record for most punts in a game with 15 in a game against the Giants in 1987.

Kick Returner—There were a few choices here. Wilbert Montgomery actually led the NFC in returns as a rookie. Derrick Witherspoon had three touchdown returns in the span of 20 games.

But I went for the overall player, and that would be Herschel Walker, who actually hurt the Eagles more with his kickoff returns against them.

Herschel had great straight-ahead speed, and kept himself in the best physical condition of any player I've ever been around.

When the Eagles signed him as a free agent in 1992 he was supposed to be the answer for the backfield problems. As it turned out it he helped them more in other areas.

Punt Returner—Earlier I mentioned that in the span of 11 years, the Eagles have had just one punt returned for a touchdown, and that was by Vai Sikahema in 1992, and he's my choice for punt returner.

Sikahema came to the Eagles after an All-Pro career with the Cardinals, and after a couple of years in Green Bay, but he showed he wasn't finished.

He put up the second best career punt return average in Eagles history at 10.7 yards per return, had the most return yards in one season of any Eagle, and his 87-yard touchdown return is the longest in Eagles history.

Vai was one of the most exciting players I've ever seen. While the Eagles have had so many returners who made just catching the ball an adventure, Sikahema was a guy who you knew could take it the distance.

Special Team Player—There was nobody I've ever seen who enjoyed special teams more than Ken Rose.

He retired after the 1994 season, and went on to coach the Jets' special teams under Rich Kotite in 1995. But he was a player at heart.

Rose, who was claimed by Ryan in 1990 after he was released by Cleveland, was built like a statue. He was most remembered for a long, black pony tail that came out of his helmet, but he was also a tremendous special teams player and leader.

Since Kotite and his staff were fired, he hasn't gotten back into coaching, but he would make a great special teams coach for someone.

Around the League

Let me begin this chapter, which is a tour around the league, and its stadiums, by saying I hate domes.

I don't care if it's the most beautiful dome in the world, with the most luxurious surroundings. I hate domes. I find nothing more stifling than walking up to the stadium on a beautiful fall day, and having to go inside to watch the game. You could say what about late in December, and there's a driving snowstorm?

To me there has always been something dramatic about a game played under adverse circumstances, under stormy skies or in other crazy weather. One of the most intriguing aspects of football is that you not only face your opponents, but you deal with the conditions as well. Whether it's the frozen tundra of Lambeau Field, or the heat in the Arizona desert, or the fog in Chicago, the elements are as much a factor as the nickel defense.

In broadcasting a football game, there's that element of drama that comes with the weather, and the surroundings. I think it adds to the broadcast to say, "It's a chilly 31 degrees, and the sky is gray, as the Eagles prepare..."

With a dome there is no weather, there is no atmosphere, it's football in your living room.

That's why my Number One stadium in the NFL, the one that embodies this game more than any other is Lambeau Field in Green Bay.

You approach that stadium on a crisp Sunday morning, and you see the people outside at their tailgate parties, bratwurst on the grill, and beer in the cooler, and they're ready for football. You walk inside, and there's real grass. And the seats are close to the field, close enough that the Packers players jump into the stands after they score a touchdown.

And then there's the storied tradition. I look down on the field, and I see the ghosts. I see Ray Nitschke, and the ghost of Vince Lombardi, and at the one end zone, Bart Starr sneaking across the goal line behind Jerry Kramer to beat Dallas in the Ice Bowl. To me, Lambeau Field is to football what Wrigley Field is to baseball. And then right across the street is the Packer Hall of Fame, which I've often visited. It's just a terrific feeling to be there.

What's also nice to know is that it's still called Lambeau Field after all these years. It hasn't changed its name to some corporate sponsorship, and it still honors the man who founded, and first coached the Packers, E.L. "Curley" Lambeau.

My second favorite stadium is in Miami, and ironically it just changed its name from Joe Robbie Stadium, to Pro Player Park in a corporate decision. But Miami is to new, what Green Bay is to old. Green Bay is tradition. Miami is technology. They went out and built the perfect football stadium. There are great sightlines, and beautiful seating areas, and the prescription turf which is grass with an artificial layer to aid in drainage.

There are ideal working conditions for the broadcasters, and the media. The Dolphins public relations staff is one of the best in the league led by Harvey Greene. What the stadium lacks in history, it makes up for in beauty, and wonderful design. In my mind, it's the best of the present day stadiums.

Kansas City's Arrowhead Stadium, and Giants Stadium, up in East Rutherford, New Jersey, are very similar. They were both designed by the late Charles Deaton, a Colorado-based architect.

Both are wonderful stadiums in which to watch a game, and both are football-only stadiums.

Kansas City rated a slight edge, because the Chiefs have gone back to natural grass, and the Giants and Jets play on astroturf.

Arrowhead is just a great place, the view is wonderful, and then right across the way is the baseball stadium where the Royals play. The sad part is I've only been there twice. The Eagles played there in 1972, the first year of the stadium, and again in 1992, and that's been it.

Giants Stadium, which I also think is a terrific stadium, is a regular stop. Not only do the Eagles play the Giants once a year there, but the Eagles play the Jets every other preseason there. So I have gotten my share of Giants Stadium over the years.

And every time I walk in there, no matter if it's a hot August night for a preseason game with the Jets, or a cold windy day in December for a big game with the Giants, I still see the play. I still see Joe Pisarcik's fumble, and Herman Edwards going from right to left for the touchdown.

It's funny but I think of things in terms of right to left, and no matter what stadium I'm in, I can tell you which way a certain touchdown was scored.

Arizona rounds out the top five stadiums. I know a lot of people don't like Sun Devil Stadium, including people in Arizona who want a new stadium, but I consider it one of the best.

I like the fact that it's a football stadium. It's a college stadium, it's right on the campus of Arizona State, but I think I like it even more because of that.

We are situated very high, as high as anywhere in the league. But from that view you can really see plays develop, and to me that's a bonus. And the beauty of looking over the wall and seeing the two beautiful mountain ranges, the Superstitious, and the Four Peaks, that encompass the desert.

We've been there for some of the hottest days of the season, but it never bothered me, because I love the heat.

My only complaint comes from a Cardinal rule. I like to light up a cigar in the booth during the game, and the Cardinals do not allow smoking. We've tried to get around it for years, but Nicole Bidwell, the daughter of Cardinals owner Bill Bidwell, always seems to catch me.

Another thing I like about going to Arizona is that because the Cardinals have not drawn well, there seems to be almost as much green in the stands as there is red. It seems as if every year more and more Eagles fans make this trip.

Last year I made my first, and only, trip to Jacksonville. But the old Jacksonville Memorial Stadium renamed ALLTEL Stadium checks in at Number Six.

On the same spot that, at one time, sat the legendary Gator Bowl, is now a beautiful new stadium with top of the line accommodations.

Ironically, this stadium was built and completed in just over 19 months, and the Jaguars became the first expansion team in sports history to play in its first home game in a brand-new stadium.

Again, it's natural grass, and the sight lines are perfect. Unfortunately the only game I've seen there was in 1997 when the Jaguars simply killed the Eagles. So I don't have any fond memories, but this is a good football stadium in which to watch a game.

I was a little disappointed in the new Jack Kent Cooke Stadium in Landover, Maryland, where the Redskins now play. I still rank it as Number Seven, but maybe after all the buildup I just expected more.

This is an above average stadium. It's certainly better than the place it replaced, the old, decrepit RFK Stadium. But it's not great.

What RFK had was tradition, and great Eagles/Redskins memories. I could always sit back there and remember John Sciarra's dropping the snap on the field goal, or Randall Cunningham's great five-touchdown game. And all those great Redskins teams under Joe Gibbs.

But it was an old stadium, and the broadcast booth was way up top, and had no elevator. It was a good way to work off your breakfast, but I often wondered if Big Stan was going to make it up there.

Ironically in the new stadium we're now too low. We're just above what would be the 200 level at Veterans Stadium, and it's difficult to see a play develop, and punts can sometimes be confusing. The high ones are taken out of our view by a ledge.

The new JKC is nice. What impresses me the most about it was that the Redskins built it themselves. There was no public funding involved. And I also liked that they named it after the late Jack Kent Cooke.

Tampa Bay will have a new stadium in 1998, just south of Houlihan's Stadium, also known as the Big Sombrero.

But for now I'll keep the Sombrero in my top 10, at Number Eight.

It's a big round stadium, with a good view, and natural grass. There's nothing exceptional about it, but it's better than a lot of the others.

Soldier Field, in Chicago, checks in at Number Nine. I know the Bears are always threatening to leave, and want a new stadium, but I think this is a pretty good place to play.

The area is so big, that half of it is wasted. If they would have backed up that one wall, they could have added another 30,000 seats.

But Soldier Field has the character and tradition that I like. They have those huge stone pillars at the front. I guess I just like saying Soldier Field. It says Chicago Bears, and the Monsters of the Midway and all of that.

I still identify Soldier Field with Mike Ditka, even though he's been gone for some time now. It just doesn't seem right to me, Ditka being in a dome.

Rounding out my top 10 is Denver's Mike High Stadium. The Broncos are another team that wants a new stadium.

I love Mile High Stadium. Actually what I love is all the surroundings more than the stadium itself. You have the Rockies in the distance, and I love when they ride the white horse out onto the field before the game.

The times I've been there the Broncos have also put on a great halftime show. They have an Air Force Academy cadet come out with a trained Falcon, and they let the Falcon circle the stadium. It's one of my favorite halftime shows, it's passed the frisbee dogs.

Rich Stadium in Buffalo starts the next 10. It's always cold in Buffalo, and that's a reason to lose points. The stadium itself is also cold.

What's unique about Rich Stadium is that the field is below street level, so you walk in and you have to walk down to the field.

But the fans in Buffalo are good fans, and they're passionate fans.

New England's Foxboro Stadium, which seems to change names every season, is also a good place to watch a game. But it seems to me that it wasn't put together very well, and it has kind of a cheapness to it. It's also impossible to get to, and get out of. There's only one access road.

But it does have natural grass, which puts it above some of the rest.

I rank Dallas 13th, and isn't that ironic?

I used to like Texas Stadium a lot better. I used to enjoy the pageantry of the Cowboys Cheerleaders. I enjoyed the feeling of the fans. I didn't even mind the hole in the roof, because that meant it wasn't a dome.

Also at Texas Stadium we had the best broadcast booth in the league. It was so big that a crew of six could sit in there and have enough room for another two crews.

A few years ago when we went there one of our new engineers went to the stadium early to check things out. I saw him Saturday night in the hotel, and asked him, "What did you think of that booth?" And he said, "It's OK." I said, "What do you mean, OK?" He said, "It's OK. There's nothing wrong with it." I said, "This is the best booth in the league." He said, "It looks like any other booth to me." I was baffled.

The next day we walked in, and that big booth was cut in half. I couldn't believe it. I shouldn't have complained. The next year the booth was gone, and we were way upstairs. And now the broadcast conditions are as difficult as any in the league.

San Francisco and San Diego are the same kind of stadium in my mind.

Both are baseball stadiums that are also used for football.

San Diego's Qualcom Stadium, which used to be known as

Jack Murphy, might be a little better than San Francisco's 3Com Park, which used to be called Candlestick Park.

But what both stadiums lack in football ambiance, they make up for in their surroundings. San Diego and San Francisco are two great cities.

In San Diego you can be almost sure that the weather is going to be perfect.

That's not the case in San Francisco, but what I like most about that city is just the drive to the game, and you see the Golden Gate Bridge.

Pittsburgh and Cincinnati are also the same, and they are both just like Veterans Stadium.

They're cookie cutter stadiums.

What is nice about Pittsburgh is coming out for a night game, as we do in preseason a lot, and seeing the river all lit up and with all kinds of activities going on around it.

But as far as the stadium goes, it is nothing special. Cincinnati is basically the same, and if you've been to the Vet you've been to all three.

Oakland's Alameda County Coliseum's only redeeming quality is that it is an outdoor stadium, and I refuse to put a dome ahead of an outdoor stadium.

But that's it.

This is also a baseball stadium, and it has natural grass, which is also to its credit.

But the seats are spread out, and it is the only stadium that until baseball is over we actually sit in an area of the stands, down around the 10 yardline.

The only place I've ever worked that was worse than this was Tokyo, when the Eagles visited for a preseason game. That was the worst, because we sat two rows up in the end zone, and you couldn't see anything.

But Oakland is only a little better.

I hate to complain, because the fans never want to hear you complain about your "free seats."

I hate all the domes, but I hate Detroit's Silverdome in Pontiac the least. Maybe it's because it doesn't have the hard roof. And it seems to have more of a lively feel to it than most domes. Also the broadcast location and working conditions are so ideal it makes it somewhat bearable.

Indianapolis' RCA Dome and Minnesota's Metrodome are just your basic domes, which means I don't like them.

I dislike Atlanta's Georgia Dome because it's too pretty. It would be good for Sea World. And it's probably nice for a concert, but not for football.

The visiting locker room is fuchsia, and supposedly that was done on purpose to make the visiting team feel less aggressive. I don't know if it works on the players, but it has an effect on me.

And the Georgia Dome's surface doesn't appear to have any texture. This looks like a ping pong table.

New Orleans' Superdome is now old, and to me ranks even below the rest. I have too many bad memories of that place. There was the Caesar salad incident before the playoff game in 1992, and of course the Super Bowl loss.

But the worst of the worst is Seattle's Kingdome.

There is nothing more gray than coming from the outside in Seattle where it's always gray and raining, to the inside of the Kingdome, which is even more dark and dank. It is just one depressing place. And now they have Ricky Watters, and let's just say Ricky's disposition isn't going to brighten up the place.

I've yet to go to Carolina's Erickson Stadium, which I've heard nothing but good things about. And hopefully the Eagles will play there soon.

By the time this book is printed I will have been to the new Baltimore Stadium in the Baltimore Inner Harbor area, but as of this writing the stadium has not yet opened.

And I haven't been to the Oilers' news stadium in Tennessee yet, but then again, neither have the Oilers.

The Next Merrill

Glamour. People think this is a glamorous job. As I grew up I thought there could be nothing as glamorous as being the voice of the Philadelphia Eagles. You know what? I was right.

This is a glamorous job. And if anything, it's even more exciting, and more glamorous, and more exhilarating than I even imagined it would be when I dreamt about having this job.

There are low moments during the season, but even those are interesting, just to see how different people, and different players react to certain situations. But this is truly the dream job I thought it would be.

However, there is a lot more to it than going to games every week. I'm on pins and needles throughout the entire season. I have very little, if any, free time. I get up early. I go down to the stadium. I spend the whole day with the team. I have various shows and interviews that I have to get done. Then there are speeches and appearances that have to be met, and it's difficult to meet them all. I feel a commitment to a lot of the charities, and I feel a responsibility to help people as much as I can, but there are only so many hours in a day, and so many days in a week. Every one cannot be met, and when you decline you feel bad, and I know I've disappointed someone. But I have a family, too. I would like to be a good parent. Cindy tells me during the season she feels like a single mother.

The other side is that when you have some notoriety, some degree of fame, funny things can occur. One such thing happened over the summer. I was at training camp all day, and Cindy and the kids went to the seashore for a few days. There was a tremendous thunder and lightning storm that night, and at about 2 o'clock in the morning I started to hear a siren. I thought it sounded like a burglar alarm. I remembered my next-door neighbors were away, and I thought, "What should I do? My neighbors' alarm is going off, and they're not home." Then it got louder, and louder, and I realized it was coming from my house. Then the phone rang. It was the alarm company. I asked them how to turn off the alarm, and the women on the other end asked for my identification number. I didn't know the number. Cindy knows all of that. I tried to explain that it was me, this was my house. And she said, "Sorry, we can't do anything without your identification number." I said, "Listen, I'm Merrill Reese. I live here." She said, "We can't just go by that." I said, "Listen, first-and-10 for the Eagles, the backs are in the I..." She laughed and said, "O.K. you convinced me."

Sometimes it can work against you as well. Once after a long day I was on my way home, and I went through a light that I thought was yellow. A local police officer pulled me over and asked for my driver's license and all the other stuff. When he saw my name he said, "Oh, you're Merrill Reese, the Eagles radio guy." I smiled and nodded, and thought to myself, "Great, I've got a fan, I'll get out of the ticket." Instead, the officer replied, "I hate the Eagles. I hate that Buddy Ryan. I'm a Dallas fan." And, of course, he gave me the ticket.

There are all kinds of stories like this. But, except for the few occasions like the Dallas fan/police officer, it's good to be known. I'm delighted when someone asks for my autograph, or sends me a letter and tells me how they listen every week. And I answer every piece of mail I get.

Then there is the other aspect of the job. I don't consider myself a hypochondriac, except during the football season. In the spring, or summer, I'll play golf in the pouring rain. I don't care. During the season, I'll do whatever it takes to avoid a cold. I worry every day about my voice, and I don't want anything to happen to it. Fortunately two of my long-time friends, Mark Sussman and Dave Friedman, are physicians who also live in my neighborhood. The minute I get any sign of a cold I call them and they come over with antibiotics, or something.

Once before a Monday night game with the Minnesota Vikings I came home with the chills, and a fever, and my temperature was 103 as of Saturday night. Fortunately the game wasn't Sunday. But these guys were able to give me the right medication and I was all right for the game.

Also I'm very fortunate that my tennis partner for the last 20 years, Avi Hampel, is a doctor who is an ears, nose, and throat specialist. So the moment I even get a tickle in my throat during the season, Avi gets a phone call. I have another friend—you might think I have my own medical staff—Dr. Jeff Wachtel, who is a podiatrist.

Even with all of that, and people are going to think I'm crazy, there are times when I get up in the middle of the night before a Sunday game, and test my voice just to make sure it's there. You know how Superman was always afraid of kryptonite? I'm terrified of a cold, or a sore throat. Germs are my kryptonite during the season.

People often ask about the boundaries of a play-by-play man who covers one team. First let me say that I am employee of WYSP, not the Philadelphia Eagles. I travel with the team, and that's where the Eagles' responsibility ends. I am paid by the radio station, not the team. The Eagles have always had what is known as "right of approval" over the announcers. That's something that just about every team in the league has with its broadcast rights holder. When the games were switched from WIP to WYSP, I know Harry Gamble highly recommended to WYSP that they keep me as the play-by-play man. I've been fortunate that I have always had a good relationship with the Eagles. And all three of the owners I've worked with, Leonard Tose, Norman Braman, and now Jeffrey Lurie have always been easy to deal with, and get along with. I can say with total honestly that in 21 Eagles seasons I have never ever been told by the team what to say, or what not to say. It has never happened.

However, I take issue when someone calls me a homer. Maybe it's semantics. Maybe they mean that in a complimentary way. But I don't like the word. To me, a homer is someone who blindly looks at the team and is out to help them sell tickets. And everything the team does is right, every player they have is the best at his position. That's not my style. I try to be completely honest in my evaluation of the team. Yes, maybe I fall into that category of being overly optimistic. I've been told I wear green-tinted glasses. But at the same time if the team performs badly, I say it. If I disagree with the coach's call, I say it. If I disagree with a draft pick, I say it. In 1997, I felt the Eagles should have drafted wide receiver Rae Carruth in the first round, and people know that's how I felt. And I've never been told not to say anything.

Now, it is not my job as a radio play-by-play man to do commentary on the front office, or to get into the politics of the organization. There is a line that a team broadcaster has that a writer does not. My job is to be a critic, or commentator, on the events that happen on the field. What I have to realize is that broadcasting the games on the Eagles radio network my audience is about 99 percent Eagles fans. As a home team announcer I allow my voice to reflect the fates and fortunes of the Eagles. Naturally I can be emotional when it is appropriate. On the other hand, while I may not sound overly excited about a Troy Aikman touchdown pass for Dallas, I will describe it, and affix credit to the people who deserve it. And if the Eagles look unprepared or flat, I have no problem with saying that. I try to be totally honest about what is happening in the game. But I will do it from an Eagles standpoint. Again, since I am broadcasting mostly to Eagles fans, when I say the score, I will say the Eagles lead the Giants, 17-14, or I will say the Eagles trail the Giants, 17-14.

One thing people say to me a lot is, "you make a game more exciting." I really hope I don't. What I strive to do is convey the excitement, capture the excitement and send it out over the airwaves. If I can do that, I was successful that game. I will never try to make a dull game sound exciting. My job is to relay what is happening. I have a responsibility to the station to maintain interest in the game. The fourth-quarter sponsors pay as much as the first-quarter sponsors. So in a one-sided game late in the fourth quarter, I can't just go through the motions. I try to stay just as sharp as I was at the start of the game. And I try to find things to talk about with the color analyst that will keep the fans' interest and keep them tuned into the game. But I don't want to create false excitement. A bad game is a bad game. If you fake excitement, you cheapen the truly great moments. If I were to get hysterical after every touchdown, the great touchdowns would get lost.

Radio is also much different than television, and even though people tell me they turn down the sound on the television and listen to us, not everyone has access to the video. I have to describe everything. I have to paint a picture. The job of the play-by-play man is to paint an accurate picture of the events on the field and then flavor it. People will talk about this call, or that call, or how they loved a certain touchdown, that's all well and good. But the most important part is giving the listeners the information, keeping them in the game.

I have a formula that I call S-T-D-D—score, time, down, distance. At all times the listeners have to be apprised of the score of the game, how much time is left, and the down and distance of the play. There is nothing more frustrating for a listener than to turn on a sports broadcast and not know the score, or not know what quarter it is, and how much time is left. Red Barber, the Hall of Fame baseball broadcaster, suggested that you should bring an egg timer, and turn it over and before the sand runs out you should have given the score. I have my own egg timer, Joe McPeak. I tell Joe that if he doesn't hear me say the score, to flash me the card with score/time on it.

Consistency is also important. Like Charlie Swift told me years ago, you talk that long and say so many things, you are going to make a mistake. It happens. None of us are free of mistakes. But the broadcasters who are consistent are the ones who make it. The ones who always keep the people informed, and in the game, those are the good broadcasters. The great touchdown calls, the thrilling and exciting calls, that's all wonderful, but the basics are what you must have first. If you get away from the basics, you'll be lost.

I probably get hundreds of letters a year from young people who want to get into this business. What should I study? What kind of classes should I take? How do you get there? They all ask. They want to be sportscasters. It's a longshot. It really is. It's the needle in the haystack. I found that needle. It's just like the millions of kids who want to play in the NFL. It's a great dream, and a great goal, but you can't depend on it. Some are going to make it, but so many others are going to fail. You need something else to fall back on in case you're one of the many who don't make it.

I'm not saying that you should not pursue your dream, but just keep in mind that it's a longshot. That's why I tell young kids to get as much education as you possibly can. And I tell them not to major in communications. I majored in communications, but I was very lucky. Had I not been so fortunate, and been in the right place at the right time I would have been prepared to do nothing else. I know a lot of colleges who prepare communication majors are not going to like seeing this, but I say major in something that translates into a more conventional job, and take the communication courses as electives. Work as much as you can in the field. Get on the student station, get internships in communications. And when you get out of school be prepared to work at a small radio station, or a small television station for a couple of years. Do whatever you can to get ahead, and work hard at it. But because you have a background in something else, if it does not work, you can fall back on your major.

There is an exception. I would tell someone who is in love with the entire communications field to major in communications. If you would be happy being a newscaster, a reporter, a writer, a producer, any of the other jobs that are involved with broadcasting. But if your desire is strictly to be a sportscaster, or strictly to be a play-by-play man then you're making a mistake majoring in communications. If I didn't get my break, and didn't become a play-by-play man I don't know what I would have done. I had nothing else to fall back on.

What's also important is to get as much airwork as you can. If this is what you really want to do, I feel it's better to take a job at a smaller station where you can be on a regular air shift, than to take a job at a larger station and hope to rise up the ranks. It's so important to get the air time. Work at it as hard as you can; learn about the games and learn about the people. If you're broadcasting a high school game, don't just show up that day and go on the air without any information. Read up on the teams, or call the coaches before the game and get some information so when you go on the air you are prepared for whatever might happen. Don't look at it as if you're only doing a high school game, treat it as if it were the Eagles and the Cowboys.

I would read different sentences to improve my diction and go over tough word combinations, or tough letters that gave me trouble.

If you have read this far, you know what I went through in my early years. You have to sacrifice. You have to be willing to work for less money than you feel you deserve at first. This is a job that has to be your dream. It's not the kind of career you decide to pursue on a whim. For the most part, every broadcaster I know has had a lifelong love of sports. And most of us have dreamed about doing this, and have sacrificed, and have given our total focus and total attention to doing just this.

When I talk about dedication to my job at home with Nolan and Ida, Nolan usually roles his eyes and Ida says, "Here comes the Bob Saget routine." She thinks she is part of the television show, "Full House" where the father, played by Saget, lectures once an episode. But I mean it from the bottom of my heart, that whatever it is, whatever your pursuit you have to devote every ounce of your energy to it. I feel I made myself a good tennis player, not a great one, but a good one where I can compete. Golf became a new passion, and while I'm not where I'd like to be yet, I'm determined to improve every season. I'm on the course as often as I can be, and if not, I'm on the driving range. I've always been passionate in everything I've gone after. And I never had more passion than I do for football play-by-play. I went after this, and I got kicked in the teeth, and had a million doors slammed in my face, and I think back at all the people who told me "forget about it," all the people who told me "you're not going to make it." But I just picked myself up, and went after it even harder. And I feel as if I have made myself into a good play-by-play man.

If you ever read that Merrill Reese has decided to retire from his job as play-by-play man for the Eagles, it is a boldfaced lie. They will have to take me kicking, and screaming, and clutching the microphone. Because I will never willingly retire. I love this too much. I love golf. And I still love tennis. But I love this even more, and it's my job. I hope I can do this for a long, long time to come. I want to do this forever.

I want to be the guy at the game, giving you the score, the time, the down and distance, conveying the mood of the crowd, describing the color of the sky, and when that special moment comes when the Eagles kicker connects on a field goal as the final seconds vanish, allowing my voice to rise with a joyful, "It's gooooood!"

Eagles Broadcast Teams
Through the Years

WCAU

1939 — Taylor Grant, Bob Hall, Harry McTigue

1940 — Byrum Saam, Hall

1941 — Saam, Hall

1942 — Saam, Chuck Thompson

1943 — Saam, Thompson

1944 — Saam, Thomspon

1945 — Saam, Claude Haring

WIBG

1946 — Saam, Haring

1947 — Saam, Haring

1948 — Saam, Haring

1949 — Saam, Haring

WPEN

1950 — Franny Murray, Del Parks, Jules Rind

WCAU

1951 — Bill Sears

1952 — Saam, Haring

1953 — Saam, Haring

1954 — Saam, Haring

1955 — Saam, Haring, Bill Bransome

1956 — Bill Campbell, Bransome

1957 — Campbell, Bransome

1958 — Campbell, Bransome

1959 — Campbell, Bransome

1960 — Campbell, Ed Harvey, Russ Hall

1961 — Campbell, Hall, Harvey

1962 — Campbell, Bobby Thomason, Tom Brookshier

1963 — Campbell, Brookshier

1964 — Campbell, Saam, Brookshier
1965 — Andy Musser, Charlie Gauer, Stan Hochman
1966 — Musser, Gauer, Harvey
1967 — Musser, Gauer, Harvey
1968 — Musser, Gauer

WIP
1969 — Charlie Swift, Clarnece Peaks, Thatcher Longstretch
1970 — Swift, Pollard, Peaks
1971 — Swift, Pollard
1972 — Swift, Pollard
1973 — Swift, Pollard
1974 — Swift, Pollard
1975 — Swift, Pollard
1976 — Swift, Pollard
1977 — Swift, Merrill Reese, Herb Adderly
1978 — Reese, Jim Barniak
1979 — Reese, Barniak
1980 — Reese, Barniak
1981 — Reese, Barniak
1982 — Reese, Barniak, Bill Bergey
1983 — Reese, Bergey
1984 — Reese, Stan Walters
1985 — Reese, Walters
1986 — Reese, Walters
1987 — Reese, Walters
1988 — Reese, Walters
1989 — Reese, Walters
1990 — Reese, Walters
1991 — Reese, Walters

WYSP
1992 — Reese, Walters
1993 — Reese, Walters
1994 — Reese, Walters
1995 — Resse, Walters
1996 — Reese, Walters
1997 — Reese, Walters

Other Titles Published By Sports Publishing Inc.

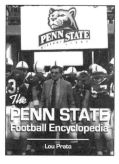

The Penn State Football Encyclopedia
by Louis Prato

In 1993, the Penn State football team played its inaugural season as the eleventh member of the Big Ten Conference, ending more than 100 years as a football independent. In *The Penn State Football Encyclopedia*, author Louis Prato chronicles 110 years of Nittany Lions football. The encyclopedia includes season-by-season reviews and player profiles of all football lettermen. Read about the team's several undefeated seasons and the exhilaration of their first National Championship in 1983, as well as the accomplishments of players like Rosey Grier, Lenny Moore, Jack Ham, John Cappelletti, Ki-Jana Carter and Kerry Collins. And no one symbolizes Penn State football more than Joe Paterno, who spent 16 years as an assistant before replacing Rip Engle and beginning his "Grand Experiment" of producing true scholar-athletes in 1966. Add *The Penn State Football Encyclopedia* to your library and take a walk through the history of "Linebacker U."

1998 • 600 pp • 300 photos • 8 1/2 x 11 hardcover • ISBN 1-57167-117-x • $39.95

Andy Russell: A Steeler Odyssey
by Andy Russell

Andy Russell, two-time Super Bowl Champion and seven-time Pro Bowler with the great Pittsburgh Steelers' teams of the '70s, writes about his career and his teammates on these great teams. Russell writes, "The stories about my teammates are not a recounting of their many records, awards, and other sporting achievements, but instead recollections of some of my personal interactions with them." Lynn Swann, Mel Blount, Terry Bradshaw, Joe Greene, chuck Noll, Jack Ham, Rocky Bleier, Jack Lambert, Franco Harris and more are included.

1998 • 250 pp • 16-page photo section • 6 x 9 hardcover • ISBN 1-57167-235-4 • $22.95

Roberto Clemente: The Great One
by Bruce Markusen

Twenty-five years ago, Roberto Clemente made baseball history when he became the first Latin American to enter the Hall of Fame. *Roberto Clemente: The Great One* explores one of the game's most dynamic players and perhaps its most selfless humanitarian. From modest beginnings in Carolina, Puerto Rico, to a legendary career with the Pittsburgh Pirates, to his tragically premature death in a plane crash, *The Great One* details the story of one of baseball's most compelling characters. Interviews with teammates Willie Stargell and Al Oliver, former major league commissioner Bowie Kuhn, and close friends of Clemente lend insight into his character and contributions. *The Great One* fully examines Clemente's legacy, at a time of unprecedented success for Latin American players.

1998 • 300 pp • 16-page photo section • 6 x 9 hardcover • ISBN 1-57167-244-3 • $22.95

www.SportsPublishingInc.com

The Greatest Moments and Players of the Philadelphia Flyers
by Stan Fischler

Stan Fischler, one of the most respected and accomplished authors in hockey history, is set to release his first book for Sports Publishing, Inc. —*The Greatest Moments and Players of the Philadelphia Flyers.* The Flyers have been one of hockey's most successful and popular teams in recent memory with an appearance in the 1997 Stanley Cup Finals and a roster filled with stars like John LeClair, Ron Hextall, Paul Coffey, and Eric Lindros. Boasting Hall of Famers like Bernie Parent, Bobby Clarke, and Bill Barber, the Flyers also are rich in history and tradition. Relive the memories of the 35-game unbeaten streak, the back-to-back Stanley Cups in mid-1970s and the legend of the Broad Street Bullies in this beautiful hardcover offering.

1988 • 250 pp • 150+ photos • 8 1/2 x 11 hardcover • ISBN 1-57167-234-6 • $29.95

Joe Paterno: The Coach from Byzantium
by George Paterno

George Paterno, the brother of Penn State football coach Joe Paterno and color analyst for Penn State football, tells the story about his legendary brother. This book is a combination of two novels — the story about an icon and national legend evoking his life as a young man prior to beginning his journey to fame. The story describes the role effect of Joe's immediate family, his relationship with them, and the importance they played in his future development.

The second part of the story deals with Joe's career after he joined Rip Engle's staff and his subsequent marriage. All of the people who helped and contributed to his legend are brought into focus for the first time.

In essence, the book is about two brothers, close but different.

1997 • 220 pages • 6 x 9 hardcover • ISBN 1-57167-153-6 • $22.95